The Global Entrepreneur

How to Create Maximun Personal Wealth in the New Global Economic Era

Ervin Williams

iUniverse, Inc.
Bloomington

The Global Entrepreneur
How to Create Maximun Personal Wealth In the New Global Economic Era

Copyright © 2011 by Ervin Williams
First Edition 2005
Second Edition 2011

All rights reserved. No part of this book may be used or reproduced by any means, graphic, electronic, or mechanical, including photocopying, recording, taping or by any information storage retrieval system without the written permission of the publisher except in the case of brief quotations embodied in critical articles and reviews.

iUniverse books may be ordered through booksellers or by contacting:

iUniverse
1663 Liberty Drive
Bloomington, IN 47403
www.iuniverse.com
1-800-Authors (1-800-288-4677)

Because of the dynamic nature of the Internet, any Web addresses or links contained in this book may have changed since publication and may no longer be valid. The views expressed in this work are solely those of the author and do not necessarily reflect the views of the publisher, and the publisher hereby disclaims any responsibility for them.

Any people depicted in stock imagery provided by Thinkstock are models, and such images are being used for illustrative purposes only.

Certain stock imagery © Thinkstock.

ISBN: 978-0-595-33037-9 (pbk)
ISBN: 978-0-595-77828-7 (ebk)

Printed in the United States of America

iUniverse rev. date: 2/11/2011

Contents

Intended Audience

There are three groups of people who can benefit from reading this book and they are presented here in order of importance. First, *nascent entrepreneurs,* who are typically working for someone else, but have a strong desire to go into business for themselves. Second, small-medium-size *business owners,* who need to expand globally to achieve organizational growth in a shrinking domestic market. Lastly, *students* taking courses in entrepreneurship, who desire to explore an international venture as a possible career option.

Nascent Entrepreneurs. Surveys show that over 90 percent of individuals currently working for others would prefer to be operating their own businesses. These are opportunity-seeking individuals who recognize that a more challenging and profitable career is possible through running their own business. However, only about 5 percent of these individuals leave their jobs and start a business. Here is your chance to act on your *dream.* This is how it can be done. We offer many suggestions and ideas for ventures that will help you start a new business. Having a global venture will enable you to travel the world, explore new cultures, and create personal wealth during the process.

Small Business Owners. Some 98 percent of businesses throughout the world are small-medium-size enterprises (SME). New start-up ventures and SMEs are the engines of economic growth worldwide. Most SMEs are local or regional in orientation, producing and selling to customers within small geographical areas. Many of these firms are limiting their growth due to the constraints of serving these markets. To achieve substantial future growth, it will be necessary for these firms to explore global expansion and to develop revenues from rapidly-growing developing countries. This book offers the SME a "roadmap" for tapping into a global marketplace through utilizing a network of associate enterprises located in other countries.

Students. There are students in more than 1600 colleges and universities in the U.S. that are taking courses in entrepreneurship. Having one's own business is unlikely to be the initial career choice for most of these students. However, knowing and understanding the dynamics of present day global business opportunities will help students to better prepare for the future through their education and work experiences. By reading this book, students can better shape their career path while keeping upmost in mind the *dream* that they too can and will have at a future global business venture.

Preface

It has long been recognized that entrepreneurship is the major engine of economic growth and individual prosperity worldwide. The Global Entrepreneur has recently emerged and this dynamic business discipline has spread as a world-wide phenomenon. The new Global Entrepreneur demonstrates how wealth-creating opportunities can occur in every corner of the globe. It is also proof that both the developed and developing worlds have insatiable appetites for an increasing amount of goods and services representing the good life enjoyed by most North Americans.

This advanced new breed of entrepreneurs has evolved as a result of the impact of four major forces in the business world: advent of globalization, the Internet/Information Age, importance of knowledge/technology, and the emergence of a new business-leadership period. Clearly, a new economic era has arrived, one in which traditional business approaches and old-line management practices are fast losing their effectiveness. However, the Global Entrepreneur thrives on the turmoil of this new era.

Global Entrepreneurs are clearly different. They are adventurous and truly *wealth-seeking individuals* as we have never seen before. These men and women are constantly acquiring new knowledge and technologies from all corners of the world. They are intensely involved in acquiring skills, abilities, and knowledge from a variety of global work experience. Global Entrepreneurs frequently operate with several simultaneous roadmaps, but their efforts are keenly *focused* on their primary goal of establishing a global venture. They are positive about their future because they believe they have the ability to shape it according to their desire.

The beauty of Global Entrepreneurship is that the process is *prescriptive, teachable and learnable.* Consequently, the purpose of this book is to assist you in taking a number of fast-forward steps toward realizing your long-term *dream*; to *create maximum personal wealth* for yourself and your associates. If you are at a critical reflection point in your personal life, or your present business is faulting, then this book offers many revitalizing "how to" suggestions, guidelines, and examples for achieving a larger *dream* - that of establishing a wealth-creating global enterprise.

1

A New Global Economic Era

"The private banks failed, the supervisory system failed,
and the politics failed, the administration failed,
and the ideology of an unregulated free
market utterly failed."

Johannah Sigurdardot
Iceland's Prime Minister

The New Global Economic Era

Two incidents occurred in America, one on 9/11/01 and one on 9/15/08, which have re-shaped the world economy more than anything else in the past one hundred years. The 2001 incident was the successful terrorist attack on New York and Washington, and the second incident was the failure of Lehman Brothers, a company holding over $600 billion in assets, resulting in the largest bankruptcy filing in American history. The latter contributed significantly to America's - and the worlds - worst recession since 1933.

It is significant that both of these events occurred in the U.S., the world's largest economic superpower. Unfortunately, it is important to recognize America contributed to the causal factors that brought about the occurrence of both incidents. The policies of George W. Bush and a necessity of protecting the oil flow from the Middle East has led the U.S. to believe it must have its military might strategically positioned and actively engaged around the world. Consequently, extremists from the Muslim faith disagree with this engagement and are fighting back, causing the U.S. to spend billions of dollars each year fighting what has been called "War on Terror."

Lehman borrowed significant amounts to fund its investing in the years leading up to its bankruptcy in 2008, a process known as leveraging or gearing. A significant part of this investing was in housing-related assets as a subprime lender, making it vulnerable to a downturn in that market. The collapse of Lehman triggered turmoil in global financial markets that was felt by millions around the world. It has also led to the bankruptcy of other firms, such as GM, Chrysler, AIG and other financial repercussions continue. Your pension fund will have a wobble, your employer's business will suffer due to a decline in sales, and you, as a home owner or entrepreneur, will have more difficulty in getting a personal or a business loan.

Just how bad the situation is was summed up by Jamie Dimon, CEO of J.P. Morgan Chase, who recently said: "I believe that in *five years* this country – and most banks – will be fine overall. The crisis will be a memory, and traditional strengths of America will show through; its ability to come together and innovate and its strong work ethic will emerge." Five years to recover – that is not something Americans want to hear, especially entrepreneurs and small business owners who get more than 90 percent of external funding from banks. Dimon goes further stating: "We all have to be humbled by the mistakes we made." Of course, one can ask at this point, were you part of the problem creating this meltdown?[1] For sure, all of us should be keenly interested in helping the country to recover, regardless of how long it takes.

Free Enterprise Capitalism Is Being Questioned

The critics of the American free-enterprise capitalistic system are abound today, claiming it to be a major cause of the current economic meltdown. But wait - a thoughtful analysis will tell you it was not the free-enterprise capitalistic system that caused unbridled market speculation on Wall Street. Adam Smith advised us in 1772 that rampant speculation in the markets could lead to this kind of "overtrading" if unchecked. Consequently, the pseudo-economic growth in the U.S. in the first decade of 2000 did indeed cause a financial "snowball" to start rolling around the world. Along its way, this snowball uncovered some severe weaknesses in the economies of other countries, such as Iceland, Greece, Ireland, Spain and Portugal. However, individuals in India and China were not hit as hard as in developed countries, because a majority of people in those countries were poor before the financial tsunami hit their country.

Critics of capitalism seem to focus on three beliefs: that capitalism degrades the quality of life; it sacrifices public good for private gain; and it may lead to unchecked economic growth, as has occurred in America. These are true to some extent, but let's set the record straight: Steve Forbes Editor, and Chief at *Forbes* Magazine, expresses it this way: "Far from having failed, democratic capitalism is the world's greatest success story. No other system has improved the lives of so many people." Also, it is not only the "rich," but people at all income levels who are doing better today as a result of our democratic capitalistic system. He further states that the current recession has to be viewed as an *interruption* of, and certainly not an *end* to, the expansion of the U.S.[2]

Perhaps the best exposé on capitalism is a book by Harold Price and his three coauthors. They discuss four types of capitalisms: the state-guided system - the state decides what to produce and provides industrial subsidies; the oligarchic - typically family-owned firms run much of the economy; the big firms - very large business groups account for most of the economy; and free-enterprise entrepreneurship - small and medium-sized businesses occupy a significant role in the economy.

The authors say that all economies have some aspects of each of these types of capitalism, but one form tends to predominate in a country. In the U.S., the free-enterprise capitalism model predominates. In the European Union (E.U.), a social capitalistic model tends to predominate; big firms are very important in Japan and Korea; oligarchy is frequently found in emerging Asian economies; and in China a strong state-controlled market system clearly predominates.

According to the authors, an overriding factor emerges from their analysis of capitalism – namely, each model results in a different economic growth rate. Those countries that stress entrepreneurial capitalism and consequently reward economic growth, have faster growth rates than countries where this is not the case. The authors are abundantly clear with their view that entrepreneurial capitalism contributes significantly to economic growth. Therefore, when economic growth is the primary goal of a country, a government should implement policies, support, and assistance to entrepreneurs that will make it easy for them to start and operate their small and medium-size enterprises. America - more than any other large nation - has recognized this premise, and its promotion of entrepreneurship has contributed to it being the world's largest economic superpower, with a $14.2 trillion annual gross domestic product (GDP).[3]

Carl Schramm, President of the Kauffman Foundation, has further emphasized the importance of entrepreneurship in another one of his books, *The Entrepreneurial Imperative.* Schramm poses and answers this question: "Why is America such a dominant economic power in the world?" Certainly it is not due to our overall level of education - we are number 12 in the world;

it is not due to our technological superiority - most technology is available for purchase in the marketplace from major consulting organizations; and certainly it is not our manufacturing capability - China and other developing countries can produce high-quality products cheaper than the U.S. If not education, technology, and manufacturing, then what explains why the U.S. has created the highest standard of living for the most people - more so than any other country in the world? Schramm concludes America's massive economic prowess is based on our knowledge, understanding, teaching, and application of entrepreneurship.[4]

Growth-Driven Capitalism

A major tenant of this book is that free-enterprise entrepreneurial capitalism will create the highest level of sustainable economic growth. In the previously mentioned book by Price and coauthors, they explains that growth-driven capitalism is desirable since it is essential for maintaining and improving the standard of living of the largest number of people wherever it is practiced. They also feel economic growth can be achieved concurrently with a balancing of environmental concerns. Obviously, there are others who disagree with this assessment. The authors believe that technological innovation and conservation can create new energy solutions and new jobs, while protecting our environment. This can work if we establish national sustainability goals and then organize the economy to provide entrepreneurs with the right incentives for addressing these environmental problems. We will examine this in greater detail in chapter ten as we discuss a more gentle form of capitalism and the need for national goals on sustainability.

The Chinese Capitalistic Growth Model

The enlightened reader may challenge Price's findings above in that free-enterprise capitalism generates more growth than the three other forms of capitalism. Surely, these authors are aware that China has averaged more than 10 percent a year in GDP growth for the past ten years. By contrast, the U.S. has averaged only a 3.3 percent GDP growth from 1947 to 2010. Consequently, China, with its state-guided-capitalistic system, is generating three times more raw economic growth than the American free-enterprise system.

China's economic performance is not only at odds with Price, it is also at odds with Adam Smith's free-market paradigm of economic success, which is rooted in two principles: less government is best, and policymakers should rely on the "invisible hand" of the market to regulate the economy, along with limited government control. Now how can these authors be so far off base? Isn't the free-enterprise capitalistic system supposed to be the most productive?

I believe Price and his coauthors were thinking of economic growth from an American perspective, meaning such growth should benefit our citizens, help society in general, and have a positive effect on our environment. On the other hand, China's growth has been a huge expense to that nation through exploitation of the lives of its human resources, the devastating consequences of constructing the Three Gorges Dam, and general degradation of the environment, both land and air. Regardless, growth is growth. China's economic performance is no flash in the pan and is expected to continue well into the 21st century, unfettered by changes in the world market, according to research by Albert Keidel. China is expected to surpass the U.S. in GDP growth by the year 2030.[5]

China's present economic growth has been achieved with a staggering cost to its population and to its physical environment. Workers in export factories work 80 hours a week in abominable health and safety conditions. Chinese peasants must pay for school, and medical services, and it is claimed that a majority of the 100 million migrant workers are owed unpaid wages, and farmers are barely paid for their land being destroyed by ravenous commercial development; and air and water pollution are responsible for the lives of 400,000 people each year. In addition, five of the ten most polluted cities in the world are in China. The Three Gorges Dam project, completed in 2006, has devastated ecosystems over a vast geographic area and displaced 1.3 million people, and submerged irreplaceable cultural sites. Many conclude China's rapid drive for economic growth and development has been a human and environmental disaster. Yes, China has had rapid economic growth, but at what cost to its people and to the country?

Since Chairman Mao's death in 1976, China has gone through four major economic changes, one each in 1980, 1990, and 2001, with a fourth phase beginning in 2008. The latter phase promotes a more promising combination of economic growth and other important goals, such as "inclusive growth." This new initiative provides for more environmental protection and social welfare for its citizens. Even when China passes the U.S. in GDP, the two economies will be equivalent in size, but not in composition. China will still have a vast undeveloped countryside, a demographic problem resulting from the one-child-per-couple policy, and a per capita income that will not equal that of the U.S. until sometime in the second half of the century. Per-capita income provides a measure of the sophistication of an economy and the quality of life of its people.

Capitalism - A Stumble, But Not a Fall

Even when taking the recent economic recession in consideration, our position is that free-enterprise capitalism is not only good, it's still the best and most productive economic system in the world for the largest number of people. However, we had some greedy Wall Street executives who almost caused a complete meltdown of our financial system and perhaps that of the entire world. The blame is clearly on America's doorsteps, landing at the feet of the president during the unbridled growth of early 2000 and his economic advisors, the Federal Reserve Chairman, the banking system, greedy Wall Street executives, all the way down to individual consumers who were enticed to use their houses as ATM machines in a period of cheap money and a false increase in real estate values. Other conditions, such as monetary globalization, facilitated this debacle but did not cause the economic meltdown. American financial institutions were able to sell and resell their over-leveraged, subprime mortgages to financial institutions around the globe thus causing worldwide financial instability. One benefit of the meltdown is that we no longer have to define the meaning of globalization.

A number of well-respected individuals believe America is still in serious trouble. Rick Karlgaard, publisher of *Forbes,* provides us with some disturbing insights. He quotes Richard Koo, chief economist for Nomura Research Institute: "The U.S. is in a balance sheet recession, marked by deflation and deleveraging that will crimp investing and spending for a decade or more." Harvard's financial historian and author Niall Ferguson says this: "Debt-laden America is past its glory [years] but will try to mask its decline by inflating away its debt problems." Also, Marc Faber, former *Forbes* contributor and international money manager and a student of the decline and fall of civilizations, agrees with Ferguson that the U.S. has passed it period of greatness.[6]

According to John Mauldin, the Federal Reserve and central banks are not quite sure to what extent the *first* stimulus package ($700 billion authorized in 2008) worked and they are not sure what the bottom of the recession will look like. Consequently, they are examining our economic system using four major economic theories: Irving Fisher (representing the classical economists); John Keynes (the Keynesian school); Ludwig von Mises (the Austrian School); and Milton Friedman (the monetarist school). Over the next few years, this grand experiment will show us which economic theory is right about our massive debt and the magnitude of the economic stimulus. Now the U.S. Federal Reserve concluded the first stimulus was "disappointingly slow" in stimulating the economy; consequently, they interjected another $600 million

(QE2) into the American economy as a *second* stimulus fund in November 2010. [7]

Our Federal Reserve has been criticized around the world for the QE2, but what it does is give the U.S. more time for finding ways of stimulating economic growth. University of Chicago economist, Raghuram Rajan, says the QE2 will not work for pumping up demand may create an illusion of growth, but will not fix a basic problem in the economy. Rajan says we do not have a cyclical problem, but it is a structural problem, resulting from a mismatch between present labor force skills and the new types skills needed for a knowledge-based economy. He also says the *root* cause of the American financial crisis was from both democrats and republicans, who agreed they could reduce the widening income gap in the country by promoting low-income-based housing loans through Fannie May and Freddie Mack as a palliative for the poor. This happed. These subprime loans helped send the housing sector into overdrive, which resulting in such loans being "re-packaged" by greedy Wall Street speculators who sold them throughout the world. When the real value of these real estate loans was discovered, the world-financial crisis began. So Wall Street just capitalized on an abundance of subprime loans created by the federal government. Very few point out this root cause of the American financial crisis.[8]

What is the best way to achieve growth after a massive recession? It is interesting to note that the U.S. is betting heavily on one popular strategy, while the E.U. zone is supporting exactly the opposite approach. Geoff Colvin discusses this in his article in *Fortune.* The U.S. is using a New World approach, or the Keynesian model, with the government pouring hundreds of millions of borrowed money into the economy to stimulate demand and further kick-start the economy. The assumption is that people will buy more, companies will expand, and the economy will start moving again. The Old World approach adopted by the E.U. is called "consolidation," which means reducing the deficit by cutting government expenses, and resulting slow or non-existing growth. In doing this, the E.U. is less apt to raise future taxes or to inflate its currency to ease the pain of repaying its massive debt. Covin says he is not sure how this ultimate economic experiment will turn out, but "it won't be good news for America."[9]

America will recover as it has in the past, but we can only expect the economy to "muddle through" what promises to be below-trend growth and a long-term secular bear market, according to Mauldin. He says, "It is not going to be pleasant or fun – there will be lots of pain – but we will get through the crisis." The real question is: "When?" At this point a substantial part of the pain is on the shoulders of entrepreneurs and small business owners, for they have been the forgotten lot in the massive bailout by the federal government. They are also the ones who generate new growth and create new jobs. The government bailed out banks and some large businesses but not start-up ventures and small Main Street businesses. Entrepreneurs and small businesses continue to be frozen out of the money market because banks had to absorb losses from both residential and commercial real estate markets.

Implications for Global Entrepreneurs

The real question for Global Entrepreneurs (G/Es) is this; just where are the largest and most likely sources of future economic growth? (Please note we will use this G/E acronym throughout the book in lieu of Global Entrepreneur.) Although growth will be the subject of chapters six and seven, we can tell you in that advance high growth is going to occur in the emerging markets, the so called "BRIA" countries (Brazil, Russia, India and China). Although the acronym includes these four countries, it is intended to mean all developing countries. Developing countries have remained rather robust during the recession. America and other rich-world developed countries have experienced a recession much deeper than was anticipated and will be slow to recover. Consequently, G/Es will find more growth opportunities for products and services in the developing world than in the U.S. or the E.U.

As an American entrepreneur, you have lots of things going in your favor even before you start your global enterprise. Sure, there are radical religious groups intent on bringing harm to our citizens and country. However, for the most part, our free enterprise system - our "American brand" - is envied around the world. The U.S. is now the most admired global country thanks largely to President Obama, according to a 2009 research report by National Brand Index (NBI), an annual measure of the global image of 50 countries. The U.S. climbed from seventh place in 2008 to first place in 2009, and is now ahead of France, Germany, the United Kingdom, and Japan, which complete the five top nations. "What is really remarkable is that in all my years studying national reputation, I have never seen any country experience such a dramatic rise in its [global] standing," stated Simon Anholt, the founder of NBI. Anholt said of the sharp contrast of President Obama's outreach to the unpopular foreign policies of President George W. Bush caused the U.S. rank to jump to the top so quickly. [10]

Our American brand includes the highest economic standard of living for the largest number of people in the world. It has also resulted in the country having premier medical colleges, top business schools, and music, movies, and innovative products that are universally admired. The world is beginning to recognize the value and importance of entrepreneurship; however, it is American entrepreneurs who are clearly the best at understanding and putting the discipline into practice. We started early in teaching entrepreneurship with the first course at Harvard University in 1964. Now more than 1600 colleges and universities offer courses in the subject, with many colleges offering Bachelor's, Master's and Ph.D. degrees in the subject.

Now, this is your challenge – as a student, entrepreneur, or small business owner; you can help your country at this critical juncture in its history. This is the first recession that most of you have witnessed, and it is likely to have lasting impact on your life as the 1933 recessions has on the older generation. Our nation and the world economy will recover, albeit slowly. It is abundantly clear that entrepreneurs will lead America out of the recession, as they have done so in the past. Start-ups of new ventures create over 30 percent of new jobs, according to the Kauffman Foundation, and existing small business, those from one to five years old, create over 65 percent of the rest of the new jobs in the economy. Therefore, bringing your invention to the forefront, starting a new venture, or growing an existing venture can mean future prosperity for you and a significant contribution to the growth of America.

For G/Es, your prospects are brighter than local or national-based entrepreneurs, since research shows those firms that engage in international trade grow faster and are more profitable than their non-international trade peers. This is true in part due to a larger marketplace, but there is another important causal factor. International trade facilitates the flow of ideas from around the world; meeting each other; they join hands, have sex and their offspring ideas from a larger collective brain result in improved knowledge and enhanced technology.

International trade facilitates the flow of ideas from around the world meeting each other; they join hands, have sex. and their offspring ideas from a larger collective brain result in improved knowledge and enhanced technology.

It is the purpose of this book to assist you in the discovery of your venture idea and to share with you essential factors required for a successful venture. Chapter two introduces the factors that enable you to be a G/E. Chapter three will help you to understand the entrepreneurial process. Chapter four focuses on knowledge and technology as ultimate wealth creation factors. Chapter five will help you discover new business ideas and opportunities arising from emerging business trends. Chapter six explores how the Information Age has helped create a new global marketplace. Chapter seven focuses on the Global Entrepreneur and how he or she is different from other entrepreneurs.

Chapter eight explores virtualization and its impact on the global enterprise. Chapter nine involves developing your management team, securing money and developing a formal business plan. Chapter ten shows how we might revive our American brand with a kinder, gentler, more compassionate form of capitalism. Chapter ten also points out how Global Entrepreneurs and their family members can be a part of a sustainable revolution that will reshape the world.

2

Emergence of the Global Entrepreneur

"Our choice is to rethink the future
or be forced to rethink the future."
Rowan Gibson

The Global Entrepreneurs

Global Entrepreneurship is not a new phenomenon. Time, location, communication, and technology separate global entrepreneurs of an earlier age from those of the 21st century. Please keep in mind that we will be using the G/E acronym as a substitute for the phrase Global Entrepreneur. A well-known G/E of earlier years was Marco Polo, even though he began his extensive travel long before the French invented the word "entrepreneur." Christopher Columbus and Vasco da Gama are also examples of historic G/Es. Lesser-known G/Es include John Raghton, Robert Chapman, and John Carlton, the British merchant adventurers of the 15th century who operated out of an ancient Guild Hall in York, England. These merchants were true G/Es, undertaking global enterprises and risking their money in extensive overseas trading. They left a lasting legacy: their medieval Guild Hall, established in 1357, with a small hospital, chapel, and one room for conducting business. Today, the ancient York Guild Hall is a beautifully restored medieval building, still owned by the original company that built it. Remarkable! During the 640 years of the Guild's existence, its G/Es were among of the dominant merchants who helped build the British Empire.

Present-day G/Es possess many traits of the British merchant adventurers. Quite visible, G/Es capitalize on emerging international opportunities, many of which they create. G/Es are able to see and take advantage of the opportunities emerging from shifting or disintegrating political, social, and economic power structures throughout the world. Viewing business ventures from a global perspective, G/Es exploit opportunities that others rarely see or think about. As a result, G/Es create new ventures that take advantage of - and frequently challenge - the old economic system. They travel to distant time zones searching for new opportunities, and they are fundamentally changing the way business is conducted and the manner in which new wealth is created.

An example of a really cosmopolitan G/E is Sir Richard Branson of England. Branson owns more than 240 companies and was knighted by the Queen in 2000 for his "services to entrepreneurship"—a high honor for someone active in a process outlawed in the Russian Republic just a few years ago. Branson has enough economic clout to team up with equity partners who essentially carry the financial risk, utilizing a process he calls "branded venture capital." He buys a company and puts his name on in it, while investors put up most of the money. His ventures span three continents and include airlines, soft drinks, trains, financial services, clothing, music stores, and cinemas. He is boastful, flamboyant and quick to say he wants his "Virgin brand" to be as well-known around the world as Coca-Cola. He is not quite there yet, but definitely he is *not* one who aims low.

Sir Richard Branson was knighted for his services to entrepreneurship.

Many people question how Branson can start so many businesses. They wonder whether he will be able to keep managing them effectively. However, unlike many Traditional Entrepreneurs who typically draw from their own limited managerial skills, Branson is backed by a strong executive team, and he uses outside consultants to bring discipline to his organization. His business selection criterion is simple: he likes to take on the well-established firms, so his central theme is to go after companies whose customers have few choices. Most of Branson's companies are private, quartered in tax havens such as the Channel Islands. Branson does not mind starting with small venture as long as he can use his personal brand to take on the established players in the name of giving customers a better deal.

Traveling the world and, taking on major corporations with clever marketing and outstanding customer services is certainly one way to be a G/E. Branson's unusual entrepreneurial flair has been successful up to this point. Some criticize his flamboyant style and wonder how long his good fortune will last. There is always the danger that today's highfliers will be in bankruptcy tomorrow. But with more than 240 companies and still growing, Branson could stand to lose a few along the way and still be ahead of the entrepreneurial pack. A prime example of the G/E, Branson operates in several countries, and he uses other people's money to finance his ventures. He enters known markets, spreads the risk over a variety of businesses, selects good partners to run his ventures, and operates from international tax havens to minimize taxes. Branson has been very successful in developing his widely recognized *Virgin* global brand. Branson's latest book, *Screw It, Let's Do It,* is a must read for all entrepreneurs.[11]

As we look beyond Branson, other factors are laying the foundation for the emergence of a new breed of G/Es. Never before have we seen so many historical convergences occurring in the world at one time, and the potential impact of each convergence creates staggering opportunities for the G/E. The savvy G/E views these major forces not as threats, but as opportunity-creating situations. Let's examine more closely some of the factors that provide profound wealth-creating opportunities for G/Es.

The Globalization Factor

Globalization is an undisputed reality today. Powerful media concerns like CNN (U.S.- based), BBC (U.K-based) and CCTV (China-based) bring world events into our homes and businesses instantly and continuously, 24/7. Now business people frequently travel the earth searching for business opportunities, production sites, and new markets for their products. Some describe globalization as "capitalism without borders." Another definition of globalization is the ease with which international competitors can enter your marketplace and score with your customers by selling products. It's not just your product and customers that are in danger—these global competitors can take your employees and eventually your business.

But the converse is also true. Globalization is the ease with which *you* can expand your business on someone else's turf. The traditional route for building an international firm is to start as a local business, grow the business regionally, then nationally, and with further growth, expand it into various other countries. Now that game has significantly changed. Some G/Es go global with the birth of their enterprises. Entrepreneurs are no longer required to follow the time-consuming, four-stage process—that of developing a local venture, then expanding regionally, nationally, and finally internationally. Enlightened G/Es don't wait—they start their business as an international venture. Entrepreneurs who continue to hold on to the old economic development mindset will be at a disadvantage in venturing into a new world marketplace. To avoid such an error, let's look at some of today's real-world examples using this new business approach.

Some Global Entrepreneurs go international at the birth of their ventures.

Heartware International Corporation became global as a start-up company. This American corporation produces a $74,000 cardiac catheter for the medical market. A Spanish doctor developed the product, and it was manufactured in Holland. The first product showing took place in Canada, and the first two sales were made in Brazil and Spain. Now the business has locations in the U.S., Brazil, and China. Ben Oviatt, formerly Georgia State University's Professor of Entrepreneurship, describes this global start-up process as an emerging phenomenon in the United States and one that will spread to other parts of the world. Oviatt says that a global start-up is "a new venture that, from its inception, derives resources from multiple countries and is geographically unlimited in its creator's vision as to its potential."[12] Starting an international venture from its inception will obviously accelerate its ascension on the world stage.

With more than 208 countries in the world, you have a big choice as to where to start your global enterprise. A logical game plan for a global start-up, or for global expansion of an existing business, is to pick three major world markets in which to consider locating the venture: namely, the United States, South America and the Far East. The U.S. is a tremendous market in itself, and it facilitates expansion into Canada, Mexico and South America. In South America, now Brazil is the up-and-coming shining star. In the Far East, China, with a ten-year 10-percent growth rate and an expanding 1.6 billion population (an estimated 2010 census number), offers substantial potential as an emerging market economy. China also offers many new opportunities for low-cost production. You may be wondering, "How can the G/E operate on two or more continents at the same time?" A good question. Developing global business partners is one solution to this problem, and this will be discussed in more detail in chapter eight, "Developing the Global Enterprise."

The G/E typically has a physical presence in two or more countries, with a networking plan to achieve further expansion. This physical presence may be in the form of an established company, a branch operation or a partnership. G/Es align themselves with people of power and connections who can make economic transactions a reality. Entry into many foreign countries will involve local politicians and business leaders who can help identify local entrepreneurs with whom the G/E can establish some form of a cooperative relationship. A number of cooperative options are available to the G/E, such as partnerships, joint ventures, cooperative agreements, strategic alliances, cross-patents and license agreements. Business partnering is one of several features that distinguish G/Es from Traditional Entrepreneurs.

Operating in other countries requires one to be culturally sensitive to the values, norms, and different ways of conducting intercontinental business. Western managers in particular seem to be rather insensitive to the cultures of other countries, according to Rahul Bajaj, Chairman of India's largest automobile company. Bajaj Auto, Ltd., has 17,000 employees, down from 22,000 two years ago. Bajaj says that most CEOs from emerging economies tend to be very global in outlook because they travel frequently and many have been educated abroad, as he was at Harvard University. Bajaj criticizes Western executives for not taking the time "to understand the rhythms and flows of social and business interactions, preferring instead to fly in and quickly fly out again, demanding their signatures on contracts in the shortest possible times." Bajaj concludes that centuries of experience has proved that lasting international partnerships can be built on collaboration, willingness to compromise, and a heightened sensitivity to the local business culture and customs.[13]

People everywhere are now aware of how quickly September 11 and September 15 changed global business opportunities. The terrorist attacks in New York and Washington contributed to massive expenditure of millions of dollars to fight terrorism around the world. The double economic whammy for the U.S. was the September 15, 2008, failure of 150-year-old Lehman Brothers that pushed the country into the deepest recession since 1933. Both events contributed to a decline in economic activity far beyond the borders of the U.S. and such business losses contributed to a global recession. Another result of these events has been a decline in U.S. foreign investment, reducing growth in Third World countries. It has been estimated that mergers and acquisitions will to fall by two-thirds as big companies shy away from planned expansion projects various Third World countries. These unfortunate factors are unquestionably creating adverse conditions for large business organizations. However, many G/Es will see this period as a ripe time for expansion of their business ventures through global alliances and partnerships. This will be discussed more in chapter eight as we explore the G/E's business vehicle.

In the same way in which the Spanish and Portuguese opened the Old World for trade, G/Es will open the New Global Economic World for unprecedented international business. G/Es will often be in uncharted waters as they bypass conventional business wisdom, opting instead for new strategies, such as going global at the birth of a venture. G/Es frequently land on foreign shores, transacting business with alliance partners and circulating freely with people from different nations and cultures. In this regard,

European and other multinational G/Es may have a substantial advantage over the more geographically restricted North Americans. To counter this, G/Es from the U.S. seem to be knocking on more global doors and seeking more international opportunities than those residing in other countries. However, entrepreneurs are present in every country in the world. Who are they? Many are entrepreneurs by *necessity*, that is, individuals living in developing countries with no source of livelihood; others are more up-scale, *opportunity-seeking* individuals who thrive on the challenges created by a turbulent, growing global marketplace.

The Information Era

The pace of business has substantially quickened in the First World as it has moved from the Industrial Age to the Information Era. The Information Era exists only in a small part of the globe, while the rest of the world is still in an industrial or pre-industrial state. Highly developed First World countries are clearly in the Information Era, but they represent only about 20 percent of the world's population. Eighty percent of the world's population lives in less-developed Third World countries. Nearly all Third World countries are struggling simply to produce enough food for their expanding populations. They need and want products and services produced by leading industrialized nations; however, satisfying those desires is a long way off for most people in the less-developed world because they lack sufficient purchasing power to meet their basic needs. Unfortunately, for the masses in most developing countries, the benefits and opportunities of both the Industrial and the Information Eras are still far removed from their daily lives.

Typically, developing countries, to some degree, have both First and Third World conditions. For example, South Africa is classified as a Third World country, but the nation is very much First World in major metropolitan areas such as Pretoria, Johannesburg, Durban, and Cape Town. The transportation, electricity, telecommunications, road systems, banks, shopping centers and housing in these cities are as advanced as those in most major cities in Europe and the United States. But just travel a few miles to the suburbs of these South African cities and you will experience some of the worst living conditions in the world, primarily among the majority, black African population. This is due to a big income disparity in South Africa—between the 9 percent white minority population and the 78-percent native African majority. Such a gap may create emerging opportunities for some G/Es to establish alliance partners in South Africa. This is particularly true as individuals from the African majority population begin to move up the scale in earning capacity.

They, too, desire all the comforts, conveniences and economic advantages being enjoyed by white South Africans and the rest of the developed world.

The possibility of having information technology (IT) available to everyone throughout the world offers tremendous growth possibilities. In the book *Future Revolutions,* David Mercer states that IT will not only help to improve persons-to-person communication, but, more importantly, it will allow "the 80 percent of humanity still living in the largely pre-industrial Third World to jump directly to a new post-industrial society missing many of the traumas of industrialization, such as urbanization, city slums, and the like."[14] I am not as optimistic as Mercer that such a giant leap will occur, but I do agree that IT is universally recognized as one of the key drivers of change and can be used to promote substantial global economic development in all countries.

From India ...

Missing the bus helped Phanindra Sama conceive his Internet-based venture. He was trying to go from Bangalore to Nizamabad for Diwali, the annual Hindu festival of lights. Tickets were only available at the bus station and had sold out by the time he could buy one. Phanindra was then an engineer designing digital chips for Texas Instruments and he thought of a solution. He created "redBus," a website and a network of kiosks, newsstands, and small retailers where customers could see schedules and buy any ticket over thousands of bus routes across India. In 2009, redBus sold 1.8 million tickets, had 200 employees and was heading towards sales of $30 million in 2010 from commissions and fees paid by bus lines. Phanindra is planning to expand his company into other undeveloped countries.

Just as the printing press helped usher in the Industrial Age, the Internet, computers and mobile phones are the basic tools of the Information Age. The use of these tools has changed the world in many ways. In particular, they have transformed the very nature of work and the way in which new knowledge is acquired. Through the Internet, anyone—even in the world's remotest locations—can obtain an unlimited amount of knowledge that can be potentially beneficial to educational, social and economic development in the area. Knowing how to use a computer and how to access the Internet in the First World are as important as reading and writing. Computers have massively increased our ability to find, develop, store, retrieve and manipulate data. Mobile phones also have accelerated the flow of information and are radically changing the nature of entertainment, business and medicine.

Companies of all sizes are using the Internet and its related tools to create new e-commerce business models. No major business or institution will be left untouched by the e-commerce era. No previous technology has ever grown and spread as fast as the Internet. The Internet encompasses the globe and makes all manner of new business contacts and opportunities instantly accessible. The Internet serves to collapse time and space between business partners. This means product development time is cut down, orders and delivery of components are sped up, inventories can be kept to a bare minimum, and customers around the world can provide instant feedback.

With the Internet, the size or location of the venture is no longer a major determining factor. With a savvy use of IT and the Internet, the smart G/E can be on an almost equal footing with giant corporations. However, the converse is true. In the book, *The World is Flat*, Tom Friedman tells us that the 19-year-old student in Bangladesh may be on equal footing with you as a student in America. So, keep in mind that your company does not have to be big anymore—you just need to possess the right knowledge base, you need to have access to a product or service desired by many, and you need to be able to entice a large group of customers to purchase your product. Flexibility and quickness to market are more important than size. What is most astonishing is the *speed* at which a Web business can develop—from concept to several million customers in a short period of time. Obviously, there must be profitable growth arising from these customers within a reasonable period of time, or investors will not continue supporting the venture. Many e-business companies have belatedly discovered this basic economic principle, which was ignored in the economic boom of the late 1990s. Profit is still very fashionable and absolutely required.

A New Management and Leadership Era

We will discuss in chapter three how entrepreneurs and business leaders are similar in behaviors and goals. Entrepreneurs seek radical business *growth* through initiating change-seeking behaviors in a small business context. Business leaders exert their personal influence in search of significant *growth* within large organizations. Managers in large firms are positioned between entrepreneurs and leaders. *Management can be defined as an orderly process of ensuring the allocation of physical resources, directing performance, and encouraging associates to achieve organizational objectives.* Traditional Entrepreneurs neither enjoy nor excel in the structured role of manager. However, G/Es are better than Traditional Entrepreneurs at the tasks of managing and leading an enterprise because of their diverse background and advanced skill base. The G/E's enterprise is typically more technically oriented, more culturally diverse, and obviously, operates over a wider geographical area. Therefore, good management and proactive leadership skills are fundamental requirements for successful G/Es.

Management is the orderly process of ensuring the allocation of physical resources, directing performance, and encouraging associates to achieve organizational objectives.

In the past twenty years, major advances have been made in the three business disciplines of entrepreneurship, management, and leadership. These advances can be seen in the development and enhancement of new *business knowledge*. In the U.S., for example, the automobile and electronic industries had to explore many new business techniques in response to Japanese competition from the 1970s to the 1990s. Warren Bennis, a leading American leadership guru, observed that during this period most American firms were "overmanaged and underled." Then U.S. businesses began to systematically employ new business techniques: downsizing, slashing levels of management, introducing cutting-edge *technical knowledge*, and searching for new top leadership in order to be more competitive in the world.

For the first time, major American firms began recruiting externally for innovative CEOs to transform their companies in order to keep pace with fast-changing domestic and international competition. A renewed emphasis on top *leadership* for U.S. businesses is very evident. Warren Bennis' assertion that American industry was "underled" proved to be right. Leadership seminars and books like *The Search for Excellence* began to flood the market, stressing the need for more proactive leadership. This seemed to have filtered through, for in the 1990s the U.S. began to recapture its world economic leadership in many industries, in no small part due to fundamental advancements in knowledge and the practice of management and leadership.

As the New Global Economic Era dawns, we find business crawling out from the weight of a first global recession. At this time, we also see a renewed emphasis on transformational leadership. We are moving beyond Warren Bennis and Tom Peters to a new generation of management gurus, such as Clayton Christensen and Jim Collins with his extensive research on leadership in corporate America. Collins's latest book is a must read for every entrepreneur – *How the Mighty Fail,* and *Why Some Companies Never Give Up.* A strong personal trait of all entrepreneurs is that of *persistence.* They follow their dreams and just don't give up. Other books by Collins – *Good to Great* and *Built to Last* - also have special relevance to entrepreneurs, in particularly those who are making and selling products. These books are about corporate entrepreneurship, personal resiliency, and the difficulty the U.S. faces in trying to reclaim its leadership role in invention and innovation. You will see in chapter three, corporate entrepreneurs and other entrepreneurs have a singular focus; that is, they all seek rapid business growth and expansion.

This renewed interest in business transformation has spread to Europe and the Far East. Businesses everywhere are searching for proactive leaders who can guide them through organizational transformation with minimum cost and disruption to their personnel. Highly successful firms are utilizing a new Renaissance Leadership Model for transforming and rejuvenating their organizations. This model crystallizes the work of high-performance managers into a simple, teachable "how to" model of performance. The model stipulates that managers must be "Hard on Performance," and, simultaneously, "Soft on People." Managers using this new Renaissance Leadership Model achieve the highest possible performance and also have the best possible people relationships. The goal for every manager and leader is to achieve this two-fold business result.

The Renaissance Leadership Model stipulates that managers should be "Hard on Performance" and, simultaneously, "Soft on People."

The terms "Hard on Performance" and "Soft on People" have specific meanings. Being "Hard on Performance" means the following: Managers must design, expect, and accept only a high level of continuous performance improvement, both incremental and radical. Simultaneously, being "Soft on People" means this: Managers must do a better job of respecting and responding to the needs, wants, rights, and culture of their associates in a nonthreatening manner. Managers have found that being "Hard on Performance" is a more normal administrative activity, and, consequently, it is *less difficult* for them to implement than being "Soft on People." The term "less difficult" is used here because neither dimension is "easy" to accomplish. There is nothing easy about achieving superior organizational performance in any business. Typically, most managers feel they should be "hard" on everything, and, unfortunately, "hard" on everybody. Unknowingly, many of these so-called "hard-oriented" managers make no distinction between these two separate, but related dimensions of performance and people.

What makes G/Es quite different from Traditional Entrepreneurs is that the G/E is likely to be familiar with emerging new *business knowledge*, such as the Renaissance Leadership Model. Additionally, the G/E is a more avid reader and a keener learner; often it is someone who has worked for the large corporation, but then left it in search of greater achievement and personal wealth. G/Es typically understand that when they use the Renaissance Leadership Model, they can achieve exceptionally high work performance and outstanding people relationships.[15]

The Importance of Technology in Creating Wealth

In a broad sense, technology can be defined as the application of knowledge to achieve some useful economic purpose. The two major dimensions of technology are *business knowledge* and *technical knowledge.* The G/E is often a master of both. G/Es understand the importance of using the most effective management and leadership advances to accomplish organizational results. An example of advances in *business knowledge* is the Renaissance Leadership Model discussed above. Of equal importance to G/Es is *technical knowledge*; they have to be on the cutting-edge of scientific discoveries of new products, services, and systems in their chosen profession. A point often overlooked is that technology refers not only to the creation and production of tangibles products, services and industrial solutions, but also to the business organization and its people management. Today technology must be viewed from a broader perspective, encompassing both *business* and *technical* knowledge. This broader definition of technology is discussed in greater detail in chapter four, "A New Wealth Creating Paradigm."

In *Powershift,* Alvin Toffler describes how the pathways of power and wealth creation in the world are being rapidly transformed. He defines power as "purposeful control over people," and he mentions three sources of power: "violence, wealth, and knowledge." Toffler points out that all three sources of power are being used in the world, but today knowledge is by far the most important source of power.[16]As mentioned above, knowledge is the key ingredient underlying the advances in technology. Other experts also share this view of the increasing importance of knowledge. In his book, *Unlimited Wealth*, Paul Pilzer states that First World countries today have an unlimited potential for creating wealth as a result of their advanced technologies. Pilzer challenges the long-held economic notion that we live in a world with a scarcity of resources. He says that, due to advances in technology, the First World has a virtually unlimited supply of raw materials and resources, which can be used to create even greater wealth.[17] This point will be discussed further in chapter four. Hopefully, G/Es and other business owners will recognize the importance of sharing the benefits of technology and wealth with less fortunate people in the world through social entrepreneurship. This sharing of technology is one way in which globalization can achieve more legitimacy in the future. Social entrepreneurship is discussed in greater detail in chapter ten.

It seems apparent that a major difference between the rich and the poor, the educated and uneducated societies, can largely be attributed to the use and/or lack of use of knowledge and technology. In this regard, Pilzer says that wealth is no longer exclusively produced by those having control of scarce resources, but today wealth is in the hands of individuals and companies possessing the most technical knowledge. Technology has substantially eliminated scarcity in First World countries. The acquisition, sharing and use of knowledge and technology in in less-developed countries can serve to reduce scarcity and make more resources available for economic endeavors. The power of technology is that it can be leveraged—the same technology can be used over and over to create more resources, or economic values, without diminishing the original technology. For example, after a diamond cutter learns to cut and polish a stone, this process can be taught to others over and over. Similarly, a leader has mastered the techniques of achieving high performance can share this process with other managers, duplicated this results over and over. This acquiring and sharing process cannot be done with tangible-hard-good resources that are normally consumed during the production process. Undeniably, technology is proving to be one of the most powerful units of production in economic history.

Economic Freedom

Individual freedom is now recognized as one of the major cornerstones in the wealth-creation process. There is a close relationship among individual freedom, political freedom, and economic freedom. As political freedom increases in a country, we often witness a parallel increase in economic freedom There is a very strong correlation between economic freedom and development of new wealth. An existing body of research shows countries having the highest level of economic freedom also have the highest per-capita income. As countries introduce and allow more economic freedom for their people, greater economic growth and development tends to follow. Individual freedom promotes individual initiative, and individual initiative serves as the basis of economic endeavors. The meaning is clear: Freedom allows for a release of the entrepreneurial spirit, which in turn, encourages individuals to establish their own businesses so they can seek maximum personal rewards for themselves and their stakeholders.

In a 14-year study of 148 nations and territories, James Gwartney and associates found Hong Kong had the highest rating for economic freedom (9.05 of 10), followed by Singapore (8.70), New Zealand (8.27), Switzerland (8.8),

Chile (8.06), and the U.S. (7.96). Following these were Canada, Australia, Mauritius and the United Kingdom – with Zimbabwe being the lowest country (3.57) in economic freedom. The research shows a slight decline in economic freedom among these countries; a first in over a decade. Nations in the top quartile of the study had an average per-capita GDP of $32,744, compared with $3,858 for those in the bottom quartile. A persistently high level of economic freedom over a long period of time leads to a higher per capita income. The per-capita income is a good measure of the overall standard of living in a country.[18]

This proven relationship between economic freedom and wealth creation is very hard to ignore. Another measure by The Heritage Foundation and *The Wall Street Journal*, the Index of Economic Freedom, also finds that the higher the economic freedom, the greater are increases in individual performance, the greater the increase in per-capita income, the more self-reported happiness, and economic freedom even serves to prevent wars.[19]

Giving economic freedom to employees will increase their performance and will also create larger per-capita incomes.

It is also possible to extrapolate links between freedoms that exist within a nation and the freedom employees are allowed to have within a company, and certainly those freedoms enjoyed by individual entrepreneurs. Research studies show that the greater the freedom granted to an individual, the more creative he or she will be. Finally, the more freedom an individual has, the more productive he or she will be. So, overall economic freedom in a country closely parallels individual freedom possessed by an employee or an entrepreneur. In recognition of this fact, most First World managers are actively seeking ways to better empower their employees, or to give them maximum freedom at work. These managers are searching for ways to provide employees with more opportunity for autonomous work. Individual empowerment occurs only when one has the personal freedom to take initiative and the opportunity to act with a greater degree of autonomy. The presence of a high level of individual freedom in a nation is a fundamental requirement for the flourishing of entrepreneurial activity. And it is widely acknowledged that a high level of economic activity stokes the economic growth engine in every developed country in the world.

Political Freedom

There is also a close parallel between political freedom and economic freedom. It appears that the two types of freedom represent the two sides of the same coin. The importance of political freedom is fundamentally linked to the conviction that an individual should be at liberty to pursue his or her own ends in a manner that he or she thinks fit. This is the essence of economic freedom. Conversely, it is economic freedom that makes independent political action possible. Clearly, government policy plays a preeminent role in determining the economic freedom of every country. Political freedom sets the foundation for economic freedom, but the two do not always occur in parallel timetables. In the United States, political freedom and economic freedom have gradually developed together over the past 220 years, thus contributing substantially to the country's present economic success. Unfortunately, economic success in one country cannot be easily replicated in other emerging democracies for many reasons—some of them cultural, political, and religious. Achieving a high level of economic success requires a collective effort by government, the business community and the citizenry.

To illustrate such difficulty in political and economic development, again look at South Africa. In 1994, political freedom occurred very quickly after a prolonged 50-year struggle for democracy. With the democratic election in South Africa, the native African majority gained political freedom overnight. But economic freedom remains far from being a reality for a majority of black South Africans. Economic freedom will require the government to put forth many new initiatives, better educate the population, create jobs, and train people to be productive in the public and private sector. All of this will take lots of money and a considerable effort over a long period of time. The right to vote is a single measure of freedom, but you are not really free if you cannot provide the basic necessities for your livelihood and your family.

Whether in Africa or any other part of the world, several points regarding a democratic system of government are worth noting. A Nobel Prize in economics was once awarded based upon this discovery: *Famines do not occur in democratic countries.* A second point that should be noted is that *all* highly developed countries in the world are democracies. There is an obvious, direct relationship between democracy, individual freedom and economic prosperity among the masses of people in any country. Perhaps political advisors should share these points with the autocratic leaders in the 53 African countries, only 18 of which were true democracies in 2010, up from 16 in 2005.

Two strong messages here for the autocratic leaders in the world. All highly developed countries are democracies! Famines do not occur in democratic countries!

Arrival of the Global Entrepreneur

Lester Thurow describes in detail the type of person needed for the New Global Economic Era. Thurow's description uniquely characterizes the G/E. Thurow says, "Individuals who will invest in what will probably be the most valuable skill that a person can have - the ability to operate in a global economy;" they, will be willing to "live outside the boundaries of the routine, will overcome the natural psychic reluctance to try the new in the face of a social environment that is always wed to the past, will have the ability to dream, the will to conquer, the joy of creativity, and [will have] the psychic drive to build an economic kingdom."[20] That is a fairly complete description of the new, cosmopolitan G/E. Now, the question is this: How do you measure up to these characteristics? Keep this in mind: most are "acquired" traits and not genetic qualities with which you were born. These traits are within your reach if you have a proactive mindset and a persistent determination to become a G/E.

In advanced economies, individual success has come by a fairly structured route: the individual is expected to get a college education, find a job, earn an increasing income, move up the corporate ladder, peak out, and then coast into a comfortable retirement. The G/E doesn't choose that route. According to John Kotter in *The New Rules,* today's success route is quite different from that of the past. He says that you need an entirely new success game plan because the old success patterns of the past are being replaced with individuals having multiple careers, incorporating continuous learning, and creating a life with lots of uncertainty. Now the ground rules have substantially changed and different ingredients are necessary to be successful in an increasingly competitive marketplace.[21] Kotter's new rules are major reasons for the increasing interest in entrepreneurship, in particular in the U.S. Most individuals recognize they must provide their own job security rather than relying upon a corporate "parent" to do it for them. Indeed, this is a strange and uncomfortable situation for the old guard, but is more of an accepted fact of life for the younger generation who intend to make their mark in a new business era.

The G/E is acutely attuned to this rapidly changing world marketplace. The globe is clearly the G/E's elected cosmopolitan domain. G/Es embrace the fact that the future is highly unpredictable, but is one they can shape to a large extent. They are constantly busy honing their business knowledge, developing and expanding their technological knowledge, and constantly searching for ways to put their multifaceted game plan into operation on a global basis. They are doggedly persistent, determined to be successful, and refuse to let others steal their dream. They are undaunted in their determination to excel with their global venture and to create substantial wealth. Creating *substantial wealth* is, indeed, a personal objective of G/Es. All these attributes make the new, cosmopolitan Global Entrepreneurs unique. It is my desire for you acquire these attributes for entrepreneurship is a continuous learning process.

3

Entrepreneurship and the Entrepreneur

"No one is an entrepreneur all the time;
everyone is an entrepreneur at times."
Raymond Kayo

The Engenderers

The concept of the entrepreneur is more than three hundred years old, the term having been coined by Richard Cantillon, a French banker and industrialist. Cantillon said the entrepreneur was one who engaged in the exchange process of buying and selling with an uncertainty of income. In early 1900s, Joseph Schumpeter of Harvard University viewed entrepreneurs as champions of economic development and have built businesses that are growth-oriented, profit-motivated, innovative, and involved in strategic management. Schumpeter stated that entrepreneurs are often engaged in a "creative destruction" process as they forge ahead with their new ventures. Edmund Phelps, a 2006 Nobel Peace Prize winner, takes exception to Schumpeter. Phelps says growth-enhancing entrepreneurship leads to "non-destructive creation" and not "creative destruction." Yes, I agree with Phelps on this.

Today entrepreneurship is universally recognized as being directly related to economic growth of regions and countries. The entrepreneurial wave that swept through the United States in the 1980s and 1990s helped make the nation one of the most productive and prosperous countries in the world. Donald Sexton, in his book *The State of the Art of Entrepreneurship*, says the

American entrepreneurial revolution will have a greater impact on the U.S. economy than any other event in the country's history, even more so than the Industrial Revolution. Keep in mind the growth in entrepreneurship is not just an American phenomenon; it is now becoming a worldwide movement. None-the-less, it seems the U.S. is more active than most other countries in recognizing entrepreneurship as a formal academic discipline and putting opportunity-driven entrepreneurship into practice.

Propensity for Entrepreneurship

Working for someone else is a product of an organized society and, as such, is compulsory for most people. Humans have a natural instinct for accomplishment, or a desire to use their individual talents, skills, and abilities for some purposeful activity. In Thorstein Veblen's 1899 book, *The Theory of the Leisure Class,* he said the *propensity for achievement* stays with a person forever as a pervasive trait and it shapes the individual's whole life. However, in industrialized societies, most people find it *preferable* to work for others, as an outlet for this natural instinct, rather than working for oneself. Employment by others provides the opportunity to acquire initial work experience, business skills, and a regular income. In advanced nations, more than 90 percent of the working population is employed by others. Thus, having a steady income is a stronger psychological attraction for most than starting one's own business. Nevertheless, *all people are latent entrepreneurs.* There is a strong desire in all people for maximum use of their individual talents in a chosen occupation or profession.

All people are latent entrepreneurs.

Even when presented with an opportunity, only a small percentage of people take the risk and start their own enterprise. What are the major factors that shape the decision to start and operate a business? Well, the truth is that we don't know all the factors. Entrepreneurship literature identifies a number of determinants, including the quest for personal achievement, job displacement, avoiding unemployment, a high desire for wealth, a desire for independence, perceived knowledge of a good business concept, having an active entrepreneurial role model, and social/cultural/political displacement. A combination of these factors is normally involved, but the making and timing of that critical decision to start one's own business tends to be individual specific.

Entrepreneurs as Risk-Takers

A common fallacy is the general public's belief that entrepreneurs are high risk-takers. It is simply not true. Entrepreneurs are *moderate risk-takers,* according to David McClelland's world-wide research found in *The Achieving Society.* Entrepreneurs desiring to go into business will often test the waters while remaining employed full-time. They frequently will develop a one-page business concept document and use it to get feedback from others about their prospective venture. Most entrepreneurs never gamble in real life. Why? They have no control over the outcome. Many do not invest in the public market for the same reason. Entrepreneurs appear to take huge risk in the start-up of new ventures, but most often that is done only after serious thought, study of the market and careful analysis of their prospects for creating a successful venture.

Even Bill Gates is an example of a moderate risk-taker. Bill Gates and Paul Allen went to prep school together in Seattle where they gained some early computing experience on the school's one rented computer from General Electric. In Gates' first year at Harvard, the two began discussing starting a company. In Gates' sophomore year, he and Allen built a workable BASIC computer program for the Altair 8800. At that time Gates realized the software market had been born. He waited another 12 months, until his junior year, to leave Harvard (not as a dropout, but on a formal "leave of absence" in case things didn't work out), and then they formed Microsoft. Gates was very careful to make calculated moves along the way in developing the company. He certainly is a risk mitigator and not a high risk-taker.

Microsoft's first real break came when they secured a contract from IBM to develop an operating system for the company's first personal computer. How this young start-up company was able to get such a major contract from IBM is a story in itself. Back home, Gates' Mother was the first female president of the United Way of King County; serving on her executive committee was John Akers, who later became Chairman and CEO of IBM and also John Opel, who preceded Akers in both positions. Mothers obviously brag about their children and their endeavors. So it is not who you know, but who your Mother knows that may influence your destiny.

Stages of Venture Development

Preparing to start a business typically occurs over a period of time, unless you are thrust into emergency mode by losing a job, or arriving as an immigrant in a country without a financial source of livelihood. Also, entrepreneurship is rarely a first occupation since people normally gain business experience and skills by working for others. Individuals usually pass through various stages of development in making a decision to open their own business. The venture development stages outlined below are presented in a logical sequence; however, the steps frequently overlap and do not always occur in the order presented.

Discomfort. There is discomfort in one's life due to a variety of causes such having a lousy job or no job at all, wanting to make a change in one's occupation, desiring to live in a distant location, seeking more personal and political freedom, and/or migrating to another country.

Ideation. One begins dreaming and developing ideas for a better future for oneself and one's family. Dreaming increases one's level of energy and helps to create a clear concept of a more desired future. Such dreaming includes the visualization, creation, and recognition of a number of ideas regarding creating a better lifestyle. Observing other successful entrepreneurs as role models often stimulates a dream of having one's own business.

Commitment. At some point, the individual makes a personal decision to change. This decision is the first step of a commitment to pursue a more suitable career alternative. Frequently one's commitment is formalized by sharing future intentions with associates and family members. The development of a commitment generates lots of human energy and stimulates the mind.

Development. Previous and present work experiences become more important as one prepares for their business. Closer association is made with a business-experienced family member, with business associates, and with other entrepreneurial role models. One reads magazines and books on starting a business and attends local entrepreneurship seminars. An initial business plan is often constructed at this point.

Start-Up. The business is started in a formal sense. The legal form of organization is determined and a business license is secured. A business location is determined and necessary requirements for producing and marketing the service or product are made.

Sustaining. Anyone can start a business, but the real challenge for an entrepreneur is to ensure its growth and profitability over the long run. The entrepreneur must properly execute three essential operational business functions - production, marketing and finance - in order to sustain a successful business in the long run.

Typically, a very small percentage of people actually decide to become entrepreneurs. The most often quoted figure is about five percent of the population in developed countries. Yet, a majority of individuals everywhere desire to have their own business with the idea of creating individual wealth. Most people never get beyond the discomfort and ideation stages. But the real purpose of listing the above six stages of starting a business is for you to determine which stage you are at in starting your business. A major purpose of this book is to assist individuals in moving toward stage five, that of starting their global enterprise. Now, let us take a closer look at the entrepreneur and the process of entrepreneurship.

Six Types of Entrepreneurs

The most frequently quoted definition of an entrepreneur is an individual who starts a business where one did not previously exist. This definition does not tell us much about the person, but only what has been accomplished. A better definition is this: *Entrepreneurship is a process where individuals seek to use their talents, efforts, and resources to create and/or grow ventures that capitalize on business opportunities and thereby create value.* In most instances, a person's prior work experience is the most important factor shaping the type of entrepreneur they are likely to become. Broadly, there are six kinds of entrepreneurs: the nascent entrepreneur who has business aspirations, but has yet to start a venture; the entrepreneur, a person who has started one or more businesses; and the serial entrepreneur, a person like Richard Branson, who has started and supports many ventures, or America's own Larry Ellison, an Organizational Entrepreneur who has acquired over 80 companies.

Entrepreneurship is the process where individuals seek to use their talents, efforts, and resources to create and/or grow ventures that capitalize on business opportunities and thereby create value.

We can be more specific in identifying six kinds of entrepreneurs, based on the various characteristics of the business entity they develop. The six different types of entrepreneurial entities are presented as follows:

Individual Entrepreneur. The Individual Entrepreneur is a person who decides to open and operate a small "Mom and Pop" retail trade or service business. The specific kind of business or industry chosen is not too important. The business may be a neighborhood grocery, a clothing store, a used furniture shop, a picture framing business, or a restaurant. What is important is that they are entrepreneurs operating their own business. The Individual Entrepreneur typically earns a livelihood income and rarely creates a large business. Retail trade is often chosen because of the ease of entry and small investment required. To operate such a business does not require much education or business experience. These entrepreneurs gain a limited amount of business experience, mainly through trial and error, in operating their business. Some academics consider this individual a small business person and not a real entrepreneur.

Craft-oriented Entrepreneur. Craft-oriented Entrepreneurs will start a business based on personal skill or knowledge developed over a period of years. They have limited education and are often skilled individuals, such as electricians, plumbers, carpenters or furniture makers. They typically start businesses based on producing a single product or service they have personally mastered. In some instances, Craft-oriented Entrepreneurs learn their trade from parents or serve as apprentices in local trade organizations. Their businesses tend to be small in scale, have one level of management, and lack separation of line and staff employees. Business growth is limited to the extent of the Craft-oriented Entrepreneur's personal skill and experience. The Craft-oriented Entrepreneur's firm usually does not grow into a large business, for craft-oriented individuals are often unable or unwilling to give up performing the physical work they know best.

Technical Entrepreneur. Technical Entrepreneurs move up the scale in education and base their businesses on something beyond themselves, such as an increase in technical knowledge and the use of other people's skills. Very often, Technical Entrepreneurs will have college training involving their technical specialty. Even though the venture may be small in the beginning, it has the potential for becoming a large-scale venture. Technical Entrepreneurs are likely to expand their business operations by bringing in other technical personnel, and offering additional products and services to an increasing number of customers. Sales turnover can be high as a result of added value from additional personnel and exploiting new technology.

Organizational Entrepreneur. This entrepreneur is not wed to a single technology, product or industry, but is an opportunist. Organizational Entrepreneurs use their intellectual capabilities to buy, sell and develop several business entities rather than focusing on a single business. They will develop a good management structure to ensure their various businesses continue to operate in the event of their absence, or their sudden departure from the firm. Their greatest challenge is that of finding businesses they desire, buying them, and then keeping their management team motivated.

Corporate Entrepreneur. The Corporate Entrepreneur is often referred to as an *intrapreneur* [an awkward word]. This is a person who facilitates the development of a new venture within a large corporation. Corporate Entrepreneurs actively promote introduction, development and marketing of new products and services that prospectively contribute to the firm's growth and profitability. Enterprising options for the Corporate Entrepreneur are spin-off ventures operating as an internal strategic business unit or as an independent external business. Corporate Entrepreneurs are often technical

R&D individuals, or marketing people who conceive and develop a new product not being offered by their corporate employer. They must be both manager and entrepreneur to spawn a new venture from within the corporate organization.

Global Entrepreneur. The G/E is representative of the highest level of entrepreneurship. G/Es are true cosmopolitans rather than locals. They are well-educated and have a wealth of new world business savvy. Their venture may even go global at the birth of the enterprise. They know that being big, in terms of physical resources, does not matter much anymore. The extensive use of information technology and the Internet minimizes the advantages of bigness and opens up unparalleled opportunities. They understand that business success is based much more on their mental attributes than on physical resources. Their major responsibility is to spot technology gaps in various parts of the world and to exploit them with new products, services, solutions and ideas. G/Es are uninhibited in their desire to create substantial wealth for themselves and their associates.

A world in turmoil creates ripe opportunities for this new knowledge-oriented G/E who has a strong desire for creating substantial wealth. The accelerated pace of global change that's upon us, whether political, social or economic, is very desirable for the G/E because such disturbances often create significant opportunities for them to exploit.

The six basic types of entrepreneurs are shown in Figure 3.1. Of the six, G/Es have a greater kindred relationship with Technical Entrepreneurs and Corporate Entrepreneurs than they have with Individual or Craft-oriented Entrepreneurs. G/Es often get involved in advanced technology at the conceptual and physical level, as they search for their unique business opportunity. However, most Technical Entrepreneurs are not G/Es. In some instances, the G/E may begin as a Corporate Entrepreneur, and then spin off their new enterprise as a separate business entity. The true G/E prefers to fly alone, unfettered by the boundaries imposed by a corporate parent.

Figure 3.1
Continuum of Entrepreneurship

Individual – Craft –Technical – Organizational – Corporate - Global

---

Entrepreneurship: The Process and the Person

Entrepreneurship can be viewed from two perspectives: as a *process* and as a *person*. Is it important to distinguish between the two? Sure it is. Just ask the question, "How can you tell the dance from the dancers?" In this regard, one can view entrepreneurship – the process – as the "dance" and the entrepreneurs – the individuals – as the "dancers." The entrepreneurship process is a series of creative activities that will bring about *birth* and *growth* in both *small* and *large* organizations. The entrepreneur is a person who performs specific venture-creating activities and/or promotes growth initiatives in existing organizations. Typically, the Individual Entrepreneur's normal habitat is the micro-small or medium-size enterprise, whereas the Corporate Entrepreneur's natural habitat is the large business organization.

**Entrepreneurship is the "dance"
and the entrepreneurs are the "dancers."**

Entrepreneurship as a Six-Step Process

Entrepreneurship has been sufficiently analyzed over the past 30 years that we can accurately describe it as a *process* with specific *action steps*. The ultimate purpose of entrepreneurship is to give "birth" to a new enterprise and/or to "grow" an existing business. So, the entrepreneurship process involves all the creative skills, resources and other activities a person utilizes in starting and/or growing a new business venture. The entrepreneur engages in this new-venture creating process to capitalize on one or more opportunistic ideas, and/or to significantly promote growth of an existing business.

The six action steps below describe the *entrepreneurship process*; all of them are necessary for starting a new venture.

1. *Discovery of a Business Opportunity.* Entrepreneurs are always searching for opportunities, and, consequently, they find them more frequently than others. They are looking for unfulfilled market niches, gaps in the application of technology, or markets where people are not being served efficiently and effectively. Opportunity development is discussed in more detail in chapter five, "Capitalizing on Opportunities."

2. *Definition of the Business Concept.* Entrepreneurs ask themselves these questions: "Can this opportunity be turned into a viable business venture?" If so, then, "What is my product or service, what is my target market, how can I produce the products, what technology is needed, what funds are necessary, what organizational structure is needed, and what are the personnel

requirements to start and run the business?" These questions are answered in an executive summary and a formal business plan.

3. *Acquisition of Resources.* Capital and people are the most important resources initially needed for a new venture. With these two resources in hand, the rest tends to fall into place. A sound business plan is often a requisite for resource acquisition. The business plan is the vehicle that can be used to communicate what the business is about and what resources are needed from business associates, investors, and suppliers.

4. *Start-up of the New Business.* Just as a pilot uses a checklist in preparing for a flight, so does the entrepreneur use a checklist for things necessary for starting a business. Such a checklist is normally part of the business plan. Key items are the incorporation of the business, legal requirements, accounting, insurance, personnel, location, physical facilities, equipment, Web presence, license, utilities, logo, business cards, and stationery.

5. *Marketing of Products and Services.* The basics of the marketing game plan are included in the business plan. Marketing is seldom a dominant strength of entrepreneurs. Their normal strength is making or producing the product or service. A concise definition of the product is necessary, along with an identification of the target market. As a result of market research for the business plan, customers are identified who are willing and able to purchase the product at the asking price. Identifying the "willing and able" means doing market research to ensure that potential customers both desire the product and have the money to pay for it. Otherwise, there is no market.

6. *Ensuring Business Growth.* A major purpose of every business is to generate an increasing flow of revenue into the firm. A continuous growth curve is necessary to attract competent employees and to acquire additional capital for the venture. Finally, the initial start-up plan gives way to a broader strategic plan, which delineates overall corporate expansion and market penetration on a local, national and global basis. The firm will also attempt to build brand awareness for the business and its products and services.

This six-step process is common to all entrepreneurs when starting new ventures. Each step is most critical to the success of the new business venture. Unfortunately, most entrepreneurs start their ventures without developing a business plan. Quite often, entrepreneurs will "take the exam before taking the course" – meaning they start their ventures without much experience and with little systematic preplanning. However, if one expects to induce others to seriously consider the venture for investment purposes, a good business plan is a necessity, even though few of them are read carefully. Business plan requirements will be discussed in more detail in chapter nine.

The Entrepreneur as the Person

We have reviewed entrepreneurship as a process, or the "dance." Now let us take a closer look at the individual entrepreneur, the "dancer," who actively puts this process into practice. Entrepreneurs are unique and few in number. They are different from the average person in the way they think, behavior, and in their respond to their surrounding world. Their personal backgrounds and motivation vary so much that it is impossible to predict in advance who will be a successful entrepreneur. When asked the question, "Do you want to start your own business?" Eight to ninety percent of people will answer *yes*, but only a small percentage of these actually start a business. However, the desire for self-employment seems to be universal. Having your own business is a strong personal motivator. Therefore, the motivation embodied in owning a business, coupled with an innate desire to become independently wealthy, are clearly two of the most dominant motives of entrepreneurs everywhere. People who espouse the belief that money is not a strong motivation for entrepreneurs are simply out of touch with reality.

At this point, entrepreneurs can be examined only after the fact, that is, after they have started their ventures. Many academics have described entrepreneurs in terms of their personal characteristics. Annette de Klerk, in her doctoral dissertation at the University of South Africa, searched business literature and found academic scholars had identified 71 distinct personal characteristics, or individual differences, among entrepreneurs. De Klerk ranked the frequency with which these characteristics appeared in the research literature and concluded that David McClelland's *Need-to-Achieve* motive and J. Rotter's *Locus of Control* dimension were ranked as the two most important entrepreneurial characteristics. Her research was then directed towards using these characteristics to determine the differences, if any, between existing entrepreneurs and non-entrepreneurs.[22] No known test can be reliably used to determine in advance who is likely to become an entrepreneur. Hopefully, future research will develop a predictive model of entrepreneurship. Such knowledge would be useful in career counseling and in identifying individuals who would most likely benefit from entrepreneurial training. Meanwhile, we continue studying existing entrepreneurs from many different perspectives, searching for characteristics that may be used to predict who is likely to become one. So far, none have been found. The most widely accepted psychological and behavioral description of an entrepreneur is based on David McClelland's Need-to-Achieve theory. De Clerk's recognition of the importance of McClelland's Need-to-Achieve theory was further supported by Wayne Stewart, in his extensive research effort identifying personal characteristics of entrepreneurs found in *Psychological Correlates of Entrepreneurship.*

McClelland conducted extensive worldwide research on entrepreneurs and reported his findings in many sources, including his book, *The Achieving Society,* which was mentioned earlier in this chapter. McClelland discovered entrepreneurs have four unique *thought patterns* that are expressed in the following major themes:[23]

1. *They set a self-imposed standard of excellence.* Entrepreneurs desire to set their own achievement goals rather than having others telling them what to do. That is a major reason why they prefer operating their own ventures.
2. *They have thoughts about outperforming others.* Entrepreneurs firmly believe they can operate their ventures better and more creatively than their competitors. Competitors just serve as a yardstick against which to measure their own performance.
3. *They desire to make* a *unique contribution.* Entrepreneurs believe the products/services they produce, along with their unique venture, will make a difference in the world.
4. *They seek to achieve long-term career objectives.* Entrepreneurs want their business to be successful over the long run in order to materially benefit themselves and their families.

The above four themes represent *internal thoughts* of entrepreneurs that McClelland discovered as he researched successful entrepreneurs while they were operating their ventures. In addition to the above entrepreneurial thoughts, McClelland found that entrepreneurs also have *personal behavioral patterns* that are quite different from the average person. His research showed that successful entrepreneurs seek situations they can influence and experience in the following manner:

1. *They seek personal responsibility for their results.* All the entrepreneurs preferred to own and operate their own business rather than work for others.
2. *They set moderate, but difficult goals for themselves.* Entrepreneurs are optimistic about what they can achieve. They will set tough goals they can accomplish, but not an impossible goal.
3. *They seek regular and concrete feedback regarding their performance.* Entrepreneurs thrive on business growth, and prefer immediate feedback of results, rather than waiting for long-term accomplishments.

4. *They constantly search for better ways of doing things.* Entrepreneurs are never satisfied with current results for themselves or others, and they are always seeking further improvement.

Even though these thoughts and behaviors are fairly reliable in describing existing entrepreneurs, they still are based on after-the-fact results. No one has been successful in developing these or any other criteria into a *predictive model* of entrepreneurship that can tell us in advance *who* will start a new venture. There are so many situational variables involved in entrepreneurship that a predictive model is very unlikely.

However, McClelland's Need-to-Achieve theory has been taught to existing entrepreneurs with positive measurable results. In Washington, D.C., a group of small-business people were trained to think and behave in accordance with McClelland's Need-to-Achieve theory. A comparable, parallel control group did not take the training, but as used for comparison of results a year later. The business people who had completed Need-to-Achieve training experienced greater business expansion, hired more employees, and increased sales and profits to a greater degree than the control group. A similar study was conducted in the Midwestern United States, involving business farmers. Again, those who received Need-to-Achieve training acquired more land, grew more crops, and made more money than did the control group of farmers who did not receive such training.[24]

Even though McClelland's Need-to-Achieve theory cannot be used to predict who is likely to become an entrepreneur; the importance of his theory is that we know *entrepreneurship is a learnable process.* The entrepreneurship process can be taught to individuals who desire to have their own businesses and it can be intensified in individuals who operate a current business. There are many who believe that entrepreneurs are born, and not developed through education or training. In regard to *nature* or *nurture,* entrepreneurship is unquestionably not an either/or situation. Obviously people are *born* with certain personal characteristics that will help them become successful entrepreneurs. There are also certain skills that can be *learned* that will help individuals achieve business success before and after becoming an entrepreneur. Clearly, entrepreneurship has been and can be *nurtured, supported and enhanced* through various types of formal and informal education and training. The bottom line is *yes*! You can learn to be any one of the six types of entrepreneurs.

Entrepreneurship is a learnable process that can be taught, nurtured, supported, and enhanced through various types of education and training.

The Search for Exceptional Business Growth

As a result of increasing competitive pressures in the global marketplace, many large corporations today recognize the need for more entrepreneurial endeavors. As organizations get larger, they tend to become less flexible and more bureaucratic in nature, and, unfortunately, they lose the entrepreneurial spirit of their youth. When this occurs, business leaders can rejuvenate their organizations and stimulate new growth through an internal revival of the entrepreneurial spirit that was clearly present when the firm was young. Executives in large corporations are ever mindful of the economic achievement contributed by small and medium-size enterprises worldwide. Now many such executives are seeking to bring about a similar pattern of accelerated growth in their large firms.

It is apparent that a proactive growth strategy for large American companies is urgently needed to cope with the after affects of the recent worldwide recession. Retailers have to adjust to a reduction in consumer demand as consumers reduce their personal debts, having less money to spend on goods and services. In the past 20 years personal, consumption in the U.S. has amounted to 70 percent of GDP, and in the future that figure is likely to be reduced to a 50 to 60- percent level. American manufacturers will be faced with limited growth for a number of years. Growth increases will not come from domestic consumption, but from countries like China, India, and other developing economies now growing at 8 to 10 percent a year. Major challenges are in store for large American companies as they strive to achieve significant future growth. Entrepreneurship is a tool that can be utilized to help address these challenges.

Achieving Growth Through Corporate Entrepreneurship

However, academic research shows that large, entrepreneurial-oriented organizations are not very prevalent today, even in the United States. A few exceptions are major firms like Apple, General Electric, IBM, Hewlett Packard, DuPont and Cisco. These firms are known for their strong entrepreneurial orientations. Internationally, Nokia, Michelin and Samsung are entrepreneurial leaders. In literature on the subject, The Corporate Entrepreneurship process has many labels: Motorola calls it "self-renewal," Philip Morris labels it "individual initiative," and Sony says it is being a "pioneer" again. Regardless of the label, large businesses can use the Corporate Entrepreneurship process to facilitate extraordinary growth and to energize their associates.

Reviving the entrepreneurial spirit in large corporations is a difficult challenge. It involves harnessing the qualities of bigness and smallness at the same time. Top executives of large corporations cannot simply mandate an increase in entrepreneurial spirit in their organizations. Entrepreneurship must be actively encouraged, nurtured and supported by senior management. Since Corporate Entrepreneurs are not "playing with their own marbles," they must abide by the restrictive governance of the parent corporation, which frequently dampens the entrepreneurial spirit. Coping with the corporate environment is a more difficult role than that Traditional Entrepreneurs play in owning and operating a personal venture. One can readily see that Corporate Entrepreneurs have to be a hybrid of sorts—part manager and part entrepreneur. This why Corporate Entrepreneurship endeavors are a fertile breeding ground for future G/Es.

Now, who are these Corporate Entrepreneurs that are likely to become G/Es? Well, there is no definitive route to becoming an entrepreneur in a big company. Corporate Entrepreneurs may enter the process anywhere along the line, from generating the product/venture idea to developing the product and delivering it to the marketplace. The internal entrepreneur can be the inventor of a product or service, the technician who constructs a working prototype, the champion of the idea, or the one who leads the way from initial creation to a successful product in the marketplace – or, alternatively, to a fully functioning, external business entity. When Corporate Entrepreneurs have a strong technical background, they are good at developing and promoting their products, but they often lack essential team-building skills. Such technical entrepreneurs are often short on the political skills necessary to work through layers of management, and frequently lack an understanding of marketing and business skills necessary to create a viable spin-off business. These shortcomings are also characteristic of most individual entrepreneurs starting small ventures.

At times, new product promoters will get their idea developed to the extent they are ready to be turned into an independent business. At this point, they will need proven managers to develop and grow the new venture. Very likely, the product promoter will go back to researching and developing other products. In such instances, line managers will then take over as product champion. Getting the product developed and to the market in the large corporation is not a solo effort. It includes the assistance of people in many departments. This is why successful Corporate Entrepreneurs will need a variety of management and entrepreneurial skills. These skills will serve G/Es well in operating their own venture.

We know most entrepreneurs tend to be young, but some are middle-aged and beyond. Gifford Pinchot, in his book, *Intrapreneuring* (his term was first used to describe corporate entrepreneurship), notes that one intrapreneur at Boeing Aircraft was a 63 year-old aeronautic scientist with a windmill hobby. This scientist contributed significantly to developing Boeing's 200-foot wind-power generator, even though he was nearing retirement. So, being an entrepreneur is not always a function of age or education, even though in developed countries most entrepreneurs are college-educated. Being an entrepreneur, or a corporate entrepreneur, is more of a *state of mind* than anything else. Entrepreneurial ideas and endeavors can emerge and be developed at any point in one's life, given the desire, the right opportunity and persistence.

Many G/Es come directly from corporate environments, especially from large international organizations. Through their work experience, they gain invaluable knowledge regarding products, markets and global operations. The G/E will frequently break away from his or her corporate parent with an idea for a prospective product the firm doesn't intend to commercialize. This situation is particularly common in highly innovative businesses that generate large numbers of new product concepts. In many instances, the parent firm will support the G/E with start-up resources and direct investments in the new venture.

Education and Development of Entrepreneurs

Entrepreneurship has been well accepted as a formal academic discipline, particularly in the U.S., where more than 1600 colleges and universities now "teach" the subject. At many of these institutions, one can earn a Bachelor's Master's or a Ph.D. degree in the subject. Yes, it is possible that entrepreneurship can be *encouraged*, *learned*, and put into *practice* by nearly everyone, everywhere. However, there is also no question that some people are endowed by *nature* with certain attributes that are helpful in being an entrepreneur. The same is true of physicians with a friendly bedside manner. They will be more successful and pleasing to patients than those who are abrupt and harsh in their relationships.

Entrepreneurial ideas and endeavors can emerge and be developed at any point in one's life—given the desire, the right opportunity and a conducive business climate. Again, one's age, sex, skills, education, or even where one lives in the world does not matter. It is an established fact that both Individual Entrepreneurship and Corporate Entrepreneurship are known, *learnable processes* involving an original conceptualization, development, and commercialization of innovative products or services desired in the marketplace. And today, these opportunities for entrepreneurs are more abundant than in any previous period in history.

Everyone has the capacity to be an entrepreneur at any age - *it is an individual choice,* sometimes a forced choice for unemployed individuals.

This is called "unintended entrepreneurship." In developed countries, some 95 percent of the population have been reluctant to "cut the cord" from their security blanket of regular employment and venture out into their own business. This is changing with increasing layoffs by industry. Individuals recognize they no longer have job security with big corporate organizations. Many see that owning and operating their own business is the best form of job security in the New Global Economic World.

Of the 5 percent who typically start a venture, most will fail several times before succeeding. Others will succeed beyond their wildest imagination. Several entrepreneurs who have changed our modern business world are Steve Jobs and Steve Wozniak of Apple, who were first to commercialize the personal computer, and Bill Gates and Paul Allen who started Microsoft, a company that has led the way in developing operating software for computers. Many other entrepreneurs have followed these pioneers in developing Internet information technology and innovative products and services businesses that have literally changed the face of the business world. We are clearly in a new age of discovery in all disciplines, as evidenced by the cloning of animals, the mapping of the human genome, and the capturing of images of exploding galaxies sent back from outer space by the Hubble telescope and the Mars explorers. There has never been a better time for G/Es to capitalize on the many business opportunities that are emerging in a radically changing world environment.

The Global Growth of Entrepreneurship

The most extensive international study of entrepreneurship is the annual *Global Entrepreneurship Monitor* (GEM), a comprehensive study of the status of entrepreneurship activities in 54 countries by a leading world research consortium. The 2009 study showed that entrepreneurial activities declined in most of GEM's countries due to the global economic downturn; however, a significant minority of would-be entrepreneurs in the wealthier countries saw the recession as a potential for increasing opportunities for their businesses. The GEM report is very comprehensive in its view of entrepreneurial activity and analyzes the subject utilizing different types and phases of entrepreneurship.

Countries in this research report were grouped into three stages of economic development, as defined by the World Economic Forum's Global Competitiveness Report: factor-driven economies - dominated by businesses that are extractive in nature, as in Saudi Arabia; efficiency-driven economies - dominated by low-cost, scale-intensive national businesses, as in China; and innovation-driven economies - dominated by production of new and unique goods and services, often using pioneering methods, as in the USA. The study recognized that all three principal types of economic activity - factor, efficiency and innovation-driven - are present in every country, though one tends to predominate. As countries develop, they move from one stage to the next with innovation-driven being the most advanced.

The proportion of necessity-driven entrepreneurs, i.e., people starting businesses because they had no other choice, increased in 2009. As to be expected, necessity-driven self-employment activities tend to be higher in less-developed countries. Since these countries are unable to keep pace with the demand for jobs in high-productivity sectors, many people must create their own economic activity by starting a venture. As an economy develops, the level of necessity-driven entrepreneurial activity gradually declines as productive sectors grow and more employment opportunities are developed. At times necessity-driven entrepreneurship occurs in developed countries, usually when unemployment rates are excessively high as in the U.S.

There is widespread agreement on the importance of entrepreneurship and three major components - *attitude, aspiration,* and *activities.* These three entrepreneurial components have an impact on shaping the economic development of countries, according to the authors of the GEM's report. One of the principal measures in the GEM study is what the authors define as total "early-stage-entrepreneurial activity," that is, the number of people involved in setting up a business and/or the actions of owner-managers in growing an existing business. You will recall we defined entrepreneurship earlier as those individuals involved in starting a new venture and/or engaged in growing an existing business.[25]

Entrepreneurship Slowly Emerging in Europe

The GEM report shows that North America is ahead of most European countries in the percentage of adults starting new businesses. A previous GEM study showed that one in 10 Americans were trying to start a new venture, in contrast to one in 30 Britons, one in 45 Germans and one in 67 in Finland. However, both the U.S. and the E.U. lag behind the developing Asian countries of China, Korea, India, and Thailand, as those countries are forced into necessity-driven entrepreneurship. These developing countries offer fertile opportunities for emerging G/Es and existing small-business owners.

In Europe, we find Old World attitudes that shun risk-taking are in part to blame for a lower level of entrepreneurship activities than is found in the U.S. Many European do not respect entrepreneurship a profession of choice for themselves or their children. Ernest-Antoine Selliere, president of the French employers' association, Mouvement Entrepreses de France (MEDEF), observed recently: "Most of the French education system is in the hands of socialists, and it teaches youngsters that entrepreneurship is dangerous, greedy and creates inequality." Fortunately, this condition is rapidly changing. The European Union has awakened to the potential economic growth that can be generated by entrepreneurs and their small and medium-size enterprises.

Consequently, the E.U. is now actively encouraging and funding entrepreneurship in many forms. In Lisbon, in March 2000, the E.U. set a very ambitious growth goal for Europe: "To become the most competitive, knowledge-based economy in the world by 2010." Truly, this was a very ambitious goal; however, they never achieved it. Even Russia, where entrepreneurship was previously outlawed under the old U.S.S.R. regime, now has a Russian Union of Industrialists and Entrepreneurs. France's President, Nicolas Sarkozy, is actively promoting entrepreneurship. He sponsored France's first World Entrepreneurship Forum in 2008, and his 2010 Forum had more than 100 guests from 40 countries for the event held in Lyon, France. The forum is a worldwide think tank dedicated to entrepreneurs and their creation of wealth and social justice.

Reuven Brenner, writing in *Forbes Global,* says the U.S. has stimulated economic growth better than any other country in the world, mainly through its entrepreneurial efforts. He says, "It [the U.S.] has created a system in which anyone with talent and energy has access to the financial resources needed for business success. That alone will not lead to fortune, but it pretty much guarantees that talented people do not fail for the lack of capital in starting a business." Brenner maintains that open access to capital, and not physical resources, is why the U.S. is the most economically prosperous and the most powerful nation in the world.[26] Brenner's thoughts are challenged today with a severe shortage of start-up funding. Yet no other society has so far been able to adopt the unique features of opportunity-driven entrepreneurship and the free enterprise system currently existing in the United States. Obviously, it is naive to think everyone wants to be Americanized. Most do not. But many are interested in the economic prosperity of the U.S., its movies, and music, but perhaps not the American society. For example, France's former President Chirac reflected this sentiment when he once said that he endorsed the U.S. market economy, but not its society in general. His belief was that France offered a better total quality of life for its citizens.

Entrepreneurship does not thrive well in countries like Zaire, Algeria, Iran, Syria, Cuba, and Russia. At present, Russia is still struggling economically after a decade of freedom from communism. It lacks an effective rule of law; it has an inefficient tax collection system; hyper-inflation has wiped out most individual savings; people have little inheritances; ownership of private property is limited; and there is a shortage of investment capital. In spite of all these impediments, a number of legitimate entrepreneurs thrive in Russia. But there is a slim chance that entrepreneurship will become a driving force for most Russians for a number of years, given the current conditions. However, G/Es from outside Russia, having money and associating with proactive Russian partners, can and do succeed, even in that turbulent economic environment.

From Russia …

The richest man in Russia is the 42-year-old metal mogul Mikail D. Prokhorov. Two years ago, he resigned from a leadership role at the Norilsk Nickel Company, Russia's largest nickel - producing company, and later sold his stake in the company. According to the 2009 *Forbes Global*, his net worth is valued at $9.5 billion. *Forbes* says there are 32 Russian billionaires, worth a combined $102 billion, as compared with 87 last year. Russia also has 8 (1.6 percent) of *Fortune's* 500 Global Companies. Prokhorov says he has always "had an inside desire to have his own money and to be independent." That sounds very entrepreneurial. He started very young, selling stone-washed jeans, and then made a big leap into state banking. With the bank's help, he bought Norilsk Nickel, and business increased rapidly under his corporate leadership. He once hung an organizational chart in his office, and under his name was this label – Citizen, the Russian Federation - instead of Chief Executive Officer.

Some 208 countries in the world lie in between the unlimited economic freedom found in the United States and the massive restrictions found in dictatorial countries. Many opportunities are opening up to people throughout the world. Today, there are extremely successful entrepreneurs in almost every part of the world. The important thing to remember is this: Anyone can become an entrepreneur almost anywhere in the world. The entrepreneurship process can be learned and can be put into practice. However, it is certainly more difficult to become an entrepreneur for people who they live in a country that has not and does not actively encourage, promote and support a strong entrepreneurial environment. In order to avoid insurmountable odds, some may have to start their business outside their own country, or change their residence by moving to a country more favorable to entrepreneurship.

Anyone can become an entrepreneur almost anywhere in the world.

It is a well-established fact that entrepreneurs breed other entrepreneurs. A very high percent of present-day entrepreneurs have parents who were also entrepreneurs. A few elite American entrepreneurs are taking a further step to ensure their children have a head start in entrepreneurship. They have enrolled their children in a "Kids Money Camp," where kids can learn about topics such as operating their own business, the stock market, the power of compounding, the "rule of 72," money mergers, stocks, bonds, unit trust, and even the importance of charitable giving. Susan Bradley, a self-styled financial guru in Florida, has been operating the Kids Money Camp for the past seven years, and recently she had a class of 13 kids ranging in age from 11 to 19. One of the student entrepreneurs started *her* own can-recycling business at age 7. She donates 30 percent of her profits to charity, spends 20 percent for gifts for friends and relatives, and puts the rest in her own bank account. One might say, "Only in America." Not so! Now Bradley wants to take her Kids Money Camp global. Clearly, the birth of another potential Global Entrepreneur. [27]

Start Your Engines Global Entrepreneurs

In this chapter, we have outlined the process of how you can start your own business. Just starting the venture is the easy part, but making it profitable, commensurate with the time effort and resources required, is the difficult part of the game. What is required is serious thought and preparation of a personal development plan. That plan should include becoming a G/E and creating personal wealth with a number of associates, here and abroad.

Individuals have a choice of starting their venture at any point along the continuum of six entrepreneurs—from Individual Entrepreneur to Global Entrepreneur. Existing entrepreneurs can also expand their present business into the global arena. As economic opportunities continue to unfold in both developed and developing countries, G/Es are clearly going to be first on the international stage, ready with their venture ideas for creating new wealth.

So, at this point, the questions are these: Where are you? Are you ready to start? What preparation are you undertaking? Do you have a strong desire to be a G/E? Well, the information presented in this chapter clearly indicates—*the choice is yours.* Your *persistent effort* toward the venture is the key. So go ahead, seize the moment—*start now*—or continue to be left behind while you watch the success of other venture-seeking Global Entrepreneurs as they create their wealth in a dynamic New Global Economic Era.

4

A New Wealth Creating Paradigm

"A nation's real wealth doesn't reside in forests of rubber trees or acres of diamond mines, but in the techniques and technologies for exploiting them."
Thomas A. Stewart

The Nature of Wealth

There are some exciting new views of wealth creation today. While physical limits to economic growth were previously postulated, now that view has been radically challenged. Some claim there is no conceivable obstacle to the perpetual creation of wealth in the New Global World marketplace. Today we can no longer underestimate the power of human ingenuity, particularly when it is unleashed by the incentive of private enterprise and the use of knowledge and technology. Acquiring and exploiting technical knowledge have become essential in creating wealth. It certainly seems economic growth and wealth creation can now be considered infinite—particularly, as evidenced by Global Entrepreneurs (G/Es) taking maximum advantage of knowledge and technology. In capitalism, wealth is considered the method of keeping score. Now being wealthy means not having to work. It means getting up at the "crack of noon." Cash is paid for the Rolls Royce. In addition to the main residence, a condominium is maintained on the ski slopes along with a family ocean home. A number of Rolex watches are in the family. Some family members buy fashionable clothes in Paris, and travelling around the world is paid as it is done. Millions can be given to favorite charities. The urge to spend your money is a perfectly normal human trait. Some call it conspicuous consumption; others even believe it to be sinful. Economists call it the "wealth factor."

Spending is certainly not the "in thing" for all those with wealth. There are many who have wealth, but do not flaunt it. In *The Millionaire Next Door*, Tom Stanley says many will never know some Americans are millionaires because they do not use their wealth to finance a jet-set life style. The average millionaire in the U.S. lives in a $300,000 house and drives a four-year-old American-made automobile. There is no chauffeur or even a swimming pool. Strange as it may seem, it's generally the non-rich who try to look as if they are wealthy. But, unfortunately, the more you spend on looking rich, the less you're likely to be worth, says Stanley. An important point here is not to confuse income with wealth. "Wealth is what you accumulate in assets and not what you make or spend," according to Stanley.[28] So, becoming wealthy involves planning, dedication and surprisingly, for many, a level of frugality. In Dr. Stanley's most recent book, *The Millionaire's Mind,* he tells us how Americans made their wealth in the past. I suggest you add this book to your entrepreneurship library.

One common view of wealth is having an abundance of material resources measured in monetary terms. This abundance of money means having financial security. It provides more *freedom* and *independence* for living a good life, more time to further strive for personal achievement, and the opportunity for personal exploration, travel, and adventure; it also allows one to engage in a broad range of self-improvement activities. What does it take to be classified as wealthy? Well, that depends on where you live. Wealth, like poverty, is a relative term. Wealth in Mozambique is measured in a few hundred dollars a year, whereas, in the U.S., it is measured by hundreds of thousands of dollars. The feeling of being wealthy depends on what others in the community possess. Relative wealth, what you have as compared to your neighbors, has long served as a strong motivational force in the U.S. under the label of "keeping up with the Joneses." The competition of keeping up with the Joneses continues in the U.S. today - with most people not just trying to keep up, but seeking to surpass the Joneses.

There is old wealth and there is new wealth. Some flaunt it while others choose to downplay their wealth. Many non-wealthy people dream about being rich. Today, in the developed world, an increasing number of people are reaching a position of wealth. There is an old saying that "the rich get richer and the poor get poorer." This is particularly true now, since the opportunity for wealth creation has increased as developed economies move rapidly into the Information Age. National leaders are expressing increasing concern regarding the "digital divide" - the chasm between the people who have information technology, and are reaping its benefits, and those who do not possess such technology.

Recently, the richest people in the world have gotten poorer, just like most other people in the developed world. *Forbes* magazine compiles an annual listing of the world's richest people. In 2009, the world's billionaires had a net worth of $3 billion, down 23 percent in 12 months. World billionaires are now at 793, down from 1,125 in 2008. The U.S. has slipped in recent years, but it is still dominant as a repository of wealth in accounting for 44 percent of the money and 45 percent of the listing, up 3 percentage points from 2008. Bill Gates lost $18 million, but regained his title as the world's richest man. Warren Buffett, last year's number one, saw his fortune decline $25 billion, but is still number two, and Mexican titan Carlos Slim Helu maintains his number three slot, but lost $25 billion in 2008.

The U.S. has 359 billionaires, 110 fewer than 2008, as the downturn in the economy continues to take its toll on the super rich. Discount retailing continues to be a wealth generator, with four of the top seven U.S. billionaires being direct descendants of Sam Walton of the Wallmart Corporation. If Sam Walton were living, he would be the richest man in the world. There are 21 new faces on the U.S. list, including Bloomberg's cofounder, Thomas Secunda; Philadelphia Eagles owner, Jeffrey Lurie; and four heirs to the Cargill Commodity fortune. Ted Turner did not fare so well last year, now being number 376 on the U.S. list, with 1.9 billion net worth, and Donald Trump fell to 450, nearly half of his net worth, shrinking down to 1.6 billion. It is of interest to note the largest percentage of the fortunes made by this elite group is from businesses dealing with intangible, knowledge-based assets rather than traditional, physical manufacturing assets characteristic of the Industrial Era.[29]

Shifting of Wealth over the Centuries

Wealth creation shifts from time to time among individuals as well as nations. A fundamental tenet of this book is this: a worldwide shift in the factors that create new wealth in business is clearly underway. Looking at nations over the past thousand years, we have seen a swing in global economic primacy from China, to Italy, to Portugal and Spain, to Britain, to the United States, and now a shift back to China is emerging. It is important to understand the major causes of these shifts in national wealth.

Eighty percent of the world's population lives in Third World countries, and 20 percent lives in First World countries. Most Third World countries are in the Agricultural Era and are struggling to produce enough food to feed their people. Obviously, it is impossible for a large number of Third

World individuals to create substantial wealth in an agricultural economy. A majority of established businesses in the First World countries are also struggling today—not to feed the population, but to transform themselves so they can meet the competitive challenges of the emerging Information Era. It is apparent that opportunities for wealth creation increase as a country enters the Industrial Era and even more so as it enters the Information Era. The giant steps from agriculture to information are extremely important in the wealth-creation process.

Figure 4.1
A Continuum of Wealth Creation

Third World
80 Percent of Humanity

First World
20 Percent of Humanity

Agricultural Era

Industrial Era

Information Era

Amount of Wealth Created

Low

Moderate

High

Many Third World countries are rich in natural resources, such as minerals, gold, diamond, timber and oil. Unfortunately, the extraction of these natural resources is often done by state-owned-and-operated organizations, leaving few opportunities for entrepreneurs. Typically, locals in these countries depend on agriculture for their economic livelihood since there is little industrial production. First World countries are clearly dominant in the Industrial Era, and the top 15 to 25 developed countries have moved into the Information Era. Some even predict a fourth era is on the horizon—the Creativity Era. Wealth-creation opportunities greatly intensify when a country moves from the Agricultural Era to the Industrial Era, and then to the Information Era, as is shown in Figure 4.1. This is partly because technology has a far greater impact in creating new wealth in the manufacturing and information domains than is possible in agriculture.

China is an interesting country and is now making a major transition from its past. China was supreme in creating wealth during the period of 1000 to 1500. David Warsh, in the *Harvard Business Review,* says that, during this creative period, a remarkable outflow of Chinese inventions paved the way for growth. These included paper, printing, porcelain, the wheelbarrow, the compass, gunpowder, the stirrup, and the horse collar, to name a few. But then the Chinese choked off further growth with various restrictive, state-initiated measures that dampened economic activity and inhibited the accumulation of further knowledge.[30]

Surprisingly, we see today a new China emerging as a market economy based on state capitalism. China has had an annual GDP growth rate of 10 percent for the past 10 years. The government is opening its economic doors again; in part it is being forced to do so in order to be a member of the World Trade Organization (WTO). Becoming a member of the WTO forced China to open the door, albeit partially, to foreign brands through easing its manufacturing investment rules and modernizing retail and logistic industries. Nearly everything for sale in China today is made in the country, but consumers there are expressing the desire for foreign-branded products. This opens opportunities for G/Es and other manufacturers to enter the Chinese market. An example is the 2010 Geely Automotive Group purchase of Volvo, a high-profile, foreign auto manufacturer. This acquisition supports China's ambition for supremacy in global auto making; it already has the title as the world's largest vehicle market.[31]

In major cities, Chinese workers can now buy their government-owned flats at a deep discount. State banks are providing mortgage funds, and apartments are being built by private investors. Although few in number, the more affluent Chinese are buying home furnishings at IKEA, a Swedish furniture company with stores in such major cities as Beijing and Shanghai. However, most major industries remain state-owned enterprises. The state still inhibits potential business growth on the Internet, as with Google, and puts restrictions on business ownership. Currently, China's estimated population is 1.6 billion people, representing more than 20 percent of the world's population. The big surge in China's economy has just begun. The Chinese government has put forth clear signals that its near-term economic model over the next five years is a consumer-driven one. This is great news for G/Es. Chinese officials also openly state that their country's resilience in the face of America's meltdown has vindicated China's "state capitalist" system.[32]

The E.U., with its 27 countries, leads the world in GPD (14.8 trillion), followed by the U.S. (14.2T), China (8.7T), Japan (4.1T) and India (3.5T), according to a recent International Monetary Fund report. China just moved to number two with a GDP of 4.7 trillion; it is followed by Japan, India, and Germany in the top five. Japan and Germany are good examples of how a country's status can change in a relative short period of time. After World War II, both countries incurred major damage to their production facilities, but, in the seven decades following the war, they have rebuilt their countries to become the third and fifth largest economies in the world.

The mantle of creating great wealth is shifting, but it currently belongs to the United States. It is the most productive country in the world, creating the most wealth for the largest number of people. The U.S. has the world's highest standard of living for its 310 million people. In 2008, the U.S. had an average annual household income of $50,303, which fell 3.6 percent from 2007. America does have people living in what we define as "poverty." In the U.S., poverty for a family of four people is defined as a household with an income of less than $20,025 a year. This translates to each of the four people living on $16.28 a day. Elsewhere in the world, more than half of the population lives on less than a dollar a day.

What are the Driver of Growth and Development?

What is the driving force that creates such great wealth in the United States? We cited earlier Carl Schramm's answer to this question in his book, *The Entrepreneurial Imperative.* He said our economic clout was not due to education, technology or our manufacturing capability, but to the presence of our *free enterprise system* that promotes and encourages *opportunity-driven entrepreneurship.*[33] In the U.S., a person can establish a formal corporation within hours—not months or years as is found in some restrictive economies. There is open access to start-up funds and investment capital to finance the business during all growth stages. The incentive of having one's own successful business means that there is virtually no limit as to how much money individuals can earn. The United States is a strong magnet, attracting aspiring entrepreneurs from everywhere in the world in their search for the "Golden American Dream" – the desire to create unlimited personal wealth. Supporting this spirit of entrepreneurship in the United States is an *organized society,* one which has gradually developed and been refined over a period of 220-plus years. This society guarantees one's personal safety, assures the ownership of private property, provide a strong rule of law protecting personal assets, and finds support in a unified legal system of business practice and conduct. A conducive social structure and political order provides a solid foundation for encouraging entrepreneurial endeavors in America.

The United States free-enterprise system promotes opportunity-driven entrepreneurship more than any other country in the world.

When will another major economic shift take place? How long will the United States retain its economic leadership in the world? The U.S. will retain this GPD leadership position for a number of years, according to Goldman Sachs, which predicts that China will surpass America's GDP between 2025 and 2030. However, its current 3 percent annual growth substantially lags far behind China and India. While still young in for a country, the U.S. economy is considered by some as being middle-aged; others say it is leaning towards maturity; and a few say it has clearly passed it glory years.

Michael Porter and Scott Stern, in MIT's *Technology Review,* say the U.S. may not recognize the serious threat to its long-term economic strength and growth. The authors analyzed 25 nations, including the U.S., and then developed a "National Innovation Index;" sort of a scorecard of potential future innovative practices. Porter and Stern looked at parameters such as the international patents filed, R&D expenditures, and the share of gross domestic product being spent on higher education. Their findings show that in 1998, the U.S. was clearly in the number one position in the world. But the authors predict the U.S. would fall behind Japan, Finland, Denmark, Sweden and Switzerland in innovation. Porter and Stern were correct in their projections. Many foreign companies are currently spending a higher percentage of sales revenue on R&D than are U.S. firms. Additionally, the U.S. scientific and technical workforce is declining in comparison with other nations.[34]

A real question here is whether the Porter/Stern Index is a true measure of innovation. Innovation is an elusive concept with no generally accepted definition or measure. The eight variables Porter uses are important, but they are at best surrogate indicators of innovation. There are a number of other things to consider when assessing innovation, such as: the quality of a patent, useful outputs generated, and whether the patent serves as a basis for other patents. One must consider the fact that in a knowledge-based economy, many innovations are not patentable. Measuring innovation must go beyond the big items, such as the quantity of patents and R&D expenditures. Consideration must include other factors, such as the dynamics of the U.S. entrepreneurial culture. Porter and Stern never professed to have written the final word on measuring innovation, but their research serves as a "wake-up call" to American business executives. America cannot afford to lag behind in innovation.

Now we fast-forward a few years. Porter and Stern's prediction came true. In the largest and most comprehensive world study ever conducted on innovation, America's position on innovation has dropped from number one in 1998 to number eight in 2009. Singapore, South Korea and Switzerland top the list. This 110-country study was conducted by the Boston Consulting Group, the National Association of Manufacturers, and The Manufacturers Institute, all in the U.S. They looked both at the business outcomes of innovation and at the government's ability to encourage and support innovation through public policy. "America needs a bold innovation strategy," said NAIM President and CEO, John Engler. He further stated, "U.S. manufacturing innovation is at risk. We have fallen behind East Asia and Europe." Yes, we have fallen behind for a couple of reasons. It is a combination of the U.S.'s decline in R&D spending and the fact that other nations, having discovered that innovations are the key to future growth, are substantially outspending America on innovation as a percent of GDP.[35]

To sustain long-term growth, more expenditure toward innovation and technology will be required. Our industrial challenges just a decade ago were to restructure, lower cost, and improve quality of the manufacturing process. Today, such continuous operational improvements are a given. Now companies must acquire and deploy the best, current world technology just in order to stay globally competitive. Perhaps the "America Competes Act" reauthorized by the 2010 111th Congress will help. This act is designed to promote excellence in technology, education, and science with cash "inducement prizes," starting as small as $1000, up to $15 million to design a better light bulb, and a $10 million XPrize to design a production-ready four-person car with 100-mile-per-gallon fuel efficiency. It is clear that innovation has become the most important source of competitive advantage in advanced economies. The Compete Act is an example of the American government not recognizing the nation's serious shortcoming in innovation, for it falls short of what is need in America to spur the level of innovation needed to improve our position in the world.

Capitalism and Wealth Creation

The most successful and sustainable wealth-creating system in the world is free-enterprise capitalism. Capitalism is an economic system characterized by the freedom of individuals and companies to own and use their physical and mental resources for personal gain. Entrepreneurs invest their personal time and material resources in creating businesses that compete in a free market. In a free economy, the key investment decisions regarding production, marketing, and finance are made substantially by individual owners, with little interference or restriction by the state.

In *The Future of Capitalism,* Lester Thurow observes that the 19th and 20th century competitors of capitalism, the other three "isms" - fascism, socialism and communism—are gone or in decay. Capitalism is noted for responding to individual needs, tapping into people's individuality and responding to their basic human motives. Thurow is emphatic when he says, "... no other economic system, other than capitalism, has been made to work [as effectively] anywhere." However, the Marxist argument continues to live in the world today where people feel that earning a profit necessarily means the exploitation of workers. In spite of the remnants of Marxism and socialism, capitalism remains the most viable system for creating maximum wealth for individuals, businesses and nations.[36]

Free-enterprise capitalism creates more wealth today for more people than any other economic system.

Since it took more than 220 years to develop and fine-tune the U.S. economy and its free-enterprise system, it should be no surprise to find that the system cannot be easily or quickly exported to other developing countries. Hernando De Soto of Peru provides some useful insights on this subject in his book, *The Mystery of Capital: Why Capitalism Triumphs in the West and Nowhere Else.* De Soto says the *rule of law* is one of the missing features in developing economies; this is very true today in African countries like Zimbabwe. Another factor restricting the spread of capitalism in many developing countries is an absence of *private property ownership.* Such ownership of property provides a transportable value useful to entrepreneurs. De Soto points out that the single most important source of capital for entrepreneurs in the U.S. has been the equity available in their homes.[37] In most developing countries, prospective entrepreneurs do not own homes, to use as loan collateral. China, the sleeping giant, is now awakening much faster than anticipated, since it is giving people the opportunity to own their homes and other real estate (truly a historic Communist shift). Home ownership in Russia has become more prevalent in the past 10 years. With private ownership comes the incentive to repair, remodel, and better furnish this new possession, in addition to its being a personal asset, that may be used as collateral for borrowing, as is done in America.

No system is perfect, and capitalism has its flaws. Capitalism is attuned to the concept of "survival of the fittest," meaning being the most prepared. Astute business people can amass a personal fortune while others around them may live in poverty. Capitalism promotes situations that create wide inequalities of income and wealth. This condition is both an advantage and a disadvantage. The opportunity for creating substantial wealth, greater than what others have, serves as a powerful incentive for people to become entrepreneurs. The disadvantage of capitalism is that it can create a gap between the rich and poor. Botswana and Brazil are the two countries with the greatest gap between the rich and poor in the world. This gap also represents the difference between the educated and the uneducated, those who have access to knowledge and technology as compared with those who do not. Such a situation can result in social strife and an increase in levels of crime.

A number of new thoughts have been put forth to address some of the negative by-products of free-enterprise capitalism. For example, in *The New Management,* William Halan points out that the zealous pursuit of money by some individuals under capitalism will lead them to violate the law and seriously disregard other negative social consequences of their business endeavors. Halan's 1996 prediction rang true in the early 2000s with the 2007-09 recession. As a result, he predicts a rise in democracy within business enterprises in the form of greater stakeholder influence by employees, customers, investors and the general public. Halan predicts a future economic revolution in business leading managers to act more like "stewards" in exercising new principles of corporate community. Halan was somewhat correct about the development of business stewardship and we will discuss this in chapter ten under the social entrepreneurship.[38]

Economic Freedom and Wealth Creation

There is a direct relationship between personal freedom and the creation of wealth. Economic freedom means that people have the right to own private property, and they can use that property for whatever legal purpose they desire, as long as it does not infringe on the rights of others. Under free enterprise, entrepreneurs can set up and operate a business venture of their choice to seek unlimited personal gain. In *Economic Freedom of the World,* discussed in chapter two, the authors found that countries with the greatest level of economic freedom also generated the greatest wealth, as measured by gross domestic product (GDP) per capita. It is important to note that these countries with high economic freedom also have the highest GDP per capita in the world. Furthermore, the countries with the greatest decline in economic freedom had decreases in their GDP per capita as well. Clearly economic freedom and wealth creation are directly linked.

Countries with the highest level of economic freedom also have the highest standard of living.

There is an important lesson here for business leaders, managers and entrepreneurs. The impact that personal freedom has on the creation of wealth is impossible to ignore. The greater the individual freedom one has the more creative and productive he or she will be. It is clear how personal freedom operates on a national basis, but the concept is also operative at the business level with managers and their employees. The more autonomy people are allowed in their work, the more satisfied and productive they will be. A major reason individuals want to be entrepreneurs is their desire for a high degree of personal freedom in their work situation. Consequently, they seek to be their own boss and prefer few restrictions while they develop and use their creative talents. These are known characteristics of entrepreneurs.

Democracy and Wealth

It is no surprise that all highly developed countries in the world are democracies. No dictator should ignore such a powerful message. However, not all democracies are highly developed countries. A nation can change overnight from a dictatorship to a democracy with a single election. However, it takes a longer period for an undeveloped country to change its economic system to that of a developed nation. Democracy often serves as a basis for building a new economic system, but democracy and a market-based economy do not necessarily develop in parallel. Zimbabwe has had independence from British rule for more than 30 years, but under the dictatorship of Robert Mugabe, the country's standard of living has continued to decline. South Africa became a new democracy overnight with the election of President Mandela in 1994, yet the country is still struggling economically to feed, house, educate, and provide adequate medical attention for the majority of its native African population.

Democracy and the free enterprise system do not support the notion that everyone should be wealthy, but they do provide the opportunity for this to happen. Democracy offers an equalizing framework for businesses to operate within, such as a unified commercial code, a system of business contracts, and an orderly legal process with impartial remedies for addressing violations of these conditions. Individuals will always have unequal earnings because of their unequal skills and abilities. Certain people have an athletic or "star" talent that allows them to command millions for their performances. Some people spend all of their money; while others forego consumption and invest their funds. Some people earn more because they take greater risks in starting new ventures; some people inherit money, invest it, and then let their earnings compound. Other people face unequal opportunities, at times because of race, gender, and/or religion. And, for no apparent reason, some people just seem to have more business luck than others, simply being in the right place at the right time.

Democracy allows these individual differences to influence people's earning capabilities and their creation of individual wealth. Obviously, wealth can be created under both democratic and nondemocratic conditions. However, it is apparent that a democratic environment is more conducive to the creation of wealth for a larger number of individuals, companies and nations. In the final analysis, wealth creation is mainly a product of individuals in both small and large businesses. Governments don't create wealth - they spend it. A certain percentage of people are motivated to excel regardless of their circumstances. Such individuals seem to have three things in common: an internal drive to achieve, the expertise or knowledge to do something unique, and the opportunity to create wealth from such an endeavor. This book is about those individuals who have these unique skills and abilities - they are G/Es. They, too, understand that democracy and freedom are the foundation stones for creating their individual wealth.

Some New Dimensions of Wealth Creation

Alvin Toffler says wealth was elemental in the past; you either had it, or you didn't. It was solid and material in nature, like buildings, oil, coal, and timber. The creation of wealth today in an advanced society, such as the United States, is derived mostly from businesses dealing with intangible assets like software, media, and service. Many Americans create personal wealth through holding stock shares in companies like Berkshire Hathaway, General Electric and Microsoft. Sure, stocks go down over time, but stock ownership over the long run is a major generator of wealth. As Toffler points out, these stocks simply represent "symbols" of wealth, but not the physical asset itself. So capital and wealth are changing in nature from tangible to intangible forms. Even the most tangible form of wealth—money—is changing in nature, and becoming somewhat obsolete as smart cards invade both developed and developing countries.[39]

In light of all this, creating wealth in the 21st century is quite a different process than in previous years. G/Es already recognize this. Consequently, as G/Es trot around the globe, virtually or in person, seeking to establish new ventures, they keep these significant changes in mind. Let's review some major factors affecting this new wealth creation process.

Technology Exchange. Technology exchange is a very effective platform for wealth creation in the new economic order. Firms can become more successful through their ability to acquire, utilize, store, distribute and market technology worldwide, in various forms such, as products, services, solutions, ideas, and experiences.

Marketing Intangibles. It is obvious that mass production of tangible products will continue; however, they have been surpassed in value by money-making opportunities in distribution, information sharing, knowledge and technology dissemination, financial transactions and services of all kinds.

A New Business Meta-Model. The traditional factors of production, i.e., land, labor and capital, will remain significant. However, as we go further into the Information Age, the ultimate enhancer of resources for creating wealth will be these five factors - knowledge, technology, entrepreneurship, management and leadership.

A New, Salient Organization. The traditional multi-layered, hierarchical, autocratic business organization has given way to a leaner (but not meaner), focused, flexible, entrepreneurial, customer-sensitive, networking, and virtual organizational entity.

Strategic Alliances. Teamwork, internal networking, outsourcing, and external alliances with suppliers, customers and competitors are the order of the day for successful businesses.

World-Class Emphasis. Astute executives are searching the globe for world-class business practices for promoting the highest possible efficiency and effectiveness throughout their business operations.

Arrival of E-Commerce. The old industrial giants are being outpaced by the young, wired, savvy G/Es. The Internet is exploding with e-commerce and wealth-creating opportunities.

For many existing businesses, the new Information-Era business practices have begun to overlap the organizations of the Industrial Era. Consequently, G/Es should be mindful of utilizing the full dimensions of e-commerce business techniques as they start their new global ventures. Knowing the characteristics of e-commerce and operating a virtual business entity are the rule of the day. The new 21st century business organization will be discussed in more detail in chapter eight.

The Ultimate Wealth Creation Factor

It is possible that an even more important wealth-creation factor has been discovered. For centuries the world has operated on the economic principle that scarcity increases value. A scarce resource was considered more valuable than a resource existing in abundance. However, this classical, economic *Law of Scarcity* is no longer accepted as an absolute in the Information Age. The *Plentitude Principle* has been discovered and is operative in a number of situations. This Plentitude Principle suggests giving your product away and then figuring out how to make money from selling allied support materials, attracting revenues from advertising sources and/or capitalizing on the product's newly developed, widespread market awareness. One author, Seth Godin, put his entire book, *Unleashing the Idea Virus*, on the Internet free of charge prior to publishing it in paperback. He maintains that this publicity helped him sell printed copies of his book. To be successful, you have to be creative in using new technology, such as the Internet, Facebook and the like, to get your product in front of the world's largest source of potential customers.

To further illustrate this point, Paul Pilzer, in *Unlimited Wealth,* has suggested a new economic perspective. He states that technology should be included as an overarching factor of production. Pilzer says technology has liberated us from the zero-sum game of traditional economics. He suggests the Plentitude Principle can be used as a *supplement* to the Principle of Scarcity. Pilzer claims that, as a result of advancing technology, people in the developed world are fortunate to live in a society having virtually unlimited resources.

The Plentitude Principle is a supplement to the Principle of Scarcity.

Pilzer's thoughts are provocative and very refreshing. He holds the view that we live in a society that is still dependent on physical resources, as traditional economists maintain. However, when we combine the physical resources with technology, we can eliminate *scarcity.* We can create a world of unlimited resources and, potentially, we could have a society of *unlimited wealth.* He suggests that both the definition and the supply of resources are controlled almost exclusively by technology.

For example, Pilzer poses these questions: Is there a shortage of fertile land due to insufficient rainfall? No, irrigation technology can make most lands fertile. Is there a food shortage? No, mechanized farming technology can feed the entire world. Is there a shortage of water? No, reverse osmosis technology creates clean drinking water from ocean water. Is there a shortage of oil? No, electronic fuel injection technology now gives twice the auto mileage previously attained. Is there a shortage of natural rubber? No, it can be replaced with synthetic rubber technology. This means that technology is supreme in enhancing, enlarging and expanding our physical resources, and that technology is the foundation for generating additional wealth.

The heart of Pilzer's theory is that the capacity for creating wealth involves more than just physical resources. He identifies this wealth creation capacity as a combination of physical resources and technology. He expresses his theory with the following formula: the **W** means wealth, **P** represents physical resources, **T** is for technology and **n*** stands for the exponential effect of advancement in technology.

$$W = P\ T\ n^*$$

Of the two components – resources and technology - Pilzer says that technology is by far the more important factor. Japan is strong proof of Pilzer's point on technology. Although the country lacks physical resources to build upon, since WW II Japan has used technology to move from being a war-torn country to being ranked the second most prosperous nation in the world. Pilzer states emphatically that technology is the most important factor in determining a society's wealth.[40] This is a very strong message for managers everywhere and in particular for entrepreneurs. The G/E understands this important point. He or she will recognize the use and application of technology as the most viable way of creating new wealth in the 21st century. A hallmark characteristic of G/Es is the extent to which they use technology in creating their global personal-wealth venture.

Dimensions and Application of Technology

Technology is defined as the practical application of knowledge for achieving some useful economic purpose. Large businesses have been very effective in applying technical knowledge to the production side of business to such an extent that today we have an *oversupply* in manufacturing capability in many industries. Automobiles are a good example here. The application of technical knowledge has been a tremendous driving force in the United States, thus enhancing raw material supply, increasing manufacturing capacity, and simultaneously lowering the cost of production operations. Just 25 years ago, the manufacturing cost of a typical product was approximately 75 percent of retail price, and marketing/logistics and other functions represented 25 percent. Today those cost figures are 45 percent for producing products and 55 percent for marketing/logistics and other functional activities.

Technology is the practical application of knowledge for achieving some useful economic purpose.

Applying knowledge and technology in production has reduced the cost of making products by 40 percent or more in most industries. Only a limited amount of additional efficiency can be further squeezed out of the production process. A question here: Has there been an equal application of creativity and innovation in marketing? Many experts answer this emphatically with a "No!" For sure, developing more efficient and effective strategies in marketing, product delivery, and other forms of logistics can offer significant opportunities for G/Es. Walmart is the leading company in the world for putting into practice the most advanced logistic techniques known for retail marketing. Such innovation has given Walmart a competitive advantage of being able to offer lower prices to consumers than their competitors.

A major challenge to business today is to make marketing more efficient and effective. Fortunately, Internet technology is helping meet this challenge. The Internet has resulted in a new business model—e-commerce—through which forward-looking enterprises are racing to attract new customers in more efficient (less expensive) and more effective (more personalized) ways than were ever possible under the old business model. The Internet and its related technologies are drastically changing the marketing side of the business in a bolder, quicker and deeper manner than the advances in technologies that have altered the production side of the business. Eventually, the Internet will transform the way in which all commerce is conducted worldwide.

The 21st century will not be the exclusive domain of Traditional Entrepreneurs or G/Es. Big business will still be a dominant force, even though it faces serious competitive challenges. Rosabeth Moss Kanter, of Harvard University, writes about the difficulty of "Teaching Elephants How to Dance." She suggests that large companies are obese, inflexible, and difficult to move in new directions. In *The Innovative Dilemma*, Clayton Christensen illustrates this problem from another perspective. Christensen says successful firms are great at improving present products, but not good at exploiting new technologies. He writes that new technologies are the major causes for great firms to stumble and fall. Large firms having close contact with customers continuously strive to meet their needs by making existing products *cheaper, better, and faster*. Consequently, when these improvements are implemented, it enables firms to *sustain* and *improve* their present position, which means the firm is offering the same, but slightly improved products to an existing customer base. However, in doing this, other important ingredients are missing. These missing ingredients are creativity, innovation and the adventuring aspect of corporate entrepreneurship that will create extraordinary future growth.

Christensen says the typical, moderately successful business is one in which management's focus is on conventional or *sustaining technology.* These companies just continue doing the things they know best. Additionally, the author's research shows that these large firms are finding it increasingly difficult to maintain continuous growth because they do not recognize the importance of *disruptive technology*. Being "disruptive" means exploring and developing a range of new products for a set of new customers in different markets than those being presently served. Some firms recognize the importance of disruptive technology, but they don't fund it appropriately because new markets are normally small, they are initially unprofitable, and their customers are relatively unknown to the firm.

It is most often the emerging entrepreneurial firm that will lead the way in development and commercialization of disruptive technologies. The entrepreneur actively seeks new opportunities; he or she is more flexible and maneuverable, and is willing to take greater risk, than the average person. Unlike a big company, the entrepreneur is not locked into a given product, technology, or a business model. We quite often find emerging G/Es are previous product leaders in large firms who got frustrated with their company's internal bureaucracy. So they leave. Another point from Christensen's research is profitability. He says, "Firms that sought growth by entering small, emerging markets earned 20 times the revenue of firms pursuing growth in larger [more mature] markets."[28] It is understandable that managers in large firms are not attracted to unproven products that are being directed to customer groups in markets known to be small. This is obviously risky, and managers are known to be averse to risk. However, the development of new products for unknown markets is normal territory for entrepreneurs.[41]

Christensen and his associate, Michael Raynor, followed the above book with another groundbreaker – *The Innovator's Solution.* The focus in this new book is how to create significant new growth in existing companies. Now keep in mind that this is truly an entrepreneurial endeavor. Growth is an imperative, necessary for creating shareholder value. The authors note that only one company in ten is able to sustain the kind of growth that translates into an above-average increase in shareholder return for more than a few years. Oftentimes when the core business approaches maturity investors will demand new growth, which is difficult and risky to achieve. The authors state that the most daunting challenge in delivering growth is, if you fail *once* to deliver it, the odds are very low you ever will be able to deliver growth in the future. Therefore, their book summarizes a set of theories that can guide corporate managers who need new growth coupled with a better chance of success. [42]

The Two Types of Technology

Technology was defined earlier as the application of knowledge to create some type of economical benefit or value. Within this definition of technology, two types of knowledge must be recognized. First is *technical knowledge*, which includes information technology (IT), engineering techniques, quality assurance, new manufacturing processes, and productivity improvements. The second type of knowledge is *business knowledge*, which includes business solutions arising from a simultaneous utilization of the three administrative disciplines of entrepreneurship, management and leadership. Businesses everywhere have long utilized *technical knowledge* to improve efficiency and effectiveness of the product-developing manufacturing function, but they have not fully employed the benefits of *business knowledge*. However, astute business managers recognize the necessity of both types of knowledge—technical and business.

The concept of business knowledge can be better understood by viewing the three disciplines - entrepreneurship, management and leadership - functioning as a unified whole. Entrepreneurship *creates* the business initially; as the business becomes more successful, management is needed to bring *order* and *stability* to the enterprise; then leadership is required to ensure long-term *transformational growth* for the firm. The author has developed an Organizational Meta-Model that illustrates the importance of these three disciplines and how they are collectively required in every successful large business. Firms utilizing this Meta-Model are more successful in achieving organizational transformation and long-term business growth.[43]

In the 1990s, a number of American firms were using the Meta-Model approach to radically transform their businesses. During that time period, Warren Bennis characterized American businesses as being "overmanaged and underled." Consequently, new leadership was brought from the outside to IBM, American Express, Chrysler and other major corporations, with the idea of revitalizing these corporations. Other businesses, reluctant to make such major changes, have continued to suffer adverse market consequences. For example, General Motors relied principally on inbred leadership for a number of years. GM had the most costly production facilities in the U.S., and the firm lacked style in its product lineup. These factors contributed significantly to the company's bankruptcy and restructuring in 2009.

Figure 4.2
The Organizational Meta-Model
Venture Development & Growth Rate

Entrepreneurship Stage	Management Stage	Leadership Stage
Venture Creation	Orderly Growth	Transformation
	Growth Rate	
Low	Moderate	High

In their book, *Every Business Is a Growth Business*, Ram Charan and Noel Tichy stress the importance of new leadership in making major organizational change. They maintain that new leaders often have a growth-oriented genetic code, and they should teach it to the rest of the organization. This is not an easy task—sometimes it takes years. The two elements of Charan and Tichy's genetic growth code parallel the two components of this author's Renaissance Leadership Model, briefly described in chapter two. This Model proposes that managers should strive to be "Hard on Performance," a dimension Charan and Tichy call "decision architecture," and simultaneously, managers should be "Soft on People," a dimension they call "social architecture."[44] Learning the Renaissance Leadership Model is the easy part, but implementing it is far more difficult. Every manager knows far more than he or she is willing and able to put into practice.

Other corporate "elephants" are beginning to recognize that their size can sometimes be an advantage. Dow Chemical is seeking to capitalize on its extensive knowledge base. Dow has leveraged its intellectual/knowledge assets by screening its 29,000 patents to determine which can be exploited by thru licensing and which should be permanently abandoned. As a result, the company has generated $125 million in licensing income and $40 million in savings over a ten-year period.

Consulting firms like Accenture have set up Corporate Knowledge Centers to store "know-how" developed with their worldwide clients regarding projects, implementation techniques, systems and management. Accenture's Centers collect individual technical knowledge from their consultants and compile it into a database that can be shared with their consultants worldwide. This knowledge is further enhanced and then sold to other Accenture clients.

Leaders of other large organizations are capitalizing on the emergence of technology as a major force in wealth creation. Toffler says, "As knowledge becomes more central to the creation of wealth, we [can] begin to think of the corporation as an enhancer of knowledge."[31] G/Es see information technology as a vehicle that enables them to be linked to major corporations while at the same time being connected to an ever-expanding world marketplace. The G/E recognizes the importance of technology and will use it as a substantial competitive advantage for creating new wealth in the 21st century. Large firms may be *enhancers* of knowledge and technology, but G/Es will certainly be the major *developers* and *disseminators.*

Characteristics of Technology

Technology has been cited as a significant factor in enhancing production capabilities. It has been a major contributor to production increases for centuries, but only recently has it been recognized as having such a strong impact on increasing the economic contribution of marketing, finance, human resources, and other productive business functions. This is only possible as we understand and apply a much broader definition of technology as espoused in this book: The application of knowledge to every aspect of the business organization.

As late as the early 1980s, most wealth was created by businesses involved with tangible assets, such as minerals, oil, land, building, equipment and other physical assets. In the 21st century, we see evidence of a shift in the nature of wealth-creating businesses. Business fortunes today are being made more frequently in media, finance, marketing, software, the Internet, and other intangibles. General Electric (G.E.) is well-recognized for its production of tangible products; however, that face is changing as the company has disposed of appliances and sold its lighting division. As wealth-creating businesses move from the physical to intangibles, G.E. is adapting to the changing world. For example, G.E. launched "Ecomagination" in 2005 as a commitment to build innovative technology that helps customers address their environmental challenges, as well as assisting the company in accelerating its growth. G.E. set a revenue goal of $25 billion by 2010, and was well on the way to meeting that, with a portfolio of 80 products and revenues of $17 billion in 2008.[45]

A strong case can be made that knowledge assets are first and foremost found in the experience, expertise and initiative of the entrepreneur. However, the business firm itself provides a socioeconomic structure in which knowledge can be developed, utilized, stored and shared. The firm can be a repository for knowledge, but such knowledge is often deeply embedded in business systems, practices and products. When an opportunity is sensed, it needs to be seized upon. This is where the G/E excels over the large formal organization. The G/E, with his or her nimble, virtual organization, can make immediate decisions and take swift action as is demanded in a new Information Era. Michael Dell and others illustrate this daily.

Alvin Toffler points out some of the unique features of technology that apply to our two-part definition of technology, i.e., *technical knowledge* and *business knowledge.* Toffler says that technology is literally *inexhaustible*; whereas land, labor, raw material and capital are consumables, therefore more finite in character. Technical knowledge and business knowledge can be *produced, utilized, catalogued* and *transferred* across organizations and geographic boundaries, in *unlimited quantities,* and *technology never gets "used up"* when it is applied in the business process. The same technology can be *used by two people or two hundred people simultaneously* in different locations, and it is still available for further usage.[46]

Technology is limitless, inexhaustible, never gets used up, and can be used simultaneously by many.

Perhaps the most significant feature of technology is that it challenges a classic economic theory, namely, that scarcity creates value. Technology itself is not considered a scarce resource. *The more technology is used and shared, the more it proliferates and creates additional technology.* This highlights another unique feature of technology—*its plentitude creates value.* This is why Shareware and other firms give away their software, so they can sell supporting materials for their products. Place your product on the Internet, *the world's largest learning and copying machine,* and then figure out a way of getting a flow of revenue from it. Place a provocative summary of your book on the Web, and then entice people to buy it from Amazon. Making technical knowledge widely available to others often increases knowledge and further enhances its value.

Toffler is adamant in stating the most important economic development of our lifetime is a new system of creating wealth. The system is not based on muscle, but on the mental knowledge one has and the technology solutions it produces. Knowledge can be defined as a *mental state of being acquainted with, and/or having an understanding of, a science, an art, or a particular useful technique.* Toffler goes further in stating that *knowledge is the ultimate amplifier of power and wealth.* Such knowledge was once believed to be an exclusive monopoly of upper management, and many managers still believe this to be true. Managerial treatment of employees in that era was called "mind over matter" – "I don't mind and you don't matter." Today, enlightened leaders know that the utilization of the skills and abilities of their knowledge workers can make the difference in the success or failure of the business.

Knowledge is a mental state of being acquainted with, and/or having an understanding of, a science, an art, or a particular useful technique. It is the ultimate amplifier of power and wealth!

But today, expert knowledge is available to any person, anywhere in the world. In 1995, Nonaka and Takeuchi stated that "the world is flat again," not because of ignorance, but because knowledge has made it a level playing field. Later Tom Friedman recognized the global importance of this idea and wrote a whole book on the subject – *The World is Flat.* All one has to do is to search the Internet to find information on virtually any subject. For the first time, there is readily available access to knowledge that will allow individuals and nations to achieve almost anything they desire.[32] However, only advanced nations have the advantage of achieving "almost anything they desire;" for they have an educated workforce, a large knowledge base, lots of technology-embedded products and equipment, a supportive business infrastructure, and ease of starting a new venture. This combination of business-enabling characteristics is uniquely part of the American-enterprise culture more so than in any other country of the world.[47]

The well-educated G/E has at his or her disposal the ultimate tools - *knowledge and technology* - which are the two major factors for creating wealth today. In a world where there are few working theories, the primacy of knowledge and technology makes lots of sense. In *Future Revolutions*, David Mercer emphasizes this reality when he notes that, because of technological advances, the future of humanity is no longer constrained by a shortage of resources. What is emerging in the 21st century, in almost every field, is a widespread potential for the application of emerging and established technologies. Present technology allows us, in the advanced world, to achieve almost anything we desire, anywhere in the world. Therefore, it is very likely the G/E who will recognize the importance, use, and transfer of technology as a primary tool in creating wealth.[48]

Fortunately, knowledge and technology can be shared extensively with others at a very low cost, and its dissemination does not minimize or reduce the value of the original knowledge source. This means that new knowledge can be acquired, utilized, catalogued, shared and transferred to other productive applications within and across organizations and geographic boundaries. It is more likely to be the G/E, and not the large organization, who will quickly recognize emerging opportunities and the potential applications of knowledge and technology throughout the world.

Developmental Insights for the Global Entrepreneur

A number of things mentioned in this chapter underscore the meaning of the phrase," New Global Economic World." The accepted old-school Law of Scarcity is no longer considered absolute today. A new postulate, The Plentitude Principle, reveals how creating an abundance of an item actually enhances its value. And the new-age Internet serves as the speeding vehicle spreading the word to millions regarding the abundance of an item. This would have been radical thinking only a few years ago.

There are other significant items in this chapter that every G/E should fully understand. One is the shift away from tangible wealth-creating factors of the past, namely, buildings, machines, oil, coal and timber, to the new-age wealth-creating factors found in intangible assets, such as software, information, media, and services. This economic transformation is reflected in the fact that 80 percent of America's GDP is now in services. Being aware of, being part of and being in the transformative flow of economic activity increases your chances of business success. Clearly, a major route to riches is providing services.

Another discovery is recognizing the two major driving forces in the new wealth-creating process. They are the understanding and application of knowledge and technology. Technology is defined as the practical application of knowledge in order to achieve some useful purpose. Knowledge is the position of being acquainted with, or having an understanding of, a science, an art, or some particular useful technique. Through the smart usage of knowledge and technology, we can create unlimited productive resources for businesses, then manufacture products cheaply and distribute them globally, thus improving the economic well-being and the quality of life of many throughout the world. What a great contribution that would be for America to present to the world. Global Entrepreneurs will have the unique opportunity to utilize these driving forces to benefit mankind, as well as creating substantial wealth and happiness for themselves and their worldwide associates.

Chapter Endnotes

Routes to Riches ...

So You Want to Be a Billionaire. Just what does it take to become a millionaire or a billionaire? Obviously it is not easy for everyone in a developed country like the U.S.; otherwise, everyone would be a millionaire. However, the number is increasing overall for many reasons pointed out in this book. Becoming superrich often requires intense dedication to seven basic "Money Rules," according to Keith Bloomfield, President and CEO of Forbes Family Trust, and Russ Alan Prince, President of Prince & Associates, Inc. After an in-depth ethnographic study of the superrich, especially those who were seeking billionaire status, they developed a set of seven "rules of conduct" that described the mind-set and behaviors most regularly applied by this superrich class of individuals.

The seven basic rules of conduct Bloomfield and Prince have identified are the following:

1. They commit themselves to extreme wealth; creating wealth is regularly the top priority and overarching motivation for these individuals.
2. They engage in enlightened self-interest; they make sure they are winners, strategically or financially, in every meaningful situation in which they are engaged.
3. They put themselves in the line of money; they pursue only those activities that have significant probability of generating above-average financial returns.
4. They engage in nodal networking; they build strong relationships with a handful of strategically valuable associates.
5. They handsomely reward associates and business partners; they ensure each affiliate party is duly compensated for his or her contribution.
6. They use failure to improve and to refocus; failure is dissected closely, used as a learning experience and as a motivator.
7. They stay highly centered on the few things they do extremely well; they concentrate on their strengths and delegate everything else.

OK, Mr. or Ms. G/E, there is no secret knowledge here. It is just a matter of your mastering these seven wealth-creating rules, for they can be used by almost anyone to significantly increase net worth and create personal wealth.[49]

How the Rich Think and Act. One thing for sure, the rich are different; but in what way other than having monetary income and assets? If you know the difference, then it may be helpful to you in your search for wealth. Ann Kadet of *Smart Money* magazine helps us understand how those in the $5 Million Club "think and behave." This elite group represents only one percent of the U.S. population and has quadrupled in the past 10 years to more than 930,000. Here are some highlights of her findings:

1. Only 10 percent of their wealth came from passive investments. Real wealth follows radical action, meaning the rich had to create their own wealth in some type of venture.
2. Being lucky helps, but research shows that luck is largely a matter of one's own making. Those who describe themselves as lucky have common traits; they are friendly and fond of new experiences, traits that put them on a collision course with new opportunities, and lucky folks simply have higher expectations of success.
3. The vast majority (80 percent) either started their own business or worked for a small company that saw explosive growth. And almost all of them made their fortune in a big lump after many *years* of effort.
4. The vast majority of the rich made their fortunes after they made up their minds to solve a problem or to do something better than it's been done before, i.e., some type of radical innovation. This means they were true entrepreneurs.
5. Getting rich also requires a certain amount of stubbornness and clarity of purpose. Sam Walton was like a cruise missile aimed at knowing everything possible about retailing. He was a sponge soaking up ideas everywhere, whether from his first job at K Mart or drivers of his rigs that brought products to his stores.
6. Becoming rich is rarely a solo endeavor. Having a team of three who share a common vision has a 50 percent chance of being successful, whereas a solo entrepreneur, even with a great idea and hired guns as partners, has only a 10 percent chance of being successful.
7. The rich are always talking about and keeping an eye out for opportunity. They are also very creative in developing such beneficial opportunities. One Atlanta entrepreneur found an office and rented it during off hours at a substantial reduction. He ran his business as a night shift from 8pm to 7pm for a year until his money flow began.
8. The rich act and feel like they are already wealthy. When you have confidence in your venture, it shows in your voice and your gestures.

> You can pitch the craziest idea to a group of people, and they will jump on board to support you if you are highly committed and enthusiastic.

So being rich means freedom to spend your time as you please, to pursue your real interests and to take a chance without risking utter ruin. This often means acting as if you already have that freedom. Now that you know this secret, you have that "freedom" as a prospective Global Entrepreneur.[50]

5

Capitalizing on Opportunities

"Good people can make any idea work.
Inept people will ruin the best of ideas."
Wendy Grossman

The Intellectual Advantage

Globalization has indeed opened up the world as a giant marketplace. But where will the next big idea emerge? What are the major opportunities for creating wealth? There is an entrepreneur in England who sells used submarines, but don't bet on the sub as a big money-making idea in the new millennium. There is a clear indication in the New Global Economy that wealth is going to be created through the use of intellectual capital, the sharing of knowledge and the application of technology. Organizations owning tangible assets such as land, plants, equipment, minerals and commodities are declining in value relative to emergent organizations in the new, knowledge-technology economy. Emerging e-commerce and Internet-related businesses are a fundamental part of the industrial complex and are gaining in status relative to blue-chip companies manufacturing durable goods.

Organized knowledge, both technical and business knowledge, is the key to wealth creation. This intellectual advantage is well-known to the Global Entrepreneur (G/E). Today's new business model uses fewer material resources by substituting knowledge and technology for traditional factors of production. The smart way to get into business today is to develop knowledge-related products and then market them directly via the Internet to a world audience. The world is opening up to commerce ventures of all kinds, and the Internet is becoming a dominant vehicle for getting products into the global marketplace. You must first develop a great idea for a world-class product that will serve as the basis of your new venture. But, remember there are very few original ideas. You can be assured that, if you are thinking of a new product, someone else has also had the same idea. Don't let that disturb you. You should get a bit worried when there is no one already in "your" chosen business. If no one is selling your product/service, then there may not be a present market for it. When a market doesn't yet exist, it will be time-consuming and costly to attract customers to your product. Just keep this in mind: it is less difficult to enter an existing market than to create a new market.

The Spectrum of Ideas

Just what are "great ideas" depends on one's perspective. We typically think of ideas from a business perspective, such as advances in "things" - products, technology, processes and services. Meaningful ideas can be about more abstract things - theories, laws, principles, paradoxes, aphorisms, constructs, complexes, fallacies, and even outrageous claims. For example, the discovery of Archimedes' "Eureka" Principle is an idea that explains the principles of hydrostatics, i.e., the science of how solid bodies behave in liquids. In a like fashion, Pythagoras' theory (the Pythagorean Theorem) is a provable idea, as are as Newton's Laws, and Adam Smith's "Invisible Hand." The idea of "conspicuous consumption" is so pervasive now that it may be surprising to learn someone actually invented the term. Thorstein Veblen wrote an essay on it in his book, *The Theory of the Leisure Class.* You will find an excellent exposure of abstract ideas in Michael Macrone's book entitled *Eureka!*[51]

Now, back to the physical world of business. The recent economic recession provides companies with lots of reasons for increased interest in creativity, developing new ideas, and innovative products to help kick-start additional growth. Truly innovative individuals and companies can build strength during such slowdowns and downtimes, and some of them emerge stronger than ever. Under such extraordinary conditions, Shira White discusses the necessity of "leap innovation" that is, developing entirely new products, services and process by moving into the unknown or unexplored. Clayton Christensen calls this "radical innovation." Leap innovation can happen anywhere in the universe of an organization, in any business function – research, new product development, recruiting, management information, financing creative projects or improving the work life of employees. Such big leaps can transform a whole company, as has occurred at Corning, which now helps customer to be more efficient, innovative, and sustainable in the new world economy. This new type of innovation inspired Frank Gehry to design the magnificent titanium curves and twists of the spectacular Guggenheim Museum in Bilbao, Spain. While visiting Bilbao, I felt the museum was more impressive than its contents. The impact of Gehry's brilliant design reached far beyond a local art museum – it reshaped the whole northern Basque coast into a modern metropolis and cultural center. White's "leap innovation" and Christensen's "radical innovation" are indeed powerful ideas.[52]

Idea Sources

There is absolutely no shortage of new business ideas in the world. Whether you are in an undeveloped or developed country, ideas are plentiful. In the underdeveloped countries of Africa, there is a great need for basic business ideas for providing more food, housing, medical care, education and jobs for an ever-growing population. In developed countries, like the United States and Japan, there is continuous pressure on business managers to find more productivity improvement ideas to maintain and enhance market positions.

Research shows close to half of new business ideas arise from a person's own work experiences. Carl Vesper studied more than 3,000 independent entrepreneurs in the United States, and his study reveals the following sources of business ideas among his samples (see Figure 5.1).[53] Vesper's findings are supported by *Inc.* magazine, which publishes an annual listing of the fastest-growing private companies in America. In 2009, *Inc.* found that the majority of America's fastest-growing firms began with some kind of proprietary competitive advantage, such as the founder's technological skills, some kind of process expertise, or the right to intellectual property embedded in a product or service. More than 80 percent of the *Inc.* 500 CEOs had even offered their winning idea to their previous employer, and a sizable percentage of these were turned down by their firm. For example, David Glickman, the prosperous owner of Justice Technology, a *Fortune* 500 fastest-growing company, offered his telephone switching technology to his employer, American Express, and it was turned down.

Will reviewing the fastest-growing businesses give you some ideas about future opportunities? Absolutely! The *Inc.* magazine listing of the top *500* fastest-growing firms represents "hot" product ideas. Could these companies represent a trend or direction for a world business in developing countries? Yes. It is very common for innovative business ideas and world-class business practices to be developed first in mature markets and later transferred to other developing economies. An emerging trend in America is for large companies to develop simple, basic products in less-developed countries and explore how demand for such products can be cultivated in the developed world. Business and consumer services continue to be rapid- growth areas in these fastest-growing companies.

Figure 5.1
Sources of Business Start-up Ideas

Sources:	Percent of Businesses:
Previous Work Experience	43%
Hobbies & Personal Interest	18%
Chance Events	10%
Someone Else's Idea	8%
Education Class	6%
Family Business	6%
Friends & Relatives	5%
Other Sources	5%
Total	100%

Most new business ideas are derived from a person's work experience.

The 2009 *Inc.* 500 fastest-growing private companies have good reason to be exuberant with their aggregate revenue of $18.4 billion, compared with $13.7 billion in 2008. Median growth is down from 1,046 percent to 880.5 percent - and that is without accounting for the worst effects of the recession. Their total employee count of 57,310 is up by almost 6,000 over the 2008 count. Looking across the 2009 *Inc.* 500, you see the future of the economy. In health care, businesses are moving forward on cancer and stem-cell research (Nexcelom Bioscience), clinical trials (DSG), and mediation management (MedVantx and Millennium Pharmacy Systems). More than 25 percent of the companies in the energy sector focus on solar and other alternative sources. Other leading companies were in advertising, software development and technical services to the federal government. Less than a third of retailers in this group have a single brick-and-mortar store.[54]

From America ...

Dale Buss tells us about million-dollar businesses you have never heard of. Rico Elmore, who weighs 300 pounds and has a big head to match his frame, had to set up his own business to supply stylish sunglasses for him and other big guys. Dave Marcks has a Geese Police squad – a group of intelligent and persistent collies that are great at banishing big birds from golf courses and other expensive watering holes. Jule Cole solves Moms' problems of lost jackets, shoes, and book bags at school with a durable, dishwasher-proof, microwave-safe, personalized, permanent label for kids' stuff. Samuel Liechti will ship you a batch of Italian-made, knee-high or calf-length cotton or cashmere/silk dress socks, automatically, several times a year, starting at $89 for nine pair. He includes a calculation of how much time you save by not purchasing socks - about 12 hours each year. His latest product is subscriptions for underwear.[55]

How to Discover Ideas

Some people seem to generate an endless supply of new ideas, but most people struggle to come up with anything new, creative or out of the ordinary. Frank Smith, President of FedEx Corporation, says to find a new idea requires one to have "the ability to think beyond relatively conventional paradigms, and to examine traditional constraints by using nontraditional thinking." Art Fry, the developer of 3M's Post-it Notes, says ideas and innovation "require a fresh way of looking at things, an understanding of people, and an entrepreneurial willingness to take risks and to work hard." Vinton Cerf, Vice-President of MCI WorldCom Inc., says ideas occur when "you invite your brain to encounter thoughts that you might not otherwise encounter—by letting your mind wander, mixing ideas freely, looking for unexpected juxtapositions from connected subjects that are not necessarily related." Douglas Engelbart, the inventor of the computer mouse, has a different opinion about ideas. He says, "The problem is not how to create new ideas and innovate, but it is how to get society to adopt the good ideas that already exist." It took Engelbart 20 years to get the computer industry to use his mouse.[56]

Generally, new ideas do not reveal themselves with a single brilliant flash in a person's mind. More likely, new ideas are triggered by something already existing in the conscious mind. Remember the old proverb, "There is *nothing new* under the sun." Many aspiring entrepreneurs feel their new product idea is original. While a young Japanese student was taking my course in entrepreneurship, he showed me his idea for easy-to-use chopsticks. He connected the two chopsticks with a round ring, making them easier for non-initiates to hold. I mentioned the proverb to the student and suggested that he conduct a computerized patent search at the university library. When he searched, he discovered 18 existing and pending patents for easy-to-use chopsticks very similar to his. Remember, it is rare to discover a really new business idea today. Anyway, *most new businesses are started with old ideas.* So, even with what is believed to be an "original" idea, you can almost be assured that someone, somewhere, is already operating a business based on that idea. That is all right, for it means that others will help you develop a market for your product and that will make market entry for your new venture easier, cheaper, and quicker.

Most new businesses are started with old ideas!

Consequently, do not be disturbed when a proposed "new" venture already exists in the marketplace. Wendy's and Burger King still sell lots of hamburgers even though McDonald's was there first. If someone else is already in the field, then it is more likely a market for the product is being developed. On the other hand, there are times when one may develop a really innovative product and may deliberately desire to be first to market. Some experts say to let a competitor spend the big money and time in developing a new market. Then introduce a superior product or service, coupled with doing a better job of marketing and managing the company - a strategy practiced by Sony. Coming in late means one will have to differentiate the product, making it more attractive and more valuable to the customer than your competitor's product. The real challenge is always there - to make the product more enticing so customers will buy it from you rather than a competitor. There are obvious strategic considerations about which route you should take to the market – should you be a leader or a follower? Peter Drucker always maintained that the advantage lies in being there "firstest with the mostest."

The Idea Factory

In an era when technology proliferates and markets shift rapidly, we find some companies whose sole purpose is continuous innovation and creation of new business ideas. One such firm is The BrainStore, operating in Biel, Switzerland, the home of Rolex and Swatch. Their central position is this: If you are short on having those "eureka moments," then you can certainly rely on a steady flow of "manufactured ideas" from their BrainStore. Clients seek out The BrainStore for all sorts of ideas: Novartis, the pharmaceutical giant wanted new food products; the Swiss Cancer Association sought ideas about how to promote sun-protection products; Nestle, Credit Suisse and the Swiss Railway also contracted with Brainstore for new ideas. The BrainStore has a secret weapon for generating ideas: it has a global network of 1,500 individuals—mainly young people from 13 to 20 years old—to assist them. The BrainStore mixes kids with clients and their own professionals to develop the end products—lots of new ideas.[57] The idea factory itself is a great idea.

The BrainStore is similar to Thomas Edison's original idea factory of the 1800s. In one year of operation, Edison's laboratory generated important ideas that had a profound revolutionary effect on industries such as the telegraph, telephone, phonograph and incandescent lighting. Edison was committed to bringing about rapid and cheap inventions; he had a personal [actual] output of one minor invention every 10 days and a major invention every 6 months. Now that is innovation, par excellence! There are a number of firms like BrainStore that act as "knowledge brokers" by selling their ideas to the highest bidder. These knowledge brokers span multiple markets and technology domains and innovate by brokering knowledge from where it is known to where it is not. Such firms achieve a strategic advantage by gaining access to a wide variety of industries and then selling their ideas to others. Other examples of knowledge brokers include Accenture Consulting, Edison and Company's Menlo Park Laboratory, Lucent/Bell, and Elmer Sperry Company.

Short on business ideas?
Use an idea factory.

One of America's leading idea design firms is IDEO, located in San Francisco. Tom Kelley, CEO of IDEO, doesn't think it is the lone genius working in isolation that comes up with the best ideas. He believes that everyone can be creative. It is the goal of his firm to tap into a wellspring of creativity among his staff and to generate a never-ending flow of business ideas. The approaches used by IDEO have enabled the firm to win more awards in the last ten years than any other idea development firm. By fostering an atmosphere conducive to free expression of ideas, and by breaking the rules and freeing people to design their own creative environment, IDEO practices what it preaches to others. Several factors contribute to IDEO's success - a deep appreciation of individual observation, a focus on teamwork in developing breakthroughs, a quick turnaround brainstorming process, and building of prototypes for real-world testing.[58]

Being Creative Helps Generate New Ideas

In most instances, idea development by entrepreneurs tends to be a solo effort. There is a substantial body of academic research showing that entrepreneurs have a low need for affiliation, moderate social skills, a high need for achievement and a strong need for autonomy and control. Consequently, Traditional Entrepreneurs in general are not good team players or team builders, nor are they good managers. These characteristics restrict the flow of good ideas and business input from others. However, entrepreneurs make up for these inadequacies, in part, by being more creative than the norm and being highly *persistent.* They intuitively use the creative process to generate ideas and to develop solutions to their business problems. Fortunately, the G/E does not fit this Traditional Entrepreneurial mold. He or she is very creative and is also a strong networking team player and an excellent leader. The G/E has or will be developing the necessary skills to be a dynamic contributor in the new Creative Era.

At times it may be necessary to deliberately engage in the creative process as a means of generating new business ideas. The creative process can be used to enhance existing ideas. Some people are brought up and educated in an environment that fosters creativity. For others, the creative process is not part of their nature, so they must develop this skill or get others to do it for them. Research shows that there are similarities in the mental processes through which outstanding ideas are developed in many fields, including entrepreneurship. In reflecting on these similarities, Durako and Hodgetts suggest a four-step creative process.[59]

Step One: Preparation. Investigation and information gathering characterize this stage of the creative process. A person should be involved in extensive reading, conversations with knowledgeable people in their field, attendance at relevant courses and workshops, and general absorption of data on the various idea(s) being pursued. Such investigation provides entrepreneurs with a variety of perspectives needed to develop a product or a new business.

Step Two: Incubation. Being creative requires time to think and mull over large amounts of data gathered in the preparation stage. Often incubation occurs when a person is engaged in activities not related to the subject being pursued. These activities include taking a shower, or even sleeping. Allowing for time to get away from the subject enables the subconscious mind to function in a creative mode. Incubation can be facilitated by exercising, playing sports, working around the house and or just relaxing in general.

Step Three: Ideation. After long periods of thinking, reflecting and frustration, then, piece by piece, things begin to fall into place. An overall pattern of events and activities emerges. It becomes clear what must be done.

Answers to the pieces of the puzzle come incrementally, but the whole picture is there. Slowly but surely, the person begins to formulate the viable idea. Then, all at once, it happens - this is it!

Step Four: Implementation. Planning is much easier than execution. The entrepreneur knows what has to be done, but it takes courage, self-discipline and perseverance to do it. Some ideas emerge from step three are in a rough form and have to be modified prior to and during implementation. Many things just will not work as planned. Entrepreneurs may take an idea in a completely different direction than initially planned, and they may well discover new and more workable solutions during the implementation stage. In spite of obstacles that may be encountered here, things will begin to take shape, and this provides incentive and encouragement to the entrepreneur. It is happening. The venture's idea is coming into fruition, and the entrepreneur will move forward with great speed.

This creative process is a proven methodology that can be used to help entrepreneurs generate and modify their business ideas. The four steps frequently overlap each other and may be utilized in a different order than presented. If you cannot find the solution in step three, then go back to step one and start the process anew. If your ideas are not flowing, just slow down a bit and give the process a chance to function. In knowing this process, you can deliberately use it to generate ideas and potential solutions to business problems. You can further enhance the above four-step creative process by practicing the following suggestions:

1. Keep a pad handy by your bedside, and record all new business ideas that come to mind.
2. Seek new ideas from other people and other business-related activities, such as trade shows, newspapers and business magazines.
3. Do not attempt to criticize, evaluate or test the value of the business ideas as they are first recorded.
4. As business transactions are experienced at work, think about how that work could be done better and with fewer resources than are being currently utilized.
5. Reach out beyond the ordinary in your search for new venture ideas. Brainstorm with others.
6. If you do not have a number of crazy ideas on your list, then you have not searched far enough.
7. After you have collected 10 to 20 really new ideas, a reality check is necessary in regard to each of them. Determine the two or three ideas

on your list that show promise of being the best business opportunity for you.

8. Talk to friends who are in business or to others who operate their own business. Share with them your aspirations about starting a business. Ask for their opinion regarding your selected business ideas.
9. Listen to the advice of others, but do not let their personal comments discourage you if their views are negative. Keep on thinking about and seeking new venture ideas. Remember all those experts who said man would never fly and there would never be a use for a home computer.
10. Keep looking. Dedicated and deliberate searching for ideas is proven to increase the rate of new ideas discovered in every instance.
11. Persistence. True entrepreneurs never give up. They continue trying until they find the right idea for their new business venture.

This last suggestion of *persistence* is a major factor in the success of many creative people, and not just entrepreneurs. Edison, Einstein and other great discoverers were doggedly persistent in their efforts. In the idea-generation process, persistence is evident when one about the idea over a period of time. So, if you want to start your business, you must be *persistent* and keep searching for ideas that can be turned into a viable business. It will eventually come to you, probably while you are on vacation while lying on the beach.

Fostering Creative Ideas From Within the Business

Entrepreneurs often have difficulty generating innovative ideas, for most begin their careers by working in established corporate environments. In big businesses, you are taught to follow ingrained precedents and to do things in the proven ways of the past. Unfortunately, this practice does not stimulate creativity and innovation. Knowing this to be true, Robert Sutton drew on extensive research in behavioral psychology to develop eleven "weird ideas" for fostering creativity and innovation.

1. Hire "slow learners."
2. Hire people who make you uncomfortable, even dislike you.
3. Hire people you probably don't need.
4. Use job interviews to get ideas, and to screen candidates.
5. Encourage people to ignore and defy superiors and peers.
6. Find some happy people and get them to fight.

7. Reward success and failure; punish inaction.
8. Do something that will probably fail; convince others it will not.
9. Think of something ridiculous to do, then plan to do it.
10. Don't try to learn from people who seem to solve your problems.
11. Forget the past, especially your company's successes.

Sutton says these weird ideas work because they help increase variance in knowledge; they help people see old things in new ways and also help companies break from the past. Furthermore, he says they are grounded in academic theory and research - and have actually been used by successful companies. Most companies will continue to devote the lion's share of time and effort to supporting the established routine, but trying some of Sutton's ideas will clearly stimulate innovative actions.[60]

Now, wouldn't it be nice if you as an entrepreneur or manager had a "predictable process" that could be used to launch disruptive change? Clayton Christensen and his co-authors say they "hope" they have exactly done this in their book, *Seeing What's Next.* They state their book "will help readers to develop an intuition for how to use the theories of innovation to predict industry change," and "if you know where to look and what to look for, you can spot industry-changing firms before they emerge." In order to fully understand what these authors are attempting to do, one must have an understanding of the three important theories of innovation in Christensen two previous books: *The Innovator's Dilemma* and *The Innovator's Solution.* These books can provide useful information to the G/E for understanding the theory and practice of *sustaining* innovation and *disruptive* innovation. The latter, disruptive innovation, is the normal domain of the G/E.[61]

Historic Flow of Ideas from Business

Small businesses have long been recognized as the major domain of innovative ideas and business growth throughout the world. You would normally think most innovation comes from the large corporations, but that is not true. The original source of new ideas is most often the individual—not the idea factory, nor the large corporation. Even when innovative individuals work in large companies, they often do not share their ideas with their employer. This individual innovative trait is reflected by entrepreneurs all over the world as they establish their small businesses. For example, William Bygraves took a close look at the U.S. Small Business Administration data bank of all small-to-medium-size enterprises and found the inventions in Figure 5.2 below emerged during the 20th century.[62]

Figure 5.2
Major Inventions by American Small Businesses

Acoustical Speakers	Heart Valves
Aerosol Spray Cans	Heat Sensors
Air Conditioning	Helicopter
Airplane	High-Speed Computers
Artificial Skin	Hydraulic Brake
Assembly Line	Learning Machines
Automatic Fabric Cutter	Polaroid Camera
Automatic Transfer Equipment	Prefabricated Housing
Biosynthetic Insulin	Pressure Cellophane
Continuous Casting	Quick Frozen Food
Cotton Picker Rotary	Oil Drill Bit
Fluid Flow Meter	Safety Razors
Geodesic Dome Soft	Contact Lens
Gyrocompass	Sonar Fish Monitoring

Ideas and businesses developed by entrepreneurs are certainly the engines of worldwide economic growth. Many developing countries are just discovering this phenomenon and are beginning to encourage entrepreneurship as a teachable process. Many newly formed market economies, such as those of post-Communist countries, are realizing the important role entrepreneurship can play in stimulating economic growth. Consequently, privately sponsored entrepreneurship programs are now even being offered in Russia, China and many other developing countries.

Ideas in a Changing Business Environment

New ideas and business opportunities often emerge with political upheaval and major social changes in a country. For example, the democratic election in South Africa has brought about major economic changes in the country. Citizens there are discovering new opportunities as the country forges ahead to provide houses, jobs and a better quality of life to the previously-deprived black majority. Change causes chaos, confusion, inconsistencies, information gaps and many vacuums in the marketplace which are quickly seized upon by entrepreneurs. Such changes often have a negative impact on existing businesses and individuals who lose their jobs in the transition. Entrepreneurs are able to create economic value out of such chaos, so they welcome radical change.

Other more developed countries face difficulty in growing their economies. One example is Chile, which has a shortage of entrepreneurs. In 2010, the government funded a $1 million Start-Up Chile program to woo foreign entrepreneurs. The aim of the program is to put Chile on the map as an innovation hub in South America by addressing what President Sebastian Pifinera calls, "a dearth of [local] entrepreneurs." Twenty-five entrepreneurs were selected for 2010, and each will receive a $40,000 grant, a one-year residency visa, and hands-on assistance from a seven-person local business team. More than 150 entrepreneurs applied, with ideas ranging from software to solar panels to gadgets that use radio-frequency ID technology. If you missed the first cut, try in 2011 when the program budget is being increased to $5 million.

But you don't have to go to South Arica or Chile to discover new business ideas. They are probably sitting at your back door, or at least across the street. An increasing number of private firms, large companies and government organizations are downsizing their operations today. Outsourcing creates many small business opportunities. Outsourcing occurs when an existing firm hires other businesses to provide goods or services previously produced by the firm's own personnel. Very often the outsourcing firm is a smaller, more specialized business. Examples of opportunities arising from business outsourcing are printing, call centers, IT support, maintenance, security, cafeteria food, short-term secretarial work, and even sub-assembly of core products. Porsche, Daimler Benz and other automotive companies are outsourcing some of their core assembly operations to smaller firms. G/Es should keep close contact with executives of large businesses located nearby. You may be able to discover new business ideas and/or get such firms to outsource some of their activities to your firm.

Your acre of diamonds may be in your own backyard.

The strategic choices for existing businesses are these: search for breakthrough technologies, exploit emerging information technologies, seek to become a world-class producer, optimize your present business operations and secure a global competitive position, or settle for being a local niche operator in an increasingly threatened and shrinking marketplace. As large firms strive to achieve these goals, many small businesses will be in a position to capitalize on emerging opportunities arising out of this process. The profound effect of information technology is that companies are using it to offer customers greater individual attention and personalized services. Companies are seizing the initiative, transforming their operations, and seeking to delight their customers as never before. G/Es need to reflect on this point: What is your distinctive specialty, or what breakthrough technology do you possess that can be offered to big business? Will your product or service create excitement in the marketplace and a profit for you?

Creating Business Opportunities

A good idea and a viable business opportunity are quite different. An opportunity is based on an idea that will create economic value. An opportunity exists only when a good idea is combined with other requirements: the presence of potential consumers who desire your product and have the ability (money) to make a purchase, and positive conditions facilitating start-up of a new business. Also, it is important not to confuse apparent needs with viable opportunities. Certainly, the presence of needs and wants are the basic requirement for a successful business, but needs and opportunities are not the same thing. In Third World countries, there are many apparent needs for housing, transportation, medical care and education. But entrepreneurial opportunities in these areas are limited in these countries since people there have little money to make purchases beyond basic survival needs. Under these conditions, entrepreneurs are often limited to micro-business opportunities.

An opportunity is an idea that results in creating value.

In some instances, opportunities are *created* by introducing a new product for which there is no existing demand. When Daimler-Benz and Ford first introduced motor-powered automobiles, there was little demand because the cost was high, fuel was scarce, and roads were few. When the telephone was first introduced, there was little demand, because unless others had a phone, there was no one to talk to. When Steve Jobs and Steve Wozniak started selling personal computers in the early 1970s, there was little apparent demand. Just a few years earlier, in 1943, Thomas Watson, then Chairman of IBM Company, said, "I think there is a world market for maybe five computers." As late as 1977, Ken Olson, the founder of Digital Equipment Corporation, mentioned that he "saw no reason why anyone would want a computer in their home." When an American entrepreneur first introduced the Pet Rock, there was no demand. After seeing it, some thought it was "cute"; others noticed it did not eat very much, and it became a craze. It even had brisk sales for a short period of time.

A viable entrepreneurial opportunity exists when these conditions are present: a *market demand* exists for the product; there are potential *consumers who desire the product* and have the *ability to purchase it*; and there is a relative *ease of entry* for the entrepreneurs who start the venture. The absence of any one of these three conditions will either keep you from starting the business or make it difficult to be successful after it is initiated. As the entrepreneur becomes successful, different problems will emerge. For example, when others notice the attractiveness of your venture, i.e., how much money you are making, you will certainly have competition.

Challenging Ideas for the Global Entrepreneur

Often G/Es have little interest in conventional business opportunities; instead they are attracted to ideas they can build into significant businesses, and concepts that will have worldwide appeal. The following areas may have high appeal to G/Es.

There are untold entrepreneurial opportunities as we enter the "Third Wave" of ubiquitous computing, that is, when we see computers distributed throughout our public and private space. They will be embedded in everything in our lives—cars, houses, clothes, cell phones, televisions, appliances, boats and most other objects we use.

Having an opportunity to help shape the "*e-corporation*" is an imminent challenge to G/Es. New kinds of virtual organizations and virtual products are being spawned daily through the use of information technology—the Internet and enterprising software are creating a new industrial order that is nothing short of an Info-Tech revolution.

Material research is attempting to decipher the chemical codes of all the tangible items in the world so that chemical elements can be reassembled into new and improved items, such as metal alloys that can repair themselves and smart materials that recognize and respond to their environments. These new materials will be stronger and tougher, and they will emit less pollution than before.

The earth itself presents some unique opportunities: harvesting the sea, not for fish, but for anticancer, antiviral, heart-stimulating, nerve-blocking properties of everything from deep-sea sponges to sea cucumbers to starfish; exploring the tropical rain forest in search of rarely seen flora and fauna, as well as other staggering treasure troves including timber, fruit, spices, and plants and animals whose secret compounds are being used for fighting against AIDS, malaria, cancer and obesity. The Amazon jungle is home to unusual fruits and vegetables, and these are being marketed to developed countries where exotic products are always in demand.

The salient revolution of "mass customization" is now reshaping the way products are produced and delivered to customers. Large firms with thousands of customers are starting to build their products so they are customized for each person; Dell will assemble a computer to your exact specifications and Levi Strauss will tailor a single pair of jeans to exactly fit your body shape.

The search for Extraterrestrial Intelligent Beings (EIB), probing the skies and *now* even our Earth for evidence of intelligent life other than known species, has become a compelling pursuit. In 2010, NASA scientist Felisa Wolfe-Simon led a research team in a discovery that could rewrite the rules of life. Until now, all organisms were thought to have six essential elements in common: oxygen, hydrogen, nitrogen, sulfur, carbon and phosphorus. The research team was successful in substituting *arsenic* in lieu of the sixth element of phosphorus in growing live laboratory bacteria. If this new finding holds up, scientists will have to add a noxious element 33 to the construction kit for human existence.

Exploring the field of genetics and scrutinizing the brain more closely may open the field of discovery linking individual genes and the hope of cures for cancer, multiple sclerosis and Alzheimer's disease. Knowing the function of specific genetic codes will allow pharmaceutical firms to develop drugs to neutralize dangerous genes and substitute vital proteins missing in aberrant genes.

Exploration in human cell growth could result in the ability to regenerate missing or damaged organs and body parts in humans. Biotech firms are eagerly searching for ways to repair, renew, or produce new tissues. This has huge implications for repairing damaged hearts and other body organs.

It is now possible to establish your own NetCard Company, offering a standard Visa card - along with favorite airline and rent-a-car company rewards - via the Internet. Personalized statements of expenses are available on NetCard's Website, and the account, as well as others, can be paid by automatic bank transfer.

Just read any issue of the publications *Fast Company* or *Wired,* and you will discover ideas that are stimulating and challenging to the G/E. These entrepreneurs are interested in things on the cutting edge of their discipline and ideas that offer worldwide development opportunities. Operating someone else's franchise pizza outlet does not excite the G/E. Many successful executives have completed the corporate route and are seeking an entirely different career experience. They are asking, "What else can I do for intellectual stimulation, to develop a greater challenge in my life, and to create even more wealth?" Becoming a G/E is one answer to that challenge.

How Ideas Shape Opportunities

A good entrepreneurial idea is the starting point of a new venture. A question that students frequently ask every entrepreneurship professor is this: "Can you suggest a good business for me to start?" There is no easy answer to this question because each person is different. Also, most new business ventures are *not* based on an "original" idea, but are based on the skill and abilities of the individual entrepreneur - something they are presently doing. Good ideas alone do not make for a successful business. In addition to the idea, a number of other things must be considered and put in place for a new business venture to be successful. First is the business plan, which banks and investors expect from entrepreneurs. Preparation of the plan ensures that the entrepreneur understands and considers all the requirements for starting and operating a successful venture.

Entrepreneurs tend to set themselves apart from other people by thinking about personal achievement and about operating their own business. Entrepreneurs will conceive and develop a number of ideas leading them towards the start-up of their own business rather than working for others. Idea development is a fundamental part of the entrepreneurial process, as is shown in Figure 5.3.

Figure 5.3
The Entrepreneurship Process

A Trigger Event	The Idea Development	The Business Opportunity	A Venture Start-up

In a person's life, there are often triggering events—both internal and external—that encourage him or her to think about self-employment rather than working for others. Among them are frustration with one's present job, the loss of a job, boredom, religious and/or ethnic persecution, governmental restrictions, or simply a long-term desire to be self-employed. When these trigger events occur, individuals begin to visualize the possibility of starting their own business. Most business ideas come from within the individual—from what they do with their hands or mind, at work, at home, or as a hobby. These ideas flow rather spontaneously since they represent current skills and abilities that are used frequently by the G/E.

Equipped with a good idea, these business hopefuls are ready for a reality check regarding their proposed venture. A logical next step is to test the market and see if there are a sufficient number of people who desire the product and are able to buy it. A viable business opportunity consists of three things: the good idea, a desire for the product, and a sufficient number of people who are able to purchase the product. All three must be present for an idea to become a viable business opportunity. Assuming these three factors are present, does the venture start at this time? Well, that depends on whether you are in a country like Zaire or Iran with little economic freedom, or in Singapore or the U.S., which have maximum economic freedom. A venture start-up in Zaire will take months or years, whereas, in the U.S., one can start a business within a few hours if desired.

Virtualization: The Organization and Products

Today's entrepreneurs are increasingly using virtual organizations for their start-up ventures. Such an organization exists only in the mind of the entrepreneur and is created upon need. When one goes to knock on the door, no one is at the office. Likewise, virtual products are also offered to customers and they do not physically exist at the time they are sold either. The product concept, as well as its design, how it will be produced, exists only in the mind of the G/E, or the G/E's associates, who have to convince customers to purchase it. Virtual products are not new. For years, business consultants have sold their virtual service products, then produced and delivered them. However, now major firms are engaged in virtualization as they produce and sell their tangible, hard-good products. A good example is Dell Computer. Dell is most efficient and effective with its instantaneous development of products based on a customer order. Orders are assembled in accordance with customer specifications and then are delivered. In-house raw materials and finished-goods inventory is measured in minutes and hours, not in days or weeks. Parts are ordered for just-in-time assembly, and then the finished product is promptly shipped to customers - frequently on the same day of order and assembly.

A virtual product is one that does not physically exist when sold.

A new form of virtualization has emerged – *virtual manufacturing*. Chris Anderson, Editor in Chief at *Wired* says, "the era of the huge conglomerate is over. The future of business will be more start-ups, fewer giants, and infinite opportunity." He says the Web will be taking globalization to the extreme. According to Anderson, a major result of the recession is the rise of the "next new-new economy," one which will clearly favor the small. New ventures can tap into the best of breed anywhere creating "flash firms" of workers and suppliers who come together to create one product and then re-form for another venture. The webification of the supply chain and today's outsourcing opportunities mean that even the tiniest company started by a G/E can now operate globally, very much like large firms of the past.[63]

G/Es will view their competencies, and those of their international network of partners, as potential sources for creating global knowledge products for their ventures. They will identify potential knowledge products by thinking about how their networking team can enhance existing products and/or how they can create entirely new products for customers. One can *distill* knowledge by developing an entirely new product and enticing customers to purchase it. In Europe, for example, a liquid ice has been developed; it is superior to regular ice because it is easier to store, takes up less space, and has a quicker freezing process since objects such as fish can be completely covered. One can also *instill* knowledge into existing products, thereby making them more valuable to customers. For example, a Seattle, Washington, company has created a method of treating textiles that kills bacteria that cause clothes to retain odors. With this new, knowledge-based chemical treatment, clothes can be worn, if desired, for days without having an odor. Shirts are currently being sold in Japan and other countries with this type of permanently embedded deodorant. Just think how much better the world would be without smelly shoes and socks!

The New World of Mobile Phone Applications

The mobile cell phone has become one of the most successful inventions in the 21th century, thanks to Dr. Martin Cooper of Motorola who invented the device in 1973. In the late 1990s, mobile phones became one of the major communication devices. Today it is unbelievable how integral mobile phones have become in our daily lives. Not only are our lives enriched by having the ability of constant communication anywhere in the world while on the go, but an increasing number of benefits arise daily and even hourly from having the personal mobile device. A seemingly endless, expanding universe of mobile applications (apps) provide a plethora of useful services to individuals. At the beginning of 2011, Apple, Inc. has close to 300,000 apps for sale in its stores alone compared with 140,000 a year ago. Tomorrow it will be 500,000 plus apps available for every conceivable thing the mind can imagine.

Interactive mobile apps residing in the cell phone itself offer many marketing opportunities for *businesses* to connect directly to consumers. Such direct, real-time connection can create unprecedented advertising, sales and revenue opportunities. On smart phones, these apps can contain on-demand streaming video as part of the total app "experience." Such video content is refreshed frequently, encouraging consumers to use the app every day, throughout the day, with various consumer incentives such as coupons for goods and services.

Mobile *entertainment* for users is a big success because such entertainment offers enjoyment in remote places, on long trips, or even at a bus stop. A variety of experiences can be offered - music, lifestyle information, news, blogging, gaming and driving directions, to name a few. Various fun applications can be downloaded from the Internet and transferred to one or more mobile phones.

Mobile *learning* is a fast-growing, relatively new side of cell phone application development. This interactive way of assimilating useful information is becoming very popular with users of all ages. Go Test Go offers a wide range of mobile learning applications in the U.S., for example, whether you are preparing for an SAT exam, a driver's license exam or getting ready to explore the cultures of a different country.

From America …

Your wait is over! Eric Adler and Julien Chabbott at Babson College may have developed an app to help solve a very frustrating problem for just about everyone – waiting in line. They developed Line Snob, a free iPhone app that gives real-time information about lines and wait times, plus rewarding users (through points that can be redeemed for coupons) for reporting on lines they are standing in. Participating businesses pay a monthly fee, and Line Snob also makes a commission with in-app promotions, which lead users to make purchases at the venues. For example, users in the Washington, D.C., area can use Line Snob to get $1 off a salad at Sweetgreen restaurant.

Apple's App Store dominates the headlines and airwaves, with consumers downloading in excess of 100 million free and premium applications each month; they are arming their iPhones with the latest in navigation tools, friend finders, utilities and games. Apple's problem is that most of its apps are exclusive to the iPhone platform, and this may restrict its international growth. Nokia and other major cell phone companies offer apps from across competing platforms, including Android, BlackBerry, Symbian and Windows Mobile, spanning some 1,700-plus mobile phones in all. Now the question for the G/E is: Where to place your mobile app? Apple dominates the U.S and is increasing its 17-percent world share of smart phones, whereas Nokia is dominant in Europe, Asia, and developing countries with its 35-percent world share.

The app world is an exploding opportunity for G/Es. If you have a stellar application idea for business, entertainment, or learning, and you do not have the skill to develop your own app, there are a number of firms that will help you to develop and market the app. You may want to look at Application, LLC, in Houston, Texas, which has a high rating in this area. A search of the Internet will reveal a number of other firms that can assist to you in developing your app. Alternatively, Google has a new App Inventor that lets business owners create their own free, targeted app solutions optimized expressly for their staffers, their customers or even their own private use. However, it is only for smart phones running the Android operating system, not for BlackBerry or iPhone users. This gives app-making a do-it-yourself spin.

Is the mobile app an opportunity for the G/E to make money? The answer is yes, but it is becoming an increasingly crowded field with many people being willing to offer free apps just for fame, recognition, or capturing lots of users. It is easy to see that most cell phone apps are much more than fun distractions during a consumer's busy day. They now represent major business opportunities. Being successful moneywise comes down to basic execution: a great concept, a good user experience, tight marketing and a smart distribution plan. There are obvious money-making opportunities with puzzles and games, but the app market is a "hit-driven industry," and the total market revenue is frequently concentrated among a few big winners in each category.

Creating the Social Network Venture

The phenomenal growth of social networking has certainly captured the attention of entrepreneurs since they tend to follow the marketplace in terms of rapid growth and development of organizations. G/Es are likely to be fans of social networking websites such as Facebook, Twitter, Linkedin, and hundreds of new ones being launched. One simply cannot ignore these online portals that get literally millions of visitors on a daily basis. Social networking will be discussed more in chapter ten. It is important for the G/E to consider marketing his/her product or service in a social networking domain. Even if you are not looking to build a network of friends online, you can develop a professional network of prospective colleagues, customers, partners, and industry peers that will help you in many ways.

G/Es are creating social network sites to make money and to gain experience in the domain. It is a lot easier than you think, and it can be done with little expense. Ning originally offered entrepreneurs the opportunity to develop their own social networking company free of charge, but now is charging for that service. There are full-featured, leading-community-building platforms (starter-kits) that can be fully customized. You may want to visit a couple of places such as KickApps.com/SocialNetworks, and Ning, which has launched do-it-yourself social network platform called Social Networks for Everyone. Ning says, "…by designing your product the right way, you can build a billion-dollar business from scratch. No advertising or marketing budget, no need for a sales force, and venture capitalists will kill for the chance to throw money at you."[64] Every entrepreneur would like that very much.

Emerging Trends Shaping the World

We started this chapter by asking, where are the next big ideas coming from? There are currently some major trends developing in the marketplace. These include many "smart" products: hand-held devices, mobile phones, intelligent instruments in autos, and even home appliances that can be accessed through networks and the Internet. Increasingly, firms have entire electronic communities using the Internet, intranets, and extranets, so that people inside and outside the company throughout the world can share needed information.

Advances in voice recognition technology are making computers and other devices easier to use. The ability to give verbal commands to the computer, the cell phone and other gadgets in the home may make life simpler. The use of satellite and wireless technology will become much more prevalent among firms, travelers, boaters and consumers. Telecommunication firms will continue to merge and strive for a greater market share so they can serve their consumers with an increasing menu of products for personal convenience, entertainment and business purposes.

Wouldn't it be nice to have a crystal ball that foretells future trends? If one could do this, it would be a sure way for entrepreneurs to capitalize on emerging opportunities. While such soothsaying is not possible, MIT's *Technology Review* does give us the next best thing. Each year, editors at Massachusetts Institute of Technology ask some of the top technology experts in the world to select emerging areas of technology, those which will soon have a profound impact on the economy and on how we live and work. Below are the high-impact technological ideas that MIT's experts have agreed upon for the past two years.[65]

The 10 Emerging Technologies of 2010

Social Networking is Changing the Way we Find Information. Real-time search for all kinds of information is a response to a fundamental shift in the way people use the Web.

Designing the Perfect Renewable Fuel. By manipulating and designing genes, Flagship Ventures has created photosynthetic microorganisms that use sunlight to efficiently convert carbon dioxide into ethanol or diesel fuel.

Smart phones will take 3-D Mainstream. The Samsung B710 phone does something unexpected when the screen is moved from a vertical to a horizontal orientation: the image jumps from 2-D to 3-D.

Engineered Stem Cells. Cellular Dynamics has developed a way to make stem cells from adult cells by adding just four genes normally active in embryos. These cells can reproduce themselves many times over, and they can develop into any cell type in the human body.

Light Trapping Photovoltaics. Kylie Catchpole discovered that depositing nanoparticles made of silver on thin-film photovoltaic cells increases the cells' efficiency and possibly can make solar power more competitive.

Social TV. A scientist in MIT's electronic research lab is working on a way to seamlessly combine the social networks that are boosting TV ratings with the more passive experience of traditional TV viewing. Opening TV to social networking could help provide personalized programming.

Making Green Concrete. Novacem, a London-based start-up, found when water is added to magnesium concrete compounds without Portland's limestone in the mix, it still makes a solid-setting concrete that does not rely on carbon-rich limestone.

Implantable Electronics. Tufts University scientists found they could use silk as the basis of implantable optical and electronic devices that will act as a vital-sign monitor for blood testing and an imaging center – and will safely break down when no longer needed.

Cloud Programming. Joseph Hllerstein at UCLA has been able to modify existing database programming languages so they can be used to quickly build any sort of application in the cloud – social networks, communication tools, games and more.

Dual-Action Antibodies. Germaine Fuh, senior scientist at Genentech, has been able to combine the action of two antibodies on one molecule. Having a single drug hit cancer from multiple directions would simplify treatments.

The 10 Emerging Technologies of 2009

New-Generation Search. Scouring the Web for information is becoming faster and easier. Could this new rise in search tools and navigation technology be a threat to Google's dominance?

Technology Market Searching. Tracking innovative technologies appearing in commercial products can lead to development of other products.

Your Next Cell Phone. Every day, new phones and new announcements purport to redefine how we will use our cell phones – from the latest GPS-enabled application to social computing. It is remarkable how the cell phone has expanded with hundreds of potential consumer usages.

Better Batteries. The lack of efficient and dependable batteries limits the development of everything from electronics to hybrid vehicles. The search for new designs that offer better, safer, and longer-lasting alternatives is on.

Solar Power. Researchers are creating novel types of photovoltaic devices that could finally make solar power a broadly practical source of renewable energy.

Smarter IT. Smarter information technology can give businesses the competitive edge. From cloud computing and new web services to greener data centers and better security management, explore the ways IT is evolving to meet demand.

Tomorrow's Car. Worries over the future of gasoline supplies and the effects of carbon dioxide emissions are driving innovators to rethink how we get around and to build electric-powered units.

Biofuels. Everyone from leading Silicon Valley venture capitalists to former President Bush is touting fuels created from biomass as a replacement for petroleum. However, new technologies are needed to make this vision economically and environmentally feasible.

Personalized Medicine. We look at how cheap, fast genomic sequencing are beginning to yield medicines tailored to your genes.

The above two-year listing of the most important technologies of our time are taken from MIT's *Technology Review* website. A majority of the ideas in these emerging technology areas are being developed in academic research laboratories and in business. Most of the idea developers are keen to demonstrate to the world the commercial value of their ideas. Some have developed their own ventures. Others have aligned themselves with large firms that provide substantial research support and an avenue for commercialization of the idea.

Most of the *Technology Review* ideas are a challenge to current industry dogma. In *Fast Company,* Rekha Balu says, "In the new world of work, you have to deconstruct the ruling dogma of your industry [or discipline] and generate heretical ideas to challenge that dogma; then build [your] strategies and brands around those [new] ideas." To be successful then, we must not be excessively consumer-led, for the world is full of constant change. *Consumers cannot possibly and should not be expected to anticipate the next big idea.* That is the role of entrepreneurs—to anticipate the future needs, wants and desires of consumers. Yes, there are a number of G/Es developing the above products and services. It is of interest to note that a majority of these inventors are internationals, and they habitually think globally. They are here in the U.S., shaping the cutting-edge technology and trends in their respective domains with the ultimate goal of commercializing their ideas on a global scale.

Fitting It All Together

A number of events, activities and functions have to fit together for a business to operate successfully. This makes life challenging for entrepreneurs because they have to "wear many hats," some of which they have never seen or worn before. Starting a business is often a major undertaking and requires considerable preparation. A properly prepared business plan will ensure that entrepreneurs know and include all the fundamental requirements of starting their own business. A business plan is like a builder's blueprint that identifies the necessary pieces to construct a successful business. The central driving force in the construction process is the entrepreneur with his or her business idea. The business plan will be discussed in more detail in chapter nine. Two other documents should precede the development of the formal business plan - a one-page business concept document and a two-page executive summary, both to be used to *pretest* the viability of the business venture before extensive time, effort and funding is spent formalizing the venture.

For a business to be successful, there must be an overall "fit" of several factors. It has been stated, "Good ideas are not worth ten cents a dozen." One must *do something* with the idea in order to give it value. To be valuable, the idea must *fit* into a sequence of events, activities and functions, and it must serve as the basis of a viable business opportunity. This pattern is somewhat like a puzzle. The pieces have to fall in place at the proper time and place in order for the business to be successful. Therefore, it is very important for the G/E to be *three people* - entrepreneur, manager and leader - all in one and all at the same time. Successfully assuming all three roles means the G/E is truly a unique person. This is also why the G/E is recognized as the highest order of entrepreneurs.

There are typically five components of the puzzle. First, the entrepreneur is the most important component. He or she starts the process and is the driving force behind the business venture. A second piece of the puzzle is finding a good venture idea. Third, one must test that idea to see if it represents an opportunity that will generate the desired profit in the marketplace. Fourth, the entrepreneur needs the ability to bring together the production, marketing, financial and management resources to start the business. The fifth, and perhaps most difficult piece of the puzzle, is "being in the right place at the right time" when starting a business. Some call this luck. But remember the old saying about luck: "The harder one works, the luckier one becomes." Obviously, persistence and luck are close relatives.

Sometimes business success comes quickly, but most of the time it occurs over a period of years. Businesses frequently fail when the entrepreneur starts a business without proper preparation. Business ideas, opportunities, markets, planning, business functions, the right time, the right place—all of these factors must be crafted together by the G/E into a coherent pattern of performance. Reading and learning the requirements for a successful business is the easy part. Putting them into practice with *patience, persistence* and *pursuit* is far more challenging and rewarding. That is the ultimate goal of the Global Entrepreneur.

6

The Global Marketplace

"It is possible today, to a greater extent than at any time in the world's history, for a company to locate anywhere, to use resources from anywhere, and to produce a product that can be sold anywhere."
Milton Friedman

Emergence of the Global Marketplace

A fundamental fact of our new economic era is the emergence of a global marketplace. In the past, most businesses have been linked to specific geographical locations. Individuals, too, are reluctant to migrate far from their home or work. For example, some 78 percent of North Americans do not possess a passport. Often, those who do not travel abroad are prone to have a narrow perspective of the world and a limited knowledge of geography. Usually they speak only one language. People are strongly attracted to their native land. Even when a country is ravaged by war, such as Afghanistan, or when an earthquake destroys a complete city in Iran, many displaced people actively seek to return to their native land, declaring they want to be there. After all, it is "home." We noted earlier how Traditional Entrepreneurs tend to be locals rather than cosmopolitans, generally for the same reason. Home and work make deep impressions on one's locality. The human tendency toward being narrow and local imposes serious limitations on business opportunities, and this severely restricts the market for products and services.

The first concrete evidence of a global marketplace occurred when many large U.S.-based organizations expanded overseas during the 1960s. With a slowing of economic growth in their domestic markets, U.S. firms were increasingly attracted by opportunities in affluent markets of Europe, Latin America and Asia. In the 1970s, the world witnessed the entry of major Japanese firms into foreign markets, particularly in the U.S., and they were soon followed by European companies responding to the North American threat. Europeans took this global threat seriously. During the 1970s, the Frenchman J. Servan-Schreiber expressed his concerns in a book, *The American Challenge*, where he warned that American multinational firms would take over the world economy. In the 1980s, Schreiber posted another warning in another book of his, *Japan as Number One*, stating that the U.S.'s position was being taken over by Japan. The Japanese "take over" did not occur as predicted, and America still dominates the world economy. However, major Japanese firms are gaining market share and are surpassing America in a number of industries, such as electronics and automobiles.

Others perceived a more recent economic threat to America from the European Union (E.U.) The E.U. was established in 1957, when six European countries formed the European Economic Community. Today the E.U. has 27 member states or countries primarily located in Europe. The entity was formed as a political and economic community with intergovernmental features, such as a president and other official administrative officers. The enlarged E.U. has been a driving force behind global cooperation through the G20 group of countries. However, the E.U. has been slow and sluggish in responding to the current recession, and member states had to bail out Greece with its financial difficulties. There is some concern that other member states will need a stimulus and bailout, as was the case with Greece and Ireland. Overall, the E.U.'s single market concept and the euro have yet to reach its original intended goals. It failed to meet its 2000 Lisbon target growth goal of being the "most competitive, knowledge-based economy in the world by 2010." In spite of a lackluster performance, Jose Manuel Barroso, the new President of the European Commission, is optimistic and says, "The commission has put forth detailed proposals for a new European and global supervisory architecture to be in place in 2010." It is expected these changes will help to identify new sources of economic growth for Europe.[66] The E.U. is not likely to be a major challenge to the U.S. for at least another decade taking in consideration their difficult response to the recent world financial crisis.

Then there is Japan and the rest of Asia. Japan has been struggling for the past 15 years to get its economic house in order. Signs of significant economic improvement are evident there for this geographically small country; however, its economic ranking has slipped from third to fourth largest economy in the world. Asia is no longer lagging behind the Euro-American regions in total economic prosperity, for it is increasingly turning toward market capitalism and has some of the fastest growing economies in the world. America faces serious economic challenges from Asian countries.

How People and Places Shape the Global Marketplace

There are a number of ways to describe today's global marketplace, such as in people, clusters, centers of excellence, economic zones, fastest-growing cities, hotspots, and countries. One will obviously find some overlap in the classifications; for example, a city may also be listed as a hotspot. So let's first see how certain types of people shape the global marketplace.

Thinkers, Makers, and Traders: Rosabeth Moss Kanter at Harvard finds that marketplaces develop preeminence based on certain characteristics of people as *thinkers, makers,* or *traders.* The thinkers are mainly conceptual and develop world-class products and/or services based on their specialized knowledge and technology. University laboratories are a good source of thinkers. Thinkers use proprietary knowledge to secure a niche in a world market. As their innovations become more diffused in business, thus losing their unique differentiation and price advantage, thinkers move in a different direction. A good example here is a recent spin-off firm from the University of Washington/Caltech, the Impinj Company, whose cofounder, Carver Mead, has 21 previous start-ups under his belt.[67]

Makers focus on producing world-class products through cost-efficient operations. Their global production operations are usually supported by strong local supplier networks, advanced technology and good sources of labor. Makers tend to be very visible and their products are shipped throughout the world. Consequently, areas where they are located tend to attract considerable domestic and foreign investment.

Traders are those who specialize in selling in the global marketplace. Kanter sees traders in cities that are posited as the "crossroads of culture, helping to move goods and services from one country to another, and managing the interactions." Miami, Florida, USA, with its strong connections to South America, is a leading international trade center in the U.S. Singapore and Hong Kong are strong trading cities linking the East with the West, Kanter says. "What distinguishes the world-class from the merely good is the ability of a global center in thinking, making or trading." World-class regions demonstrate excellence in at least one of the three domains.

Clusters: It has proved important to be among "clusters" of other organizations in your industry. For example, to be world-class in microelectronics, it is essential to be located in the Silicon Valley cluster; likewise, to be world class in tufted carpeting, it is imperative to be near Dalton, Georgia. In the past, size of the enterprise used to be far more important than it is today. For G/Es, the size of the enterprise can be small if located near a "cluster" of like manufacturers, or some recognized center of excellence. In so doing, the G/E can be a part of a local business community, share in the available infrastructure, have key suppliers, and access the most advanced technology, machine tools, raw material, and labor from various industry support firms. Such clusters of excellence give the small G/E a scale and operational scope not otherwise possible.

Centers of Excellence: Having the primary location in a center of excellence allows G/Es to focus on their unique position, or the particular niche they have chosen to serve exceptionally well. Contrary to prevailing thought, the larger the global marketplace, the greater is the necessity for G/Es to specialize, or narrow their product/service offering, in order to be successful. Therefore, it is not advisable for G/Es to consider a wide range of products: leave that to large firms with more resources. G/Es should concentrate on becoming world leaders by developing their core competence with a very narrow product/service *focus*. Understanding, finding, and then developing one's core competences are of particular importance to G/Es. This is facilitated by locating near a technical center of excellence, accumulating as much expertise and knowledge as possible, and optimizing the business through a network of global partners.

Economic Zones: The global marketplace, with its free flow of economic activity, has created a "new borderless world," according to Kenichi Ohme in his book, *The End of Nation States*. In this borderless world, specific regions have emerged as major economic zones and are real havens for entrepreneurial development. These economic zones, although small in size when compared to national states, are immense in relative economic importance. You can find these zones in various parts of the world: the Research Triangle Park, North Carolina, USA; the Cambridge/Oxford area in Britain, with its 1,200 technology firms; northern Italy; Baden Wurttemberg, Germany; Fukuoka and Kitakyushu in Japan; the Growth Triangle of Singapore; and the city of Dalian, Liaodong Peninsula, China.[68]

Fast Growing Markets: The Alibaba Group has developed a Speed of Change Index, which ranks the world's fastest growing markets. The top ten fastest-growing markets are listed here: Bosnia (100 Points) is rapidly changing as it propels itself out of a war and decades of communist rule; Albania (86 points) didn't end communist rule until 1991, and is busy transforming its economy into a market-oriented system; Taiwan (84 Points) has the distinction of being the fastest-moving wealthy country on the Speed of Change Index; China (76 Points) has much more social and economic freedom than 20 years ago and is looking to continue its 9 to 10-percent growth in GDP for several more years; Cape Verde (75 Points), the former Portuguese colony of

10 islands in the North Atlantic, is bearing fruit from its economic reforms launched in 1991; and Mozambique (73 Points), the poorest country in the world, finally ended its civil war in 1992, and is showing signs of sharp growth, mostly in the agricultural area.[69]

Cities: Major cities such as New York, London and Hong Kong, have long been recognized as global hotspots favorable towards business development. They are no less important than Stockholm, Cambridge/Oxford, Geneva, Amsterdam, Milan, Helsinki, Munich, and Paris. Lesser-known hotspots are Bangalore, the technology capital of India; Taipei's Hsinchu Science Park, home to dozens of high-tech companies, Tokyo's Olympus Basic Research Institute, with dozens of companies and research facilities; and Israel's Bioinformatic Start-up Compugen in Tel Aviv, which supports high-tech ventures. Russia is getting into the high-tech game and is trying to duplicate Silicon Valley with a number of secret scientific cities deep in the Ural Mountains. One such city is located in a small village outside Moscow where security is so tight that children have to wear security badges. Victor Vekselbert, project co-director, says the country is trying to diversify its economy away from oil and to duplicate the vibrancy and entrepreneurial spirit of America's technology hotbeds. On a smaller scale, Boulder, Colorado, has become the top U.S. city for technology start-ups. That is largely because of a bottom-up revolution led by an influx of techies; Boulder has the highest concentration of software engineers per capita in the nation.

Now we have new kids on the block as the fastest-growing cities in the world. First is Beihai in China, which has been named the fastest-growing city worldwide. Beihai has grown from a small harbor to a modern city and is a hub city connecting the southwest of China to Southeast Asia. A second newcomer is the Indian city Ghaziabad, located in the Uttar Pradesh state and which has a number of flourishing industries, such as high-tech, diesel engines, and even liqueur. Next is one of the oldest cities in Arabia, the 2,500-year-old-city Sanaa, the capital of Yemen, which is the commercial center a fruit-growing and the political capital of the country. From these cities, we go next to Surat, the eighth-largest city of India; Bamako, the capital of Mali; Lagos, the most populated city in the largest African country of Nigeria; Faridabad, India, known for producing vehicles, tires and shoes; Dar es Salaam in Tanzania; and number ten is Chittagong, the second-largest city in Bangladesh. Truly, we have a new world order developing in the fast-growing cities and their respective countries.

Perhaps you as a G/E can help shape cities of the future, which are likely to embrace these following trends, according to *Fast Company:* smart energy grids; a venture capital mind-set; cultural centers; a renaissance of older neighborhoods; open-source city government; car sharing; incentivized teachers; urban farms; zero-emission public transit; artists as residents; and broadband everywhere for everyone.[70]

Countries: Today BRIC is a wide-used acronym for the four countries of Brazil, Russia, India and China, a dynamic growth area. BRIC represents all developing-growing countries of the world and not just the four mentioned. Many experts consider Russia a developing country, but not one that is growing rapidly, as the other three BRIC countries are. China, India, and Brazil, in that order are truly growth economies. The increase in Asian growth is particularly evident in the automotive segment. This is where the traditional U.S. big three firms continue to lose market share, not only to Asians, but also to European firms. China has become both the largest automobile producer and the largest auto market in the world, with its massive growth surge in 2009.

There are individual countries that stand out for being more favorable towards promoting entrepreneurial endeavors than others. In its fourth annual Best Countries for Business Index in 2009, *Forbes* ranks countries having the best start-up business conditions in 127 economies. Topping the list for 2009: Denmark, for a second straight year, takes the number one spot. The U.S. is up two spots to number two; Canada is up four spots to number three; Singapore is number four; and New Zealand is number five. Big movers include New Zealand, which moved up seven spots; Australia, number eight, up five spots; Jordan, now 33, moving up 28 spots; United Arab Emirates, now 46, up 28 spots; and Malaysia, number 25, up 13 spots. Keep in mind these are not economies with the highest GDPs. *Forbes* just wanted to share with entrepreneurs and investors information regarding dynamic national economies that are most favorable for entrepreneurs starting new ventures.

The United Arab Emirates, in particular, has made strides in protecting intellectual property rights through initiatives like educational seminars for thousands of students, with support from corporations like Procter & Gamble, Estee Lauder and General Motors. New Zealand has improved its free-trade ranking by pursuing talks with India, Korea and Hong Kong. The China agreement was a "first" for a developed nation to establish a free-trade deal with China.[71]

Entrepreneurial hotspots include small towns, large cities, geographic regions, and whole countries around the world.

The researchers at *Forbes* cite six characteristics that promote countries as entrepreneurial hotspots: Having top academic or commercial research facilities; an appropriate number of entrepreneurs serving as role models; liberal tax policies, especially regarding stock options and capital gains that encourage entrepreneurs; an infrastructure of professional service companies; an outward-looking commercial tradition; and a pool of local investors that specializes in financing early-stage technology companies.[46] The global marketplace has truly arrived, and millions of eager consumers everywhere are open to new products and services. Needless to say, this global marketplace creates enormous opportunities for G/Es.

Major Contributing Factors Shaping the Global Marketplace

Nations tend to rise or fall, depending on how they develop, use, and adapt to new knowledge and technology. Political development tends to lag behind business development. Politics is inherently local, and business is becoming increasingly global. An established political order is very slow to change; however, business models change frequently. For example, the traditional Industrial Era paradigm is no longer the operative model of the New Global Economic Era. The large organization of the Industrial Era is becoming outdated and dysfunctional due to its size, structure, and inherent cost. There is a definite trend in the devolution of large, permanent business organizations. Most large organizations today are in transition, or certainly need to be, in moving towards a more flexible, temporary network of individuals capable of better serving both local and world markets.

The arrival of the New Global Economic Era, and the resulting global marketplace, is the product of four economic forces. The combined forces of *globalization, technology, the Information Era*, and the *Internet* all shape the global marketplace and the new economic order. Small and large firms are struggling to adapt to the rapid changes and opportunities in this new economic order. Who will be the most likely winners? It will be the bold, those who start early, those who learn the fastest, and those who get there the quickest with the best customer value. The new global marketplace is not confined to large multinational firms, or even to the smaller mininationals. For sure, this global marketplace is the choice domain of the G/E.

Globalization of Markets

From a business perspective, *globalization* can be defined as the ease with which a competitor can enter your market with world-class products and offer them to your customers at lower prices. In a somewhat broader view, globalization means a common viewpoint, a set of values and aspirations shared by people in many countries throughout the world. These common aspirations held by many are constantly stimulated by satellite television transmitted to the remote regions of China, India, and Africa and into other developing economies. The New Global Economic Era of the 21st century will include the 80 percent of the world's population living in the Third World—and some say that within three decades it will be dominated by them.

Globalization is the ease with which a competitor can enter your market offering world-class products to your customers at lower prices.

Globalization allows product knowledge to travel around the world in a matter of days, and copies of products can be on the market within weeks. This is particularly true with fashion items like clothing; for example, Zara, women's apparel, has reduced its lead time on clothing from nine months to seven days. It can occur with other products and services as well. It took Gillette three years to develop its first Mach3 razor. Copies of its three-blade razor were on the markets within a few months. New ideas, songs, unique dance crazes, and other social concepts are quickly diffused worldwide without regard to physical distance or national borders. The global marketplace is open to new ideas that have intrinsic power and value. Globalization touches all phases of a business organization and it has made profound, irreversible changes in how business is conducted. Complex organization networks are required to manage the geographic diversity of business operations, including alliances for R&D, production, marketing, licensing and outsourcing of services.

Technology Shapes the Global Marketplace

The recognition that *technology* is a key determinant in expanding one's productive resources has enormous global implications for both First World and Third World countries. From a business perspective, technology emerges in two forms—physical and conceptual. The physical aspect arises from the application of *technical knowledge* to enhancing and developing new products, processes and production solutions. The conceptual dimension arises from the application of *business knowledge* that is concerned with how things are organized, how they operate and how they function within the business organization. G/Es understand they must have a competitive advantage to be successful in the marketplace. This competitive advantage will come just as often from the use of *business knowledge* (the conceptual), such as having an advanced distribution system, as it will from having tangible, world-class products (the physical), which arise from the application of *technical knowledge*. All too often, business managers view technology from a narrow perspective, primarily from a physical standpoint.

All too often managers view technology from a narrow perspective, primarily from a physical standpoint.

Advances in technical knowledge have contributed to the development of new medicines from the rain forests of South America. Such advances have substantially increased rice and corn yields needed to feed the hungry in Asia and Africa, and they are creating new markets for existing products through technological transfer. Advances in business knowledge are generating radical, new organizational forms and many other innovative ways of managing the enterprise, to such an extent that academics are being forced to rewrite their business textbooks. An absolute imperative for every G/E is to view technology in its broadest context.

The Information Age and the Global Marketplace

Our entrance into the 21st century marks four decades of the computer era and 21 years since the Internet was invented. The computer has ushered in the first *Information Age* for the developed world. In business, as in war, information is vital. In the Persian Gulf War, Allied troops had a far better communications network than did Iraq, and they managed information more effectively. The Allied satellite and reconnaissance information provided great detail about Iraq's static defenses and troop locations. The Tomahawk cruise missiles were programmed so they could follow streets directly to their targets. Iraqi soldiers carried messages by hand, while Allied soldiers used hand-held satellite transmitters to pinpoint targets in the field. Having, using, and then denying information to Iraq paved the way for an unparalleled victory for the Allies in the war. As in war and so in business, those with the most information and knowledge are the ones who dominate.

As in war and so in business, those with the most information and knowledge are the ones who dominate.

A strong case can be made that the essence of business is having and using knowledgeable information. The success of your global business will depend on your ability to gather and process massive amounts of information from international constituents. The most revolutionary development of the Information Age is that the exponential growth in our ability to communicate with others on a worldwide basis. The use of teleconferencing, view-data, e-mail, faxes, international courier service, and other network computing makes communications between countries like Germany and South America as easy as it is from London to nearby Liverpool. It's clear, today's communications revolution continues to radically shrink our world as we move further into the 21st century. This vast, quick, inexpensive ability to communicate 24/7 throughout the world is an enormous asset for G/Es.

The new Information Era makes it possible for the writer-consultant John Naisbitt to operate his company, Megatrends, Ltd., with 57 joint ventures in 42 countries; and he has only four employees including Naisbitt. "He" is indeed a multinational firm; also, Naisbitt is a *prime example* of a small G/E. The term "Multinational" is certainly acquiring a new meaning. The traditional view is that a multinational has to be a large global company. However, a multinational can be a small number of people networking for a common business purpose in several different countries. Small entrepreneurial companies are now creating the global marketplace as well as the *Fortune* global firms. More than 50 percent of U.S. exports are from companies with fewer than 20 employees. Now that size and location of business have shrunk in importance; speed and flexibility are becoming increasingly important competitive advantages. These two attributes are the hallmarks of the G/E.

More than 50 percent of U.S. exports are from companies with fewer than 20 employees.

James Davidson and William Rees-Mogg, in their recent book, *The Sovereign Individual*, comment on this issue by saying this: "The processing and use of information are rapidly replacing and modifying physical resources as the most important source of wealth creation." The significant factor today making all this possible is not production, finance, marketing, or even the customer—it is *information technology*. What makes the information-driven global economy different from the Industrial Era is a significant proportion of the values of local goods and services will come from creative new ideas and shared knowledge. Obviously, the Internet is a major tool that is facilitating and supporting this wealth creation process.[72]

The Internet—A Global Marketing Tool

The Internet and the World Wide Web started with a group of U.S. scientists searching for an alternative source of communication in case of a nuclear war. It is only in the last decade of the 20th century that the Internet has been recognized as a viable business tool. Now literally thousands of business organizations, highlighted by such firms as Amazon books and Charles Schwab brokerage, have started Web businesses. Some experts say that e-commerce is poised to capture 20 to 50 percent of the market is certain industries, such as computers, software, automobiles, and books. David Mercer, in his book *Future Revolution*, says the biggest advantage of the Web is "hyperlinking," a seamless switching among Web sites, e-mail, CD-ROM and a variety of other media. This hyperlinking will allow all of an organization's constituents—employees, customers, suppliers, stockholders, and partners around the world—to switch with ease from the firm's mainframe computer to the company's Web page, then to warehousing inventory, to manufacturing, to the credit department, and to any other operation of the business. Within this extended global enterprise, a seamless network of business information can be retrieved in minutes without ever talking to an individual.[73] You do not have to be Amazon or Schwab to take advantage of such communications technology. A venture can operate as a four-person, global networking organization like that of John Naisbitt, a trend-seeking informational consultant.

In order to successfully compete in a local or global marketplace today, small businesses must establish an online presence. The Internet has transformed how, where and when business is conducted, thus creating opportunities for savvy entrepreneurs and leaving disconnected companies lagging behind. Setting up shop online provides a number of advantages, including the following major business boosters: broadening your potential customer base by selling your goods and services online; allowing for more local targeting based on demographics and psychographics; creating a new delivery system by having customized e-learning courses; and shrinking marketing expenses by providing seminar materials and other information online. The Internet has become a primary marketing tool for many firms, and traditional marketing expenses have been cut in half by many organizations.

The Use of Intranets and Extranets

The Internet allows a firm to link its entire supply chain together, and it facilitates the development of a virtual, global, online trading company. Companies are discovering how to extend corporate information to customers, partners, suppliers and other constituents via the *extranet*. For example, Walmart is known for having the most advanced logistic systems in the world; providing a unique competitive advantage that contributes significantly to the company having the lowest distribution cost in the retail industry. Now Walmart is using that core competence to assist their upstream product suppliers in lowering their distribution cost. Quite naturally, this means

Walmart will request a share of that savings in lower prices on products from these participating "extranet" organizations.

Internally, organizations are using the *intranet* to seek ways to cut costs and to improve communications among employees. In the emerging Internet Era, firms are no longer restricted to physical showroom space to exhibit their products. The G/E's "showroom" can exist solely in virtual space. Mercedes has iPad-equipped salespeople who are able to show payment schedules and initiate loans from any Wi-Fi location. Their virtual warehouse can stock an unlimited inventory and can be infinite in size. Business suppliers can receive orders, ship direct to the customer and then bill the customer in the firm's name without company employees ever seeing the product.

A study by the U.S. Commerce department found that 26 percent of Americans were using the Internet in 2000; then it jumped to 143 Million, or 54 percent, in 2001; and in December 31, 2009, some 76.2 percent of 310 million Americans were Internet users. Internet use in other countries is: Oceania/Australia, 60.8 percent; Europe, 53.0 percent; Latin America/Caribbean, 31.9 percent; Asia, 20.1 percent; and Africa at 8.7 percent. Official statistics show China's Internet users reached 384 million (24 percent) by the end of 2009; that is some 80 million more than the total population of U.S. The Internet is the major tool for G/Es reaching their customers in the global marketplace. Some of this potential is presented in the Net-Centric Business Model presented on the following pages.[74]

The Net-Centric Business Model

Understanding how an Internet economy is going to shape your current business model and everything you do is critical to business success. Unquestionably, the Internet has fundamentally altered the way many firms are organized and how they operate. These changes will impact the relationship between business producers and consumers more profoundly than one can imagine. The question is, will you or your company be in the driver's seat in this new Net-Centric industrial order, or will you be a casualty of this radical change?

In addition to fundamentally changing the way businesses operate, the Internet has introduced a host of new digital companies to the business world in a short period of time. This means business competition has intensified across the board – from small to large businesses. Gary Hamel and Jeff Sampler challenge every business manager with this provocative comment: "Somewhere out there is a silver bullet with your company's name on it and there is a competitor, perhaps unborn and unknown, which can render your business obsolete."[75] Many corporate CEOs frequently ponder this comment, wondering if a "silver bullet" is on its way to their company.

Figure 6.1
The Net-Centric Value Wheel

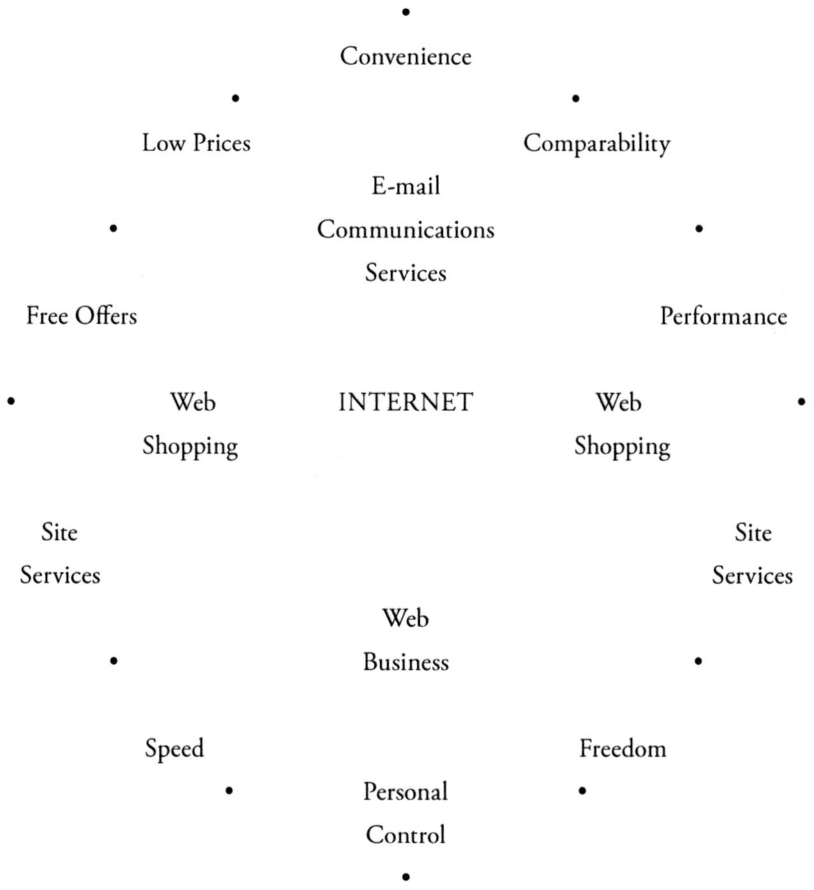

The race is on. Who is going to get there first and with the most customer value? Today it is Amazon.com, but tomorrow it may be Buy.com, a firm that began selling consumer products on the Web in 1996. Buy.com began selling products below cost to create a company brand loyalty synonymous with having the lowest prices. Buy.com sells computer products, and books, with plans to offer many different consumer products. It has purchased more than 2,000 domain names that begin with B-U-Y and has a new Web site named www.10percentoffamazon.com. Does Buy.com have a "silver bullet" marked for Amazon? It certainly seems they are aiming in that direction. The many ways the Web can be used to tap into the global marketplace is illustrated by examining the Net-Centric Value Wheel shown in Figure 6.1. Starting at the center of the Value Wheel, the Internet is essentially a *service product*, a delivery vehicle, which can create an array of desired customer values. Hopefully, it will generate more profits for sponsoring businesses.

In designing a Web business, you will need to think about your service offering at three levels. The most fundamental thing to understand is the core service itself, the technology of the Internet. Business leaders will have to ask this question: What are the advantages and disadvantages of using this new technology in my business? In experimenting with online sales, Levi Strauss discovered that the Web increased sales of their jeans when customers knew exactly what they wanted, while customers who are undecided and not sure of the fit still come to their stores. However, Levi has dropped its online sales and now allows retailers (Macy's, etc.) to sell their product online. The Gap has had better success selling online. For a while, Polo only sold its products through retail outlets, but it too has started online sales so it would not miss out on this new avenue of reaching thousands of customers online.

The second level of the Net-Centric Value Wheel reveals more tangible Web service products: *e-mail, general information, business information and Web shopping services.* Each of these service areas can provide useful benefits to Web users, who as a result, frequently return to the Web. Just twelve years ago, only 4 percent of the U.S. population used the Internet daily. Now more than 75 percent of its citizens are logging on each day. This is a very powerful world-wide trend; consequently, the Internet is an awesome tool for G/Es to use in their businesses to reach consumers. In discussing the e-corporation, Hamel and Sampler state that this is more than just a trend. Rather, it is a "tidal wave," and there is no other business venue available where sales are growing anywhere nearly as fast as on the Web.[76]

On the outer edge of the Net-Centric Value Wheel is a range of third-level customer benefits that further differentiates Web services from services normally received in the traditional marketplace. Online consumers have *convenient shopping, low prices, free samples, quick service, extra freedom, more means for comparison, neutral advice, personal control and access 24 hours a day.* These benefits are the epitome of values desired by millions of consumers, both online and offline. The Web will not replace offline retailing, but its impact is going to be much greater than many present non-users seem to believe.

To survive in the new Net-Centric world, firms will have to offer products and services representing incomparable values to customers. Customers will be "king" as never before. They will possess substantially more product knowledge and access to price comparisons from around the world as they shop on the

Web. Consumer expectations will be heightened in regards to *speed, convenience, availability, comparability, level of service,* and *price* as they explore the Web. Offline businesses will feel the impact of this as their Web-oriented customers impose their newly acquired Web experiences, i.e., speed, lower prices, and high levels of service expectations, to traditional non-Web businesses. This new form of competition will be a rude awakening to many traditional businesses.

An augmented Web service product serves all three levels of customer benefits in the Value Wheel. By understanding this range of benefits, the G/E can better customize his or her offerings on the Web. In discussing the e-corporation, Hamel and Sampler state, "If you don't believe deeply, wholly, and viscerally that the Net is going to change your business, you are going to lose. And if you do not understand the advantages of starting early and learning fast, you are going to lose."[77] Clearly, we live in a new point-and-click world that generates income, wealth, and opportunities never before possible. It is not only the vanguard Internet companies like Yahoo, Amazon and e-Bay that are profiting from the use of the Web; literally thousands of smaller companies are seeking their fortunes on the Internet.

An Expansion of the Internet World

Allow me to share with you this scenario from Chris Anderson: Individuals start and end a normal day on the Internet, but not on the World Wide Web. You wake up and check your email on your bedside iPad – an app. During breakfast you browse Facebook, Twitter and The New York Times – three more apps. While driving to the office, you listen to a podcast on your cell phone – another app. At work you scroll through RSS feeds in a reader and engage in a Skype conversation – more apps. As the day ends, you listen to Pandora a bit and then watch a movie on Netflix's streaming service. All of this is done on the Internet, but not on the Web. The significance of this is we have moved from the wide-open Web to closed and/or semiclosed platforms that use the Internet as their transportation vehicle. This is a new world where Google cannot reach or search, nor will HTML rule.

Chris Anderson says, "Two decades after its inception, the World Wide Web has been eclipsed by Skype, Netflix, peer-to-peer sharing, and a quarter-million other apps." This is a big-time move and consumers love it. They are choosing dedicated platforms because they work better, they relate more to daily life, and the stuff comes to you rather than you having to go to the PC screen. Anderson says, "The Web [its many sites] is just one of many applications that exist on the Internet." The content Web sites you see in your browser account for less than a quarter of Internet traffic. The rest of the traffic on the Internet comes from newer Net applications: mobile devices, email,

Skype calls, peer-to-peer file transfers, online games, Xbox Live, iTunes, voice-over-IP phones, iChat, Netflix movies, and the list gets longer each day. Again, all these devices are using the Net, but not the Web. Today the Internet hosts an increasing number of closed gardens, and the Web is now an exception, not the "ruler." A key factor driving this fundamental shift in the digital world is that it's easier for companies to make money on the emerging new platforms. Flexibility, accessibility, and quick problem-solving capability (most apps are designed for a single purpose, i.e., traffic directions, etc.) are also reasons why millions are flocking to the new digital-world media.[78]

An Emerging Virtual Business Organization

The Organizational Entity: A new hybrid organizational entity is emerging in the New Global Economic Era. This new organization will be unlike the old in that it will appear less as a discrete enterprise and more like a constantly changing cluster of networking-related activities. The Internet, intranet and extranet will provide the tools for a seamless communication link with all of the firm's constituents. The new hybrid organization will maintain some of the features of the earlier pyramid structure, but will clearly be different in size, scope and operation. Its overall aim is to be very efficient and highly responsive to a global marketplace. This organization will be discussed in greater detail in chapter eight.

Quite often G/Es will have prior work experience in large corporate organizations. They understand that the large corporation is slow, cumbersome, inflexible, and not designed for the fast-paced changes of the Information Era. The G/E's 21st century firm is likely to be a "virtual organization"—a business *without* physical buildings and heavy equipment. The virtual organization will appear seamless, permeable; it will frequently reflect a continuous, changing network of company associates, suppliers, manufacturers, customers, stockholders and outsourcing entities.

The G/E's company of the 21st century is likely to be a "virtual" organization, a firm without possession of physical buildings and heavy equipment.

The formal pyramid organization is characteristic of the Industrial Era and is still used by most large firms. These organizations show line and staff business functions under titles such as Vice Presidents of Production, Marketing, Finance, and Human Resources. This pyramid organization structure has served business organizations well for many years. However, the concurrent revolutions occurring in manufacturing, marketing, finance and management are changing the rules, especially in international engagements. Most astute business leaders today recognize that the top-down, dictatorial leadership approach used during the Industrial Era has serious limitations: it is not an effective operative approach for knowledge workers. Networks and virtual entities are now replacing old organizational models. The traditional line functions of production, marketing and finance are undergoing dramatic changes. With the world now opening to a global marketplace, it is certainly anything but business as usual. Let's look at a few changes taking place in these organic line functions and how they affect entrepreneurs entering the global marketplace.

Emerging New Manufacturing Concepts

Production: Although America's manufacturing base is shrinking, it is still the largest in the world. It is just the big firms that are shrinking. The time-and-motion-assembly line techniques, characteristic of the Industrial Era, have been replaced with mass-customization, best-practice benchmarking, outsourcing, core competencies and other innovative ideas. Many major automotive firms perform the core tasks of designing, engineering and marketing their cars. But often everything else—including final assembly—is outsourced. The Porsche Boxster is assembled by Valmet, an engineering firm in Uusikaupunski, Finland. BMW is outsourcing the engineering and production of its X3 compact sport-utility vehicle to Magna Steyr in Austria. As the world marketplace opens up to business, business has opened up to the world in its search for global strategies that lead to superior performance. Clearly, a "we-can-learn-from-everywhere" culture will predominate in business. An ever-changing international marketplace will contribute to this new learning environment.

Developed economies have excelled in using these new management technologies to such an extent that we have developed an *overcapacity in production* for most physical goods, i.e., autos, wine, food and manufacturing in general. This is great for consumers, because such abundance means lower prices. This state of affairs is also a clear signal to G/Es: Don't get caught with lots of "heavy metal" production and physical plant capacity. Remember the new wealth creation paradigm. Today it is clearly knowledge and technology, not physical assets that are the dominant value-producing components in business. Keep in mind that knowledge can be constantly generated and amplified through continuous learning, thus making it infinitely expandable.

The G/E's production capabilities should be a knowledge-based enterprise based on one to three core competencies, consisting of those things the firm does best. Outsourcing can be used to secure performance in other business areas. Typically, core competencies are not a product as such; rather, they are multifunctional activities such as product design, logistics, or a sharply honed technical skill. All of these can provide wide access to a variety of markets. IBM's major core competency now is *better customer service through informational technologies.* However, in nearly every case, one characteristic of a well-defined core competency is that it is directly related to some customer benefit. The more difficult the product-service knowledge of products is to copy, or imitate, the greater the advantage for the company. Core competencies that have applications in a variety of areas are preferred, since they do serve as the basis for expansion, which then, hopefully, can be leveraged over many countries.

The G/E may minimize his production cost by starting the venture with a *virtual product* – a product that does not physically exist and is only created when it is sold. The impact of a virtual product is evident in that you never have a costly finished-goods inventory. A good example of a virtual product is the *service* offered by a business consultant. It can also be a *product,* as Dell Computer has demonstrated by having one of the lowest-cost computer manufacturing facilities in the world. Obviously, not every product or service lends itself to being virtual. The G/E should thoroughly embrace the virtualization concept due to the significant reduction in the cost of starting and operating the venture.

In regards to production, virtualization can be taken to an even higher level – the *virtual micro-factory.* Chris Anderson, Editor in Chief of *Wired* magazine, has welcomed us to the next Industrial Revolution with his virtual micro-manufacturing concept. He says, "the tools of factory production, from electronic assembly to 3-D printing, are now available to individuals in batches as small as a single unit. Anybody with an idea and a little expertise can set assembly lines in China into motion with nothing more than some keystrokes on their laptop. A few days later, a prototype can be delivered to their door, and once it is checks out, they can push a few more buttons and be in full production, making hundreds, thousands, or more." What this means is a G/E can become a "virtual micro-factory," with a capability to design and market goods without an infrastructure, raw material or finished-goods inventory. Products are assembled and drop-shipped by external contractors who serve other similar businesses. Today these micro-factories exist across the country and are making all kind of product you can imagine.[79]

But wait! You don't have to go to China to start your virtual micro-factory. The Chinese are known for stealing your idea, especially if you send them the whole product. Just let the Chinese mass-produce a single commodity component part of your product. That is what SparkFun of

Boulder, Colorado, does. They have a Chinese partner who will make millions of small printed circuit boards (PCBs) for a few cents each. These PCBs are a basic component of a number of products made by SparkFun. Their business is global and high-tech, with two-thirds of the sales from outside the U.S. If you need a single prototype of your product, you can get it made here in the U.S. at Protomet Corporation in Oak Ridge, Tennessee. Protomet will also manufacture small batches of your completed product. Or you can rent your laser-part-cutting machine online from a Wellington, New Zealand, company called Ponoko. If you log onto Ponoko's website, you can find some 20,000 items – housewares, toys, and furniture – all available for purchase or they will laser-cut your product according to your digital design either in Wellington or Oakland, California.[80]

Marketing: The New MoneyMaker

Marketing: It was noted earlier that a worldwide overcapacity exists in manufacturing, and this situation will continue for several decades. Therefore, a key business challenge in the immediate future will be marketing rather than the production of goods and services. Rosabeth Moss Kanter describes it in this manner: "The world is becoming a global shopping mall in which ideas and products are available everywhere at the same time."[54] Milton Friedman made the same observation in his quotation that opened this chapter. In searching for world-class products, people everywhere will want access to this *global shopping mall,* and, quite naturally, they will want entry to the mall from the convenience of their home.

This desire for acquiring the best, while sitting at home, puts increasing pressure on local producers to be world-class providers to consumers, even though they may not be global in scope. Technology allows buyers to scan an immense number of outlets in search of the lowest price for world-class products. Buyers will also be able to employ such technology to easily shop across jurisdictional boundaries. For example, in Europe one can buy an item in the Principality of Andorra, avoid paying the 17-percent E.U. value-added tax, and use the item or have it shipped anywhere in the world. Of course, this transaction is available only to those visiting Andorra or those connected to the Internet. It is easy to see that one must possess this knowledge about Andorra in order to capitalize on such savings.

The desire for acquiring the best, while sitting at home, puts increasing pressure on local producers to be world-class providers, even though they may not be global in scope.

Paul Pilzer says the route to wealth creation has substantially shifted today. Most of the fortunes of the twentieth century were created from industries producing tangibles—automobiles, steel, manufacturing, oil, and other tangible natural resources. There has been a shift in the past decade to personal fortunes coming from new and better ways of marketing and information sharing. Pilzer cites the following wealth creators as examples: Fred Smith, founder of Federal Express; Ross Perot, founder of Electronic Data Systems; and Sam Walton, founder of the Walmart retail stores. Though Sam Walton is now deceased, his children and a couple of relatives are multimillionaires. *Fortune* shows daughter Christy Walton, and family are worth $24 billion; Jim Walton, - $20.1 billion; Alice Walton, - $20 billion; and Robson Walton, - $19.7 billion. Of interest, Sam had a brother, James "Bud" Walton, now deceased, who helped start the first general store in Bentonville, Arkansas. Bud Walton was generous to his two daughters who are also billionaires; Ann Walton Kroenk has $3.2 billion and Nancy Walton Laurie, $2.6 billion. All total, they have a net worth of $89.6 billion. That's amazing coming from a retail service business with a simple strategy – *buy low, sell cheap, sell in volume.*

What is the likelihood that a Walmart will work in China or India? Well, it's good in China and less so in India. Walmart opened its first store in China in 1996, and has 180-big box stores in 90 Chinese cities. India is a different story. The Indian government does not allow Walmart and other foreign companies to retail direct to consumers. So Walmart has undertaken a backdoor, or an upstream, strategy by having a 50/50 joint venture with Bharti Enterprises. The joint venture operates as a wholesaler of clothes, electronics, home goods, and vegetables to shopkeepers, hotels and other businesses. The company has made significant strides with Indian farmers by helping them improve farming techniques, by paying higher prices for their produce, and providing free transportation to retailers. Walmart has spent several years building relations with farmers, and suppliers and setting up its distribution system with the hope that someday India will remove its ban on foreign companies having retail stores there.

Firms the size of Walmart have adequate funds to conduct market research before entering a market. G/Es may not have such funding. Allow me to share a personal experience. I was invited to be a Visiting Professor of Entrepreneurship at the University of South Africa in the late 1990s. That was right after President Mandela came into office, and he had established a national goal of constructing a million new houses for the majority black South Africans. As an entrepreneur, I thought this would be a great time to help the country achieve this ambitious objective. Therefore, I researched the pre-fabricated home industry and discovered a great design for an inexpensive three or four-bedroom house that I felt was suitable for South Africa. I even contracted with two firms to ship one each of those houses to South Africa so they could be used as templates for constructing others. What a terrible mistake. Good houses in South Africa are made of concrete blocks; bad houses are made of sheets of tin or other nonburnable products. In South Africa there are no large trees, only small shrubs, most of which have been plucked for firewood for cooking and heating. Even if you imported and erected a wooden house, it would not last an hour after dark – the locals would tear it down and run off with the firewood. That illustrates the importance of having a local business partner who understands the local culture. They can save you lots of money and embarrassment.

Aspiring G/Es are faced with the difficult task of developing a global marketing strategy. This strategy will involve leveraging core competencies on a global scale and achieving synergies through networking partners around the world. The choice and number of networking partners will determine the firm's geographic market scope. It is important to remember you are marketing your core competencies, not necessarily the products. James Quinn says, "Products themselves are only physical embodiments of a set of services desired by customers."[81] McDonald's is known for its *quick service, consistent quality,* and *cleanliness*, more than for its hamburgers. A key factor for G/Es is to be a dominant global force in marketing of core competencies - those qualities that are greatly valued by customers. It other words, it won't be your hamburgers.

As China, India, and Africa with its 53 countries really start to grow, people there will want many of the goods and services that are abundantly available in the developed world. With a present overcapacity in manufacturing, some G/Es will have a field day supplying these rapidly emerging *new* markets with *old*, or existing, products. China and India offer huge potential. But it will take some time for African markets to develop large-scale purchasing power. In Africa, needs are great, but remember that needs alone do not make a market. Only when real needs are coupled with the monetary ability to purchase does a market exist. Currently, most native Africans do not have the ability to purchase more than basic survival needs.

As a G/E you will not be in the position to start your venture with the clout of a Walmart. At the very basic level, you may want to consider starting your venture with a *virtual product* – a product that does not exist until it is sold. As previously mentioned, a good example of a virtual product is the *service* provided by a management consultant. Virtualization has assisted Dell in becoming one of the lowest-cost producers of computers in the world. In doing so, Dell is an example of a new-age hybrid organization. The company had combined the components of the Information Age with the functions of the traditional business organization, namely sales, production and finance.

Financing: The Key to Entrepreneurial Development

Finance: There is a direct relationship between America's economic growth and the country leading the world in making funding available to finance entrepreneurial endeavors. Money is available to capable people with innovative ideas and a burning desire to start a new venture. This in part explains the influx of entrepreneurs from all over the world to North America. Not only does the U.S. have the most advanced private equity market, but it also has liquid markets (albeit too liquid in the early 2000s) for a wide range of securities, from high-yield bonds to employee stock ownership plans. In most of the world, regulation and repressive taxation prevents the emergence of vibrant financial markets. Even within the E.U., there is a shortage of venture capitalists and angel investors as compared to the U.S. In developing countries such as Russia, Syria and Cuba there are few venture capitalists available to provide financing for aspiring entrepreneurs. Therefore, it is easy to understand why entrepreneurship does not flourish in repressive economies and why economic growth in such countries is restricted.

However, the above money flow to entrepreneurs in the U.S. came to a screeching halt in 2009-10, resulting from the worldwide recession. At the beginning of the recession, the federal government was forced to bail out major Wall Street banking institutions to forestall a total collapse of our financial system. The government also provided huge sums of money to General Motors and Chrysler to keep these businesses alive through a structured bankruptcy. What the government has failed to do as of late 2010 is to provide substantial funding for start-up ventures and to Main Street small businesses. Entrepreneurs rely on community banks for more than 90 percent of their external funding to start new ventures and fund the growth of existing businesses. Reserves for lending by community banks have been shattered with homeowner bankruptcies and the commercial real estate crisis has further diminished bank reserves. It is not realistic to expect commercial banks will open their purses again to entrepreneurs until 2012-13 and even beyond. There has been minor improvement at the margin to free up funding for entrepreneurs. The SBA is making more money available with better terms, but most of this comes through the already strapped banks. The government has offered some minor end-of-the-year tax relief if a business hires new employees, but that is little help for entrepreneurs with start-up ventures. It is difficult to understand why there is not a massive federal program for start-up ventures that create 30 percent of the new jobs and for existing businesses that create another 65 percent of all new jobs.

Increased use of information technology has reduced the cost of starting a new venture. Additionally, the use of virtualization of products, organizations and manufacturing has further reduced the capital requirements for potential G/Es. The establishment of a global network of partners will take considerable personal time, or "sweat equity," on the part of the G/E. Banks often avoid early start-up ventures because of the high risk involved. Thus, entrepreneurs must rely on their personal funds, and money from friends, relatives, family and individual investors. In the U.S., there are more than 300,000 "business angels" - a very special group of individuals who provide their own private funds as seed money for early start-ups of promising ventures. We will discuss angel investing more in chapter eight, but note that they currently invest in less than one-half of one percent (0.5) of American start-up ventures. This means that the "good" ventures need not apply; you have be a "great" venture to get funding from angel investors. We also discuss in chapter eight whether entrepreneurs should invest personal funds in a new venture, even though this is a common, expected and often a required practice. Our advice is to avoid it whenever you can.

Examples of Small Global Internet Businesses

The Internet is *not* a business model in itself. It's just an interconnection of a large number of computers through which individuals and businesses can communicate in various ways. The advantages of the Internet are immediately available to all businesses, regardless of size. Just notice how some *small-scale* G/Es are promoting their business on the Web.

The Cigar Box: Keir Sword of Edinburgh, Scotland, offers good Scotch whisky and cigars from the Royal Mile Whisky Company, where he is director. Customers were constantly asking for a larger selection of cigars, so he launched The Cigar Box on the Web in 1999. After two years, his venture became Scotland's largest Cuban cigar specialist, attracting cigar aficionados from around the world. His annual turnover has increased by 25 percent to more than £1 million ($1.45 million), largely due to his online presence. He customized the site by offering information about cigar production and even showing a Havana mansion where some of the world's finest cigars are produced.

Teddington Cheese Company: Perhaps you do not know the difference between Cornish Yarg and Stinking Bishop. Well, just visit this site – www.teddingtoncheese.co.uk. Doug Thring and his partner set up their site in 1995, and now they receive more than 120,000 hits per month with orders averaging £30 ($44). This portal has enticing photographs and facts on the history behind each cheese. Their clients hail from Moscow to Singapore, and the site frequently receives hits from New Zealanders with a penchant for Stilton.

The Wedding Ring Workshop: Vincent Seymour and a partner own a High Street jewelry store in London. They set up their Web site hoping to augment sales in their main store. The site includes photographs of diamonds, cuts, color, clarity and information on carat weights. Now their online presence is responsible for 60 percent of the company's turnover. Orders have come in from places like the Grand Canary for a £10,000 ($14,500) gem. One customer flew in from Nigeria after seeing the Web site. The partners have two more Web portals in the pipeline.

Sykes Cottages: Cive Sykes founded his U.K. Company in 1991 and took it online in 1997. He offers an online database of holiday cottages in several countries. Interested parties can access pictures and information on the cottages before deciding to book them. They can select their cottage by country, region, number of bedrooms, length of stay, and they can even specify amenities such as an open fireplace. Fifty percent of Sykes' business is generated online. He is currently developing his site so it will be updated every ten minutes.

Earth Treks, Inc.: Do you know what it feels like to scale Mount Everest's 29,035-foot summit, laboring to find enough oxygen while battling a blizzard? You can find out from Earth Treks' new online climbing center and professional guide service based in Columbia, Maryland. Earth Treks brings these experiences directly to you on their Web site. Since the company launched its Web site in 1999, guides from all over the world—from Ecuador's Cotopaxi volcano to the Himalayas' Mount Everest—have regularly posted journal entries online about their on-high experiences. One climber commented, "Eighteen hours of snowfall makes Camp Two on Everest a living hell." Revenue for Earth Treks has doubled over the past two years.

These small Internet businesses are operated by G/Es searching for additional growth and expansion in the international marketplace. Note that each business has a clearly defined *focus* - cigars, cheese, diamonds, vacation cottages, climbing experience - and uses the Internet medium to take the product to the various corners of the world.

Future Internet Trends Shaping the Global Marketplace

So what are the experts projecting will be the Web trends, at least for the next year or two? Wouldn't that be nice to know. We are not predicting; however, there are some near-term Internet trends worth reviewing below.

The Mobile Web. Every web-savvy business knows smart phone usage is on the increase. Entrepreneurs are increasingly developing Web-based businesses that are specifically used for handheld devices. G/Es must develop their Website to be accessible through a smart phone or apps, or users will go elsewhere. People are going to use mobile phones in the same way a laptop was used in the past.

SEO. Optimization and SEO is changing with the rise of personalized and real-time search. The social network Twitter sparked a trend when it designed the first popular real-time search engine. When users search for a term, the site updates that search with new 'tweets" as they are made. Google has recently introduced a personalized search and a real-time search function of its own, complete with indexed tweets. All of the normal SEO things will still apply, but be aware of these changes.

Social Media. Facebook and Twitter were the standout social networks in 2009, and their popularity has surged in 2010. In early 2010, Facebook share of the Internet traffic surpassed Google's search engine. As a G/E, you cannot afford to ignore one of the biggest markets on the planet, and you are doing so if you do not have a strong presence on the world's most dominant social networking site.

Online Retailing. Online spending by consumers in the U.S. has risen to more than 7 percent of retail volume in 2010. Clearly, most smart retailers now realize they cannot operate without an e-commerce offering. Forrester Research predicts online retail sales will grow at a 10 percent compounded annual rate until the year 2014.

Advertising. The Internet advertising industry grew 27 percent in 2009 over its 2008 level, and it is expected to continue growing throughout 2010, according to the Interactive Advertising Bureau. During the next 12 months, there will be substantial expansion of mobile phone advertising with the increasing number of apps coming onto the scene. Experts in the field say businesses should consider advertising on prominent social networking sites just in order to to keep up with market changes.

Reputation Management. Firms that do operate Websites, with most major firms having them, have to be increasingly aware of how rumors and allegations can travel faster than the speed of light in the digital age. Businesses should pay particular attention to possible damage to the corporate reputation by carefully monitoring who is talking about their brand and being ready to address any negative situation that may occur. Domino's Pizza got into trouble when two employees posted a video of themselves handling food unhygienically on the Internet.

Marketing. More and more companies are using mobile phones for marketing. Firms are beginning to commission mobile apps, especially on the iPhone, for marketing purposes. Google has a system where users take a picture of a barcode with their mobile phone and use the search engine to find more information on the product, as well as locating the product itself. Clearly, mobile advertising is heating up, and businesses are developing new technologies and interesting ways to market to consumers.

Content Product. Growth of the internet has encouraged entrepreneurs to publish their own content using blogs, pictures, and videos of their product. Firms should think about creating some type of content on YouTube, for there you can possibly create a global audience. You are not going to succeed there with a blatant marketing pitch; consequently, it has to be a meaningful experience that will appeal to a wide audience.

Cloud Computing. Now more businesses are beginning to understand just what the tech-heads were talking about. Cloud computing is becoming more essential for businesses to back up their data or use a piece of software hosted by an external server. Cloud services are centered around three areas: applications/software-as-a-service, data backups, and internal services for businesses with customized programs.

Hopefully, these future trends will give you some ideas for shaping your global Internet business. We will be discussing the nature and character of social networking more in chapter 10. The rapid growth of social networking presents lots of opportunities for the G/E.[82]

Even with all of today's Internet opportunities, fewer than half of all U.S. small businesses have Websites or advertise on the Internet. However, Nelson Online reports that most consumers today search online for local shops and services before picking up the phone or leaving the house. This fact does not escape the attention of large organizations such as Google and Microsoft. Even a slew of start-ups are intensifying their focus on small businesses. Microsoft's Bing is shoring up neighborhood-specific information and business listings. Yahoo has just renewed a partnership with Nokia to power its maps and navigation services for local business listings. Google has rebranded an older, small-business service called Local Business Centers as Google Places. Google has pages with data on millions of small businesses, and some 2 million companies have added their own information to those pages. Business owners can pay $25 a month and have their listings, complete with photos, pop up with an icon and other information when consumers check neighborhood maps on smart phones and on the Internet.

An Era of Unlimited Marketing Opportunities

Never before have individuals had the opportunities that G/Es have today. You have a potential outreach to the most remote corners of the earth for tapping into 6.8 billion people in both First and Third World countries. Such scope and numbers will intimidate the less informed entrepreneur. However, G/Es understand that the bigger the pond of opportunity, the more they will have to *focus* with their product or service offering. This process can begin with self-analysis, using Rosabeth Moss Kanter's three characteristics; for example, are you a *thinker, maker,* or *trader*? You need to decide which of these three characteristics predominately describes you. This process can be a first step in helping you shape a business focus and location. There is more information on Kanter's three characteristics at the beginning of this chapter, and you may want to review her full article on the Internet.

The sheer size of the world marketplace clearly dictates to G/Es and/or small business owners they should not attempt to appeal to the entire market. Even Walmart, the largest and most profitable retailer in the world, must gradually explore ways of entering developing countries such as China and India. The magnitude of the world marketplace simply provides you with an unlimited number of options to explore. Now your question is this: What kind of product or service *niche* are you capable of developing for entering the world marketplace? You are not going to be able to appeal to everyone anyway, so you need to define that narrow product/service offering from which you can develop your primary focus. For Volvo, one can say its focus is not the automobile, but it is "safety." For BMW, its focus has now changed to the "joy of owning and driving its automobiles." For Michael Porter, his focus is "competitiveness"; for Tom Friedman it is "sustainability"; Starbucks, it is the total "experience" of visiting one of their full-service establishments; For Apple, it is "innovation"; and for Disney it is "magic." So the focus is a combination of product, knowledge, values, and attributes that an individual receives through their use and consumption.

You will be starting your business with that narrow product or service, one that fills some niche in the beginning, but has substantial scaling possibilities as you move forward into the world marketplace. Note that McDonald's mission is to offer the world's best quick-service restaurant experience. Some time ago, the firm identified three key attributes that ensures them being the best: "quality, service and cleanliness." The mission statement wasn't developed overnight, nor were these three qualities, which Ray Kroc later defined as what he wanted his restaurants to be known for. It is of interest to note that nothing is said here about hamburgers. Your service product could be as simple as a unique phone app, an Internet game, or participating in the green revolution that Friedman is predicting, which you will read more about in chapter 10. My contribution to the latter is a book now underway involving children in helping parents conserve and reduce the use of electricity in the home.

Undeniably, the biggest and most dynamic global marketplace is a reality. This market will continue to grow and expand to accommodate insatiable needs, wants, and desires of a world approaching seven billion people. Clearly, we live in a borderless world. No country, company or individual has a monopoly on business opportunities in the developed or undeveloped world marketplace. Businesses will continue to flourish in those countries and regions that best support entrepreneurship.

You can be assured of that an elite group of Global Entrepreneurs will appear in every corner of the world. Keep this in mind - entrepreneurs are emerging *everywhere*, even under the harshest economic conditions. They will be using every source of available knowledge and technology to sharpen their skills and to capitalize on emerging opportunities in the global marketplace. You can also take this unique opportunity to be a Global Entrepreneur, striving toward a personal goal of creating your individual wealth.

Chapter Endnotes

Manufacturing Resources Available to Global Entrepreneurs

Even though some 80 percent of American gross domestic product is classified as being in services, some G/Es will need to find a manufacturer abroad or even one in America. The following sources will be helpful.

Alibaba.com. Alibaba has a network of more than 850,000 manufacturers, distributors, and other suppliers from 240 countries, although many are from China. Sellers pay to be listed, but buyers use the services for free. Manufacturers post information such sales volume and factory size. Buyers can search by country and by product type. Profiles of the site's 30,000 gold members include online video tours of their plants. User forums give you access to other companies' experiences with manufacturers.

Thomasnet.net and Thomasglobal.com. Thomasnet lists more than 600,000 manufacturers, distributors, and resources in North American, mostly in the U.S. Thomasglobal lists some 700,000 manufacturers and industrial service providers in 28 countries, including China and Brazil. Thomasnet lets you submit the same bid to multiple vendors, making it easier to compare quotes.

Globalsoures.com. Globalsources has a free catalog of more than 150,000 manufacturers, predominately in mainland China, Hong Kong, and Taiwan. Some 15,000 suppliers provide extensive information, including a credit check and sometimes third-party plant inspections. To help narrow the offerings, the site lets you sort vendors by criteria such a products they make and markets served.

Uschamber.com. The U.S. Chamber of Commerce has affiliated American Chambers of Commerce Abroad in 100 countries. You can contact them through the site's online directory, and they will connect you with any of their members – typically Americans who have set up operations in other countries – who may be able to help you with manufacturing. Some, but not all, of the Chambers Abroad will charge you a fee for making the introduction.

Small Business Administration. Six Steps to Begin Exporting is the latest SBA tool in their National Export initiative toolbox to help entrepreneurs begin exporting. This practical interactive website will help connect entrepreneurs to the nearly 96 percent of the world's customers living outside of the U.S. The process begins with a self-assessment to gauge the entrepreneur readiness to engage in international trade. That step is followed by sections on training and counseling; resources to create an export business plan; information on conducting market research; assistance for finding foreign buyers; and lastly investigating financing for your small business exports, foreign investment or projects. This website is by the U.S. Department of Commerce and the U.S. Small Business Administration – www.export.gov.begin.com.

7

The Global Entrepreneur

"You have to think about making an impact in as many places as possible because everything you are can be known everywhere else."
Rosabeth Moss Kanter

Unlimited Future Opportunities

We have the business knowledge, the technical capability, and unlimited resources to achieve almost anything that society desires. However, there is one restriction: the above "we" refers to a few First World countries with 20 percent of the world's population. For the remaining 80 percent of humanity, the picture is not so bright. They are locked in an undeveloped world. A major political, social, and business challenge in the 21st century will be to share knowledge and technological resources so wealth-creating capabilities can be widely utilized in Third World countries. The United Nations and the World Trade Organizations will not provide a solution to this problem. It must be more of an undertaking by astute business leaders and social entrepreneurs who understand the importance of decreasing global poverty. Hopefully, Global Entrepreneurs (G/Es) and other business leaders will take a more active role in introducing wealth-building capabilities for the developing world.

We can begin the wealth-sharing process when business and world leaders understand they possess the potential for creating unlimited productive resources. Our current knowledge and technology required to turn natural resources into wealth seems to be "unlimited." Only when this fact is realized will the "wealth gap" start narrowing in a positive economic manner, rather than being forced to do so by local protestors and/or revolutionary means. Technology never gets used up; hence, the more you share technology with others, the more it is put to use, the more it will regenerate, and the more it will result in a further proliferation of additional knowledge and technology. G/Es can facilitate this sharing and proliferation process throughout the world and this will result in the creation of greater economic prosperity for many people in Third World countries.

A Volatile Business World

The current business world is certainly one characterized by unpredictability, volatility, and dynamism. New and varied technologies, along with globalization, are transforming markets, products, and business processes. All this is creating a new global economic order for business. This burgeoning era creates excitement for G/Es because they see many global opportunities on the horizon. They welcome globalization with open arms. G/Es not only know how the system works; they know how to work the system, and how to create dynamic wealth opportunities. G/Es function in an anticipatory mode, with a keen insight about how they can shape their own future. Consequently, the G/E moves forward with confidence and enthusiasm in developing international enterprises.

From Canada …

Bruce Poon of Trinidad is a self-reliant G/B. He has escaped from a Burmese jail, crossed a 110 degree Mongolian desert on a brass-saddled horse, and has run with the bulls in Pamplona, Spain. He has also built G.A.P. Adventures in to the world's biggest adventure-travel company, which has 700 employees, 16 boats including a now-sunk, 345-foot Antarctic cruise ship, a hotel in Ecuador, and businesses that cover seven continents. His primary business is arranging interesting and exciting journeys for people around the world. His company had $110 million revenues in 2009, according to *Forbes*.

A rapid changing environment favors the agile entrepreneur who has a clear mobility advantage over large organizations. The breakneck pace of technological change will be a boom for the G/E who mentally and structurally prepared to ride the crest of the wave. Lew Platt, former CEO of Hewlett-Packard, said, "Positioning is all-important. If you are not *first* into the market, and if you are not *first* in the minds of the Net Generation with your product concept, then you are going to have a tough time succeeding." Being first also means being fast. In the Internet world of total connectivity, speed is the key to survival. Business can be conducted with a few keystrokes, a click of a mouse secures payment, and a sale can be consummated with the speed of light. An important by-product of e-commerce is it has shown businesses how speed can be used advantageously as a strategic weapon.

The Global Entrepreneur and Leadership

The G/E has to be more than just an entrepreneur. He or she must be an effective leader. G/Es and top business leaders are both obsessed with a central objective, that is, *extraordinary business growth*, as measured in every way; sales, profits, productivity and shareholder value. Normally, the G/E creates growth in the context of a small business, whereas the leader creates growth within the environs of the large organization. But keep in mind, *extraordinary growth* is the goal of both. The opportunity for growth energizes people, provides a purpose for structuring and restructuring, delivers opportunities for wealth creation, and offers challenges and excitement for G/Es and their employees. For G/Es, their growth arena has been expanded by their search for opportunities throughout the world.

The characteristics of G/Es and top business leaders are surprisingly similar, starting with their strong emphasis on high growth, and their search for new products and expanding market opportunities. The G/E eagerly searches the world for unrecognized needs and unidentified markets that have been overlooked by others. Proactive business leaders view growth opportunities differently from many of their contemporaries. For example, they don't accept the commonly held dictum that there are no growth opportunities in mature markets. Firms like Apple and General Electric embrace the concept of *Corporate Entrepreneurship*. They have achieved significant expansion in mature markets by offering more services and products to existing customer and by expanding the pool of customers with entirely new product and service offerings. These Corporate Entrepreneurs are much like G/Es, who are constantly searching for unrecognized, unfilled needs not yet identified by competitors.

The characteristics of G/Es and business leaders are surprisingly similar – starting with an emphasis on extraordinary growth by both.

The G/E is similar to the transformational leader who brings about radical change throughout large organizations. G/Es also share a number of qualities with such transformational leaders. Both are charismatic, intellectually challenging, and possess and outstanding ability to influence others. In Tichy and Devanna's book, *The Transformational Leader*, the authors' research reveals effective transformational leaders have the following attributes: they perceive themselves as change agents; they are moderate risk takers; they intuitively trust people; they have a core set of values and principles that guide their behavior; they are eager to learn from their own experience and that of others; they have good cognitive skills and use them in analyzing business problems; and they are visionaries who trust their intuitions.[83] All of these attributes are also common to G/Es. Transformational leaders and G/Es operate differently from functional manages, who act more as stewards or custodians of the business, rather than as change makers. Both entrepreneurs and leaders operate under conditions of risk and uncertainty, whereas managers seek to avoid such situations.

The Highest Level of Entrepreneurship – The Global Entrepreneur

When discussing the propensity for entrepreneurship in chapter three, we mentioned that men and women have an innate desire to personally achieve and accomplish something of significance. This search for personal accomplishment usually begins while working for someone else. In most cases the decision to work for another is based on the need for an income, rather than acquiring work experience. But working for others does not satisfy the G/E, or even the Traditional Entrepreneur. The quest for personal achievement in the 21st century has been intensified by a quadriga of forces including globalization, the Information Age, the Internet, and the use of knowledge and technology for creating new wealth. Business opportunities in which individuals can create significant wealth is a relatively short period of time have clearly emerged. These worldwide opportunities have awakened and energized a new breed of venture-seeking G/Es.

The "uber-entrepreneur" is clearly the highest level of entrepreneurship known today. He or she is well-educated and has extensive new world business knowledge. G/Es often have a business that goes global at birth. Being big, in terms of physical resources, is no longer necessary. In fact, it is a handicap, for it often restricts a business to a physical location. The extensive use of information technology and the Internet minimizes the advantages of bigness and gives the G/E international mobility. G/Es understand that wealth creation today is based far more on the mind than on muscle. Their major task is to spot knowledge and technology gaps and to exploit them. A world in turmoil generates many wealth-creating avenues for the knowledge-based opportunity-seeking G/E.

Being big, in terms of physical resources, is no longer a necessity. It is a handicap.

Traditional Entrepreneurs often go into business for themselves as a result of displacement or dissatisfaction with working for others. G/Es are more deliberate; they make an early decision to have their own business. The decision may come during college, as was the case with Johan Birgersson, a 23-year-old student, in Stockholm. Birgersson had the opportunity at an industrial seminar to present his idea to Tellie AB, the large 40,000-employee Swedish phone company. Birgesson boldly told Tellie: "The future is broadband." Tellie was not interested in this visionary business concept. So Birgersson started his own Internet consulting business – Framfab. In recent years this Swedish Net company has acquired Mindfact in Germany and Guide in Sweden, making it the world's third-largest Internet consultancy. However, problems occurred with such early, explosive growth as Famfab employment rose to 3,000. Then the business hit the wall. Excessive losses in 2001 devastated Framfab share prices, and Birgersson resigned as CEO and board member. Birgersson acknowledged he had made a number of mistakes; the biggest was not resigning earlier. Many young entrepreneurs (Birgersson was only 29 at this point) lacked leadership skills necessary for operating rapidly-growing companies during the turbulent dot.com period. Birgersoon' lack of leadership skills was no exception. Entrepreneurs are good at starting ventures, but they often fall short in providing their ventures with competent management and leadership skills required for rapid growth.

Global entrepreneurship includes people from all over the world; mostly the young, but also the not-so-young; those with businesses on the Internet and offline businesses; service businesses offering information and knowledge products, but also ventures that market tangibles products; and those with technical expert in their domain, as well as individuals with non-technical businesses.

The Global Entrepreneurship Process

In the same manner that Technical Entrepreneurship involves a process and a person, these two dimensions are present in Global Entrepreneurship. Let us examine the G/E in regards to these two dimensions. In chapter three, we explained the difference between the entrepreneurship process and individual entrepreneurs in terms of a "dance" and the "dancers." The G/E process is somewhat different from the process of Traditional Entrepreneurs even though they both seek the same end result – the formation of start-up ventures and/or accelerating rapid growth in existing businesses. The G/E process includes the following steps: recognizing and creating an international business opportunity; developing a virtual business entity; utilizing an extensive networking connectivity; the physical start-up of the global business; having a desire to achieve some type of break-through accomplishment; and ultimately, forming a public venture. Let's review this G/E process in more detail for it is indeed a *process* that one can learn.

They Recognize and Create New Opportunities. G/Es are opportunistic business people who excel in opening of new markets created by globalization and facilitated by e-commerce. Their firms create real and virtual products and services that can be instantaneously customized in response to needs of global customers. G/Es see knowledge as a product in its own right. They seek to develop knowledge products and find new ways of pricing and selling them. There are increasing opportunities for G/Es to "bundle" disaggregated services, bringing them together under their own business umbrella, and providing them in more convenient packages for international customers. The G/E possesses a state of mind that spans the globe searching for unlimited opportunities for the business. Therefore, G/Es organize and operate the business for the purpose of creating and capitalizing on unlimited growth opportunities. The G/E's objectives are to discover promising ideas for a new venture, quickly turn those ideas into viable product/service opportunities, find customers who demand such products in a profitable critical mass, fill it, and then repeat the process with those and other service products.

From China …

Yuan June started his online forum after he saw Chinese people wondering how they could "sweep their ancestor's tombs" without going back home. For 10 yuan ($1.40), his website allows mourners to set up online memorials for their late relatives, upload photos and videos of them, and burn virtual incense and make an offering of money. Page views per day reach over 10,000 during the Oingming festival, when Chinese families traditionally visit their relatives' gravesites and practice rituals such as kowtow and money offering. His customers, primarily from Japan, U.S., and Chinese coastal cities like Fujian, are those who cannot get back home during China's tomb-sweeping festival, says Yuan.

They Develop Virtual Business Entities. Being cognizant of the emergence of a new business paradigm means the G/E understands that knowledge and technology are primary factors in the wealth-creating process of the

21st century. For the knowledge and/or technology venture, G/Es will use a virtual architecture in developing their product and for the overall structure of their organization. Virtual products often exist only in the mind of the G/E before they are produced, and are instantaneously created based on customer demand.

Ordering a custom-made computer on the Internet from Dell is a good example of a virtual product. You can use the Internet today to order a Mercedes or BMW according to your specifications to be shipped from the factory within just weeks. This virtual organization design requires a minimum of people, money, facilities, equipment, and other expensive tangibles, thus allowing organizational capital to be leveraged globally. In some instances, G/Es may not even deal directly with the consumer, for this can be accomplished by partners in their virtual network. The virtual organization is one that is borderless, flexible, and continuously changing, with its many evolving interfaces among the venture, its various partners, suppliers, and customers. This new, flat, virtual, networking-type organization will triumph in the Information Age because of its agility, flexibility and economy of operation.

They Develop Networking Connectivity. An important key to establishing a global business is *connectivity.* International contacts and connections are vital to open doors and pave the way for establishing the global venture, as well as reaching customers. The power of *network connections* allows a company to grow fast. Being widely connected allows you to have greater impact in the global marketplace. Remember, *everything you know can be known by people everywhere.* Even a local business can have customers all over the world if the business has the right connections. Those connections will allow you to implement world-class business practices, innovative ideas, and technology around the globe. Creative network linkages, such as cooperative alliances, allow individuals to establish ventures without large investment, or the problem of management associated with mergers. The G/E probably has read John Kao's book, *Jamming*, where he makes this comment: "The power of creativity rises exponentially with the diversity and divergence of those connected to the network."

They Intent to Start a Global Venture. G/Es have very strong and ambitious intentions as they initially design their international ventures. Entrepreneurship research demonstrates that having such ambitious *intentions* will significantly affect the success, growth, and survival of the venture. There is no doubt that the Pygmalion effect is at work here: people with strong expectations, or intentions, usually act on those expectations. The traditional route for globalization of a business is to grow the business locally, regionally and nationally; then expand into one or more international markets. The G/E will often bypass this conventional process and initiate the global ventures with the start-up of the enterprise. In a typical scenario, a global start-up begins with a product made in one country and them markets it in or more other countries. Though outsourcing, this can be accomplished without ownership of manufacturing facilities. Nike is a good example, for the company outsources it manufacturing and other business functions with the exception of marketing. The globalization trend and the advent of e-commerce are clearly enabling factors assisting the G/E in starting a global venture

They Seek to Achieve Breakthrough Accomplishments. It has been frequently acknowledge that Traditional Entrepreneurs are a rare group. Well, the G/E is no ordinary person either. G/Es are clearly extraordinary in what they propose to do and also in what they actually accomplish in their global business ventures. One can easily make the case that G/Es have two overriding goals in life. First is that of achieving some type of breakthrough accomplishment, or an individual achievement that merits significant recognition in society. This individual achievement goal is accomplished by the G/E in developing a viable and successful global business that reflects the G/Es unique accomplishments. In spite of the prevailing views of socio-psychologists, a second paramount G/E goal is to accumulate wealth. Wealth ranks with, but necessarily *after,* the achievement goal. Wealth has to follow achievement, for wealth *results* from the successful accomplishment of the enterprise. One measure of wealth is the amount of money created (saved or invested) as a result of the G/E's business. Perhaps the greatest accomplishment of all for G/Es is to have an eminently successful global enterprise that rewards them with significant wealth.

They Design The Business as a Public Venture. Some G/Es will choose to keep their venture a private entity; however, most G/Es will elect to make their venture a publicly-listed business as soon as possible. If G/Es can get venture capitalists to concur with their intentions of going public, this will greatly enhance the growth and value of the business. Convincing investors will ensure adequate start-up and operating capital, thus allowing the G/E to concentrate on the core value-creating activities of the business. Having such backers creates the conditions for a second round of financing if the venture proves successful. Also G/Es will be able to attract more capable employees through stock options and other forms of compensation and, most importantly, G/Es will have the potential opportunity to create greater wealth for themselves and associates by having a successful publicly-traded business.

The six-step G/E process is three fold: It is *prescriptive, teachable,* and *learnable.* G/Es will not allow any of these six steps to be a roadblock to achieving their dream. They will master all the required skills and abilities, or they will purchase the services of others as needed. Their pervasive connectivity provides them with many worldwide contacts that can greatly assist in identify resources and finding information needed for their venture.

Global entrepreneurship is prescriptive, teachable, and learnable.

The Global Entrepreneur as a Person

The G/E is truly a product of the 21st century. These results from a real convergence of several interactive forces: globalization, the Information Age, the Internet, and the use of knowledge and technology. All of these forces have created an abundance of international wealth-creating opportunities for entrepreneurs. These forces, coupled with the entrepreneurial spirit of the G/E, are liberating individuals as never before. In today's work environment, individual having a high degree of motivation and education are literally creating their own future. While it is true that the G/E generally has a high IQ, being a genius is not a necessity today. We live in a special time says Gary Hamel, "Whatever you need to know to create the future, you can know. [84] This is the uniqueness of today as compared to any previous period of history. If G/Es do not have what is needed for their venture, they are confident they can master it, acquire it, or get others to accomplish the function for them.

If G/Es do not have what is needed for their venture, they are confident they can master it, acquire it, or get others to accomplish the function for them.

The G/E's tasks are far more complex than those of Traditional Entrepreneurs. Today's G/Es are adept at e-commerce; they have a very wide-angle vantage point that is needed to focus on recognizing global opportunities and have the agility to fast dance with a variety of partners. They are able to spontaneously move from the present to the future while at the same time crossing national boundaries. They have unparalleled diplomatic and political skills, yet are still able to understand the needs of the person on the street. They have powerful analytical skills and superb instincts; they know the old language of ROE and EVA, and they have a new vocabulary of Internet acronyms, like B2B, B2C and P2P. They possess strong intentions of creating something really big – a global venture. Indeed, today's G/Es are quite different; they are more adept, and much more complex, than any previously known entrepreneur. The G/E. is clearly representative of a new class of uber-entrepreneurs.

Unique Thoughts Patterns

It is possible to further analyze existing G/Es by a *process* of observing their *thoughts* and *behaviors*. Earlier we discussed the Traditional Entrepreneur as being a person – "the dancer." The G/E is also a "dancer," but he or she is a fast dancer with different dance steps, new music, and with a variety of partners. But here, too, we do not have a really reliable predictive test to determine *who* is likely to become a G/E because they can only be observed *after* becoming an entrepreneur. In the same manner, we defined the unique characteristics of Traditional Entrepreneurs in chapter three; the G/E also has *unique thought patterns*. These unique thoughts clearly differentiate G/E from Traditional Entrepreneurs. There are four mental challenges that tend to occupy the thoughts of G/Es as they contemplate their future ventures. They are as follows: a personal desire to create their own employment; a quest for achieving a breakthrough accomplishment; their desire to have a successful business on a world stage; and a strong determination to create substantial wealth. Let's look at these *thought patterns* in more detail.

Creating One's Own Self-Employment. "The greatest excitement of the future is that we can shape it," says Charles Handy (60) The G/E invents his or her future by exploiting opportunities with associates in various global domains. G/E/s seek, and are successful in capitalizing on, present discontinuities and economic upheavals underway throughout the world. They recognize that working for oneself provides a high level of job security than is present elsewhere in industry today. If there is to be individual job security in this era of unparalleled change, a period which is characterized by downsizing and rationalizing in industry, individuals must create their own self-employment. Additional changes are instigated by a revolutionary-new system of creating wealth, that is, through the utilization of knowledge and technology. Knowledge and technology are the forte of G/Es and, consequently, they never worry about unemployment. They are their own job security.

Thinking of Achieving Breakthrough Accomplishments. Creating something of historical significance is the dream of the G/E. These individuals often think of themselves as an Edison of a chosen industry, because of their many innovative ideas. They would be delighted to come up with a creative idea that results in producing a harmless cigarette, or identifying the genetic root of cancer. Nanotechnology is opening up increasing opportunities in fabricating and building of tiny communications and computing devices. Once can sense the excitement as young innovators try to exploit quantum effects – those quirky rules that govern atoms and molecules – in their search for radically new electronic devices. The Massachusetts Institute of Technology

(MIT) looked into the future through the work of more than 600 innovative entrepreneurs who were involved in computing, biotech, the Web, radical new materials, and ingenious hardware. MIT found them shaping breakthrough accomplishments in their disciplines – making breakthroughs that stagger the mind – and many of these pioneers were still in their middle twenties. Such restless young innovators are clearly the scientific and technical G/Es of the near future. We will discuss this promising group of G/Es later in this chapter.[85]

From England ...

Stelios Haji-Iannou is a Greek serial entrepreneur and is best known for starting his British budget airline, EasyJet, at age 27. When Stelios launched EasyJet in 1998, he really had to battle the big boys – British Airways and others, in order to get his firm up and running. As a son of a Greek shipping tycoon, he had a ready source for collateral funding. Now Stelios has created an EasyGroup of 16 companies. He has started a global chain of Internet cafes where customers can access his other ventures such as Easy-rent-a-car; Easy Value, a dot.com that finds deals for shoppers; and soon-to-be established EasyMoney, a cut-rate loan business. Stelios' ultimate goal is to float all of his start-up ventures in a publically traded company.

Seeking World-Class Orientation. Because of their constant search for advanced concepts, G/Es are true cosmopolitans who have a clear lead over local entrepreneurs. Such sophisticated concepts include: continually searching for the best and the latest in knowledge and advance technology, constantly enhancing their competence through their desire and ability to meet and exceed the highest standards available anywhere; and further widening their collaborative network through global connectivity, thus providing greater access to resources, people and organizations throughout the world. This global quest for the best enables G/Es to constantly expand their knowledge, for they find linkages and parallels in just about everything they see, hear, or do as they move around the world. Being able to tap into the world's best offers the G/E a clear advantage over those who are more locally restricted.

Desiring to Create Substantial Wealth. A major conclusion of most socio-psychological research in entrepreneurship is that monetary rewards are only of secondary importance in motivating individuals. This research does not reflect another branch of study, namely, research in economic theory. The G/Es desire for wealth is noticeably stronger than their entrepreneurial ancestors. G/Es are too more open in expressing their desired as illustrated in the title of a *Fortune* magazine cover article: "They're very young. They're restless. And they're ready to get rich." Unquestionably, *money is a major motivator* and is a strong underlying stimulus for venturing by G/Es. If there is doubt whether money is of primary importance, just ask any G/E this question: "Would you start this venture knowing you will earn only a modest income and have no chance of generating significant wealth?" You will get a blunt retort to such a question! If the individual's wealth-creating opportunity is taken away, economic progress will stagnate. The emergence of an increasing number of wealth-creating opportunities is apparent a result of globalization and other major economic forces shaping the New Global Economic Era. There are several reasons for starting a new venture, but nothing motivates an individual like the never-ending desire for money. G/Es will not be apologetic about their increased psychic drive to build economic wealth for themselves and others.

The four unique thought patterns are not all-inclusive, but they certainly seem to dominate G/E's thinking. Obviously, G/Es think about many other things as they contemplate their new enterprises. For example, G/Es will intuitively think of the need to develop and hone their leadership skills and the ability to communicate. These are generic skills needed by all types of entrepreneurs, managers, leaders, and other professionals. But the four thought patterns described above are unique to G/Es and do indeed further serve to differentiate them from other entrepreneurs. However, we know thoughts alone do not *maketh* the entrepreneur. Recently a venture capitalist commented that he does not invest in entrepreneurs who are just thinking about starting a new venture, he will only invest in those who are actually operating a business and are extremely enthusiastic about growing it. Obviously, *thinking* and *doing* are two separate activities. The G/E succeeds at both and their behaviors below will explain how they do this.

Personal Behavior Patterns

Thoughts precede and influence individual behavior. David McClelland illustrated this is his classic book, *Motivating Economic Behavior.* He taught the process of entrepreneurship to a number of individuals worldwide (including the author), thus enticing them to *think about the discipline*, and subsequently encouraging them *to start* their own ventures. It works! *Entrepreneurship is a learnable process.* McClelland's research revealed the more one thinks about starting a business, the more likely one is to engage in over "behaviors" resulting in creating a business.[86]

G/Es have a unique set of *behavioral patterns* that are brought into play in the creation of their global business venture: They span borders and continents with the greatest of ease; they often exhibit unconventional and disruptive behaviors; they are usually moving very decisively on a fast track, far ahead of the crowd; and they are living in a continuous learning mode, soaking in everything, everywhere. Now let's review the G/Es *behavioral patterns* in more detail, keeping in mind these too, are things that can be individually mastered over a period of time.

They Span Borders and Continents with Ease. The international cosmopolitan nature of G/Es is one of their overarching characteristics. They are constantly on the move to various parts of the world, with a couple of passports and several airline tickets in hand, heading for other destinations. G/Es make themselves available for unlimited opportunities because of their ability to utilize people, resources, and technology located anywhere and everywhere in the world. Their cultural sensitivity enables them to transverse continents and national boundaries and to be welcomed by local business people and government officials. A real key to the G/Es is their orientation to the global community. They are not confined to a particular location, as are Traditional Entrepreneurs. Such international communities are a comfort zone for the G/E.

Their Actions Are Unconventional and Disruptive. You will frequently find G/Es leaving positions in large corporation, giving up that security blanket, and searching for their own new venture. Such unconventional moves are the norms for G/Es, who will choose to change their professions several times before finding the excitement of their life in operating their own extended enterprise. G/Es know that in times of turmoil and rapid change, the unconventional often wins. They understand that they must shape the future, or be shaped by it. What makes G/Es seem so disruptive is they are continuously reinventing themselves, rapidly changing careers, remolding their thoughts and behaviors, and constantly adapting to an ever-changing world.

They Move on a Fast Track. The G/E well understands the "attacker's advantage," and knows the importance of getting there "the firstest with the mostest." Their network office may work around the clock, around the world, by quickly designing and delivering their service products. Production design may first start in America, then be off to Japan by the end of the day, on to Germany, and then back to the United States – all within twenty-four hours. He may even physically live in Hong Kong, and commutes to an office in Silicon Valley, as does Alan Wong, CEO of VTECH. Wong frequently circulates among offices in Hong Kong, the U.S., Europe and at his production facility in South China. They know in order to win in the 21st century, they must move quickly to stay ahead of the change curve, and that means they are always on a fast track.

Such speed to market with your product is highly critical today, for potential competitors will rush to the market with a product if they hear through the industry grapevine that another firm is about to release a competitive product. Knowing this, Health Discovery Corporation of Savannah, Georgia, conceived of the idea of a world's *first* mobile phone app for determining a low, moderate, or high risk assessment for having melanoma, or other forms of skin cancer. This is done through a laboratory analysis of cell phone pictures taken of the mole or skin lesion by a person in the privacy of their home. The company quickly issued a press release to ensure the claim of having the world's "first" mobile phone app for assessing the possible risk of skin cancer. Health Discovery plans to include in its service a list of cancer physicians and clinics that are closest to the person requesting the risk assessment.

They live in a Continuous Learning Mode. A legacy from Peters' and Waterman's classic book, *In Search of Excellence,* is that excellence is a constantly moving target. The future is also a moving target – nothing will ever be what it was, or where it was. Fortunately, G/Es seem to thrive on "creative construction" and future uncertainty, because that's where most opportunities reside. The G/E prepares himself or herself for a fast-moving world where everything has become, or is becoming obsolete. Their preparations are to live in a continuous learning mode. They understand that a competitive advantage is achieved by learning and implementing more quickly than rivals. It is not the idea that counts in many instances; it is how quickly you can implement it. Again, G/Es enjoy a unique advantage due to being in multiple international information exchanges, where ideas are freely shared, traded, and constructively implemented. They frequently engage in an off-balance, fast-track learning process. This is normal for a person operating at the edge of chaos, as many G/Es seem to do in their ventures.

As a result of G/E's unique behavior patterns, they have at their disposal many valuable intangible assets of the 21st century; *competence* – being able to operate in a world-class environment anywhere on the globe; *knowledge* – having the latest and best business ideas available anywhere; *technology* – knowing the best and most proven ways of achieving superior performance; and *connections* – having a superior network of associates and relationships around the world. Again, it is because they have these valuable intangible assets that G/Es have such a significant advantage over Traditional Entrepreneurs.

The wealth-creating capacity of G/Es in the Information Age will be enormous. An elite group of G/Es are incredibly rich and others are becoming so. Some are mention in this book. In another book, *The Sovereign Individual,* James Davidson and William Rees-Mogg discuss the new cyber-economy and tell us that "anyone who thinks clearly can be potentially rich." They proclaim that the brightest, most successful and, most ambitious individual in the cyber-economy will emerge as "sovereign individuals." These individuals will be liberated as never before for *their ideas will be their greatest source of wealth.*[87] These are the people who will take full advantage of the social and financial consequences of the four concurrent revolutions mentioned previously. They are the cosmopolitan G/Es.

Cosmopolitans and Locals

Another striking difference between G/Es and other entrepreneurs is their cosmopolitan nature. By contrast, local-oriented entrepreneurs do not have the opportunity to tap into the world's best people and resources; consequently, these entrepreneurs are often restricted to operating on a small scale and in a narrower geographic market. Mothers residing in the hills of north Georgia who watch their sons and daughters depart for California must understand their children will never return home. These young people often retain a nostalgic feeling for the local community in which they were raised, but due to their wide exposure to the rest of the world, they are changed forever. They are not anti-local; they simply have links to a wider world that affords them different opportunities and options. G/Es prefer their wider choices over traditional loyalties. They also have a preference for world-class standards rather than accepting a lesser quality that is often found in small localities. Consequently, locals can become cosmopolitans, but a cosmopolitan will never be local again.

Locals can become cosmopolitans, but never will a cosmopolitan be local again.

Cosmopolitan G/Es will often affiliate with locals in their network of businesses around the globe. They understand the concept of thinking globally and operating locally. An affiliate network of geographically dispersed locals allows the G/E to have the best of both worlds, that is, being open to global thinking and opportunities, and at the same time serving local markets with a keen sensitivity and understanding of the native culture. The G/E needs to make the appropriate governmental connections in the communities in which his/her business operates. In China, the G/E will hire the village elder who judges local disputes. In doing so, the G/E will cut through a great deal of red tape in opening a venture there. Business is becoming increasingly global, but politics remain local. Local politicians are always interested in showing their constituents how active they are in bringing new businesses to the community, whether this is true or not. Also, contact with government officials can help in identifying appropriate locals with whom the G/E will need as partners. So, the success of G/Es is due in part to linkage to a global network of local partners with whom they share knowledge, technology, and an array of world-class business practices.

From Japan …

Hiroshi Mikitani was in his early thirties when he picked up his English language skills while living in the U.S. and attending Harvard University. He made his first mark in his native Japan where he started a consultancy, Crimson Global, and then established Rakuten Ichiba, an Internet company that makes serious money. In 2005, Rakuten's revenues exceeded $1.1 billion. In 2008, Ratuten merged with Baidu to form China' largest B2B/B2C online shopping company. Through this online retail store, he allows his clients to pay cash upon receiving their merchandise at the local post office, a-novel distribution system.

Global and Traditional Entrepreneurs

A basic tenet of this book is that G/Es are significantly different from Traditional Entrepreneurs. A major difference is the wealth-creating potential as discussed above, but there are other differences as well. To say G/Es are wired-in members of the Net Generation is a real understatement. They view the capability of the computer and the Internet as close partners in their quest for new ideas and business ventures. It is indeed an incredible time when G/Es, with their portable computer and satellite links, can conduct their information-related, multimillion-dollar business anywhere in the world, at any time, day or night.

Table 7.1 highlights the major differences between G/Es and Traditional Entrepreneurs. In analyzing such differences, the global orientation is perhaps the most significant. Another major difference is the G/Es lack of substantial fixed investment in plants and equipment due to his or her emphasis on virtualization and outsourcing. Clearly E/Es are a new class of venture-seeking individuals.

Figure 7.1
A Comparison of Traditional Entrepreneurs And Global Entrepreneurs

Factors:	Traditional Entrepreneurs:	Global Entrepreneurs:
Orientation	Local	Cosmopolitan
Geographic	Regional/Country	Global
Alliances	One or two	Numerous
Technology	Moderate	Cutting-edge
Intelligence	Above average	Very high IQ
Patents held	Maybe one	Several
Connectivity	Single firm	Many partners
Information Technology	Uses PC & Cell Phone	Net generation user
Organization	Functional	Virtual
Careers	First or second	Fourth or fifth
PDAs	Uses one	Typically 3 or 4
Builder	One's business	Global bridges
Boundary	Regional/national	International
Reproduces	Products & sales	Self & ventures
Headquarters	Company office	Where CEO is

Selecting Future Global Entrepreneurs

What, where, and who will be developing the next big idea for changing the world? Answering that question is like picking the next stock that is going to make a million. What we can do is share with you some young innovators who are well on their way to create ventures that will impact the lives of people in many countries and perhaps the world. Below is a summary of an annual list of the most promising young innovators as identified by MIT. These are exceptional leaders in technology who are united in their urgent desire to improve what we do, how to get it done quicker and cheaper, and how to help improve our quality of life. They are building safer, simpler, speedier electronics and software; better, more resilient medical devices and treatments; and cheaper, cleaner energy sources. A few of these outstanding innovators are listed below.

Kevin Fu, 33, from University of Massachusetts, was chosen as the innovator of the year from this group with his technology for encryption software that is providing security to credit cards and to medical devices that use RF communication, such a pacemakers and defibrillators. While Ranjan Dash, 32, was at Drexel University he developed a novel chemical recipe for making a carbon material that holds great promise for energy storage for hybrid electric vehicles. Adam Dunkels, 31, of the Swedish Institute of Computer Science, has perfected a minimal wireless-networking protocol that allows almost any device to communicate over the internet. Andre Lynn, 32, in Cambridge, England, has developed a unique method of coaxing the human body to rebuild damage bone and cartilage rather than using metal joint replacements. This is just a highlight listing of these young entrepreneurs.

This is just a sampling of thirty-five young innovators working in disparate fields and places, from clean rooms and labs to factories and slums, from New England to Nicaragua. There is no question that many of these young innovators with their amazing technological discoveries are bound to be among future emerging G/Es. The complete list is very impressive. You may want to "Google" this *Technology Review* article and review the complete listing of these young innovators in nanotechnology, biotechnology, energy, software on the Internet.[88]

The Arrival of Present-Day Global Entrepreneurs

Now we move from emerging G/Es to those with established ventures. *Inc.* magazine has developed a simple way to identify global companies that are a part of their top 500 fastest-growing businesses. They measure the miles from the corporate headquarters to the most distant customer. The reach of these global companies stretches from the depths of the North Sea to the highest peak of Antarctica. Geo-Solutions below takes the first place in that its New Kensington, Pennsylvania, headquarters is 9,325 miles from its most distant customer in Brisbane, Australia. Below is a look at more global ventures and the products/services they are providing to international customers.

AdqQuest. This firm maintains offices in Bellevue, Washington, and Rio de Janeiro (6,884 miles), and helps software companies translate applications in more than 60 languages. Founder Hiram Machdo grew up in Rio de Janeiro and works out of both office locations.

Always Underfoot. This Curitiba, Brazil, firm is an importer-exporter of 40 species of South American floorboard from Brazil, Paraguay, Bolivia and

Peru. The company has shipments of a thousand truckloads each year and has logistics centers in Bedem and Caritiba.

RigNet. This Houston, Texas, firm outfits offshore oil rigs with telecommunications systems. A recent project involved linking an offshore rig off the coast of Nigeria to an office in Bedford, England.

Access Technology Solutions. American-Japanese logistic company handles more than 20,000 shipments a month. A major source of business is shipping consumer goods from the U.S. to Japan, such as baby strollers, a big staple product of the company.

Remote Medical International. This Seattle-Antarctica firm offers medical support to people in far-off locations and in dangerous situations. Last year an RMI employee led a team of climbers scaling Antarctica's tallest peak to field-test some equipment.

Milestone Metals. This Virginia-China-based firm buys scrap metal such as steel and brass, and sells it to foundries and smelters in China. A recent batch of copper was turned into an underwater communications cable.

Echo Global Logistics. This China-Utah company coordinates freight delivery around the world. One recent job involved getting a generator the size of a locomotive from the inland port of Wahan, China, to a power plant in Mona, Utah.

Geo-Solutions. This Pennsylvania-based company prevents groundwater contamination, and earns a fifth of its revenue abroad. One recent project as in Brisbane, Australia, a fast-growing container port city, where it installed a containment barrier around a large dredge.

Clear Harbor. This Georgia-based company provides service, technical support, and administrative outsourcing to U.S. clients through its facilities in the eastern Caribbean.

Celergo. This three-year-old Illinois firm provides payroll services to companies in 90 different countries.

All of these *Inc.* firms were founded and generating revenue by the first week of 2005. They are principally U.S.-based, privately held, for profit and are independent, not a subsidiary or division of other companies. Of course, this is the ultimate goal of G/Es to have such an international venture.[89]

As you can see, most of the above firms provide service products; however, there are still many thriving, growing companies that make tangible products that you can see, touch, and feel. Here are five *Inc.* 500 high-growth firms that are showing remarkable growth through the sale of their tangible products.

GATR Technologies. This Huntsville, Alabama, firm makes inflatable satellite dishes that provide high-speed Internet and phone access to American soldiers in Afghanistan. It was also part of a mobile medical unit during the earthquake in Haiti.

Rennen International. Two Chinese brothers, Takang and Weizrung Lee, started their New York auto parts business by buying accessories from China and hawking them to auto retailers. They soon found high-quality automobile wheels generated much better revenue than muffler-shaped key chains.

Clear Align. This Pennsylvania company makes custom surveillance equipment for national-security and military customers around the world, according to Angelique Irvin, founder and CEO. Their equipment is mounted on submarines, satellites, unmanned aerial vehicles, buildings and cars.

Metal Mafia. Based in New York, this firm has a 4500-item catalog that includes jewelry for navel, nose, lip, back, cheek, arm, neck, hip, wrist, hand, and fingers. Most are designed in-house and the firm sells three million pieces each year to retailers around the world, with most of the items wholesaling for less than $5.

MaxTorque. One would think that most gearboxes for opening and closing a valve would have been invented by now. Don't tell that to this Limerick, Maine, company, which has developed an improved cylindrical-worm gearbox that opens and closes valves better than others on the market. It expects to sell some 1500 gearboxes this year with prices from $500 to $80,000.

Whether you have a service or a product, one can clearly see from these *Inc.'s* fastest-growing companies that the world has truly become a single marketplace. The question for you is this: What product or service offering are you developing that can be sold in the international marketplace?[90]

From Ideas, to Ventures, to Extraordinary-High-Growth Web Organizations

The world is abound with potential opportunities, more so today than ever before due to globalization and the expansive nature of Internet technology. One amazing thing about our New Global Economic World is how quickly a previously unknown business concept can just explode on the scene overnight and become a mammoth business in short order.

Mark Zuckerberg founded Facebook in 2004, along with three other Harvard students, two of whom graduated magna cum laude. His original idea would not have won a business plan competition, for all he wanted to do was to offer a social connection, an updated yearbook, and personal homepage for a few thousand Ivey League students. In a short period of time, it exploded in popularity among American college students and other users; whereas today it has over a half million users in more than 100 global markets. Mark is the world's youngest self-made billionaire and is still is in his twenties.

Great ideas arise from strange places. Jawed Karman refused to believe the tale of the great dinner party help by Chad Hurley and Steve Chen, which

Karmin wasn't able to attend. Hurley and Chen had video proof, but no way to immediately share it with Karmin. Well, the rest is history, for these three founders developed YouTube in 2005, in California, with a little help from $11.5 million funding by Sequoia Capital. YouTube became a global phenomenon in less than a year, and today is the third-most-visited Internet site behind Google and Facebook.

Less is more, according to Jack Dorsey and his cofounders of Twitter, a social networking and microblogging service. Since its creation in 2006, Twitter has gained notability and popularity worldwide with its service that enables its users to send and receive other users' short messages (140 characters) called tweets. Twitter has more than 100 million users worldwide and is growing rapidly, with 2 billion tweets per quarter being posted by the end of 2009. Twitter has sometimes been described as the "SMS of the Internet." The basic mechanics of Twitter are remarkably simple and allow persons to know what their friends are thinking, doing, and feeling, even when co-presence isn't possible.

This decade has spawned an incredible number of fast-growing web-based companies such as: Baidu.com in 2000, China's largest search engine; RapidShare.com., a German one-click hosting website; Wikipedia in 2001; MySpace in 2003; LinkedIn in 2003; and msn.com. in 2009, just to name a few. The emergence of these and the above new-age global ventures make Microsoft, founded in 1975, and Apple, in 1976, seem like senior citizens. However, Since Steve Jobs returned to Apple in 1997, his *corporate entrepreneurship* efforts have brought about a renaissance in Apple with the introduction of iPod, iPhone, iPad, and other electronic products. A new growth phase may be emerging at Apple since it has added *services* to its product offering. Apple now has an iAd mobile advertising service and beginning clients, Unilever PLC and Nissan, have paid a cool $1 million to have interactive ads placed inside iPhone apps.

Apple is certainly one of the best organizations having developed major game-changing products. These products have reshaped Apple's business model and significantly changed the music industry. They have an amazing record of successful product introductions; however, over the past 30 years they have churned out some product flops. We can cite 10 of these products: Apple Cyberdog, Taligent, Apple EWorld, Apple Pippin, 20th Anniversary Macintosh, Motorola's ROKR cell phone, Macintosh TV, Macintosh Portable PC, Apple Lisa, and the Apple Newton. Success with new product introductions comes at a big price. Large organizations are not anymore successful in creating them than entrepreneurs – they just have more money to do it.

How the world has changed since the formation of Apple in 1976! It is hard to believe the firm started as a partnership, not even a corporation, and with three founders (yes, three) – Steve Jobs (21), Stephen Wozniak (25), and Ronald Wayne (41). Woz was an employee of Hewlett Packard and Jobs was freelancing at Atari, where he and Wayne became casual friends. Jobs wanted a tie-breaker in case of a conflict with Woz and enticed Wayne to become a partner in Apple by offering him 10 percent interest in the business. Wayne then backed out of the agreement within two weeks, after he discovered Jobs was borrowing a tidy sum of money to build their first computer order from Byte Shop in Mountain View, California. Wayne did not want to assume his share of the *risk*, so he gave up his 10 percent claim and accepted $800 as a one-time payment for his efforts at Apple. Jobs earned $8,000 on the first order and again, history was made. It was after this transaction that Jobs secured funding from investors; he then incorporated the business, purchased the partnership, and finally developed a business plan.

Once in business, G/Es frequently observe their customers and markets; they recalibrate, readjust their product offering, and make major changes in the venture during the early stages of development and growth. The founders of YouTube attempted to start a dating service before they settled on their video-uploading service. Such ventures evolve, based not on the original business plan, but more on emerging marketing circumstances, and the ability of the entrepreneur to recognize and respond to such events. Then they create new opportunities as Apple has done by expanding into new consumer markets beyond the originally-planned core business.

From Entrepreneurship to Professional Management

We have mentioned several times that the skills and abilities of entrepreneurs are not comparable with those of managers in many instances. A clear indication of this is more than 50 percent of founding entrepreneurs are replaced within a year after receiving funding from angel investors and/or venture capitalists. Many astute entrepreneurs understand this and make up-front adjustments by bringing in professional management before being asked by investors. We discuss this here, as it is easy for a G/E to fall into the trap of wanting to make lots of money and to run the show at the same time. Research by Noam Wassran tells us that it's tough for entrepreneurs to do both.

As always, there are exceptions to such research. Bill Gates and Steve Jobs have done a superb job of building their ventures from a two-person start-up to a successful global businesses. However, we agree with Wasserman that it is "tough" to do both and entrepreneurs should be aware of this. By knowing in advance this is a likely problem one can make adjustment by preparing to bring in professional management at the appropriate time to help the founding entrepreneur. Investors will be looking for this in your business plan. David Filo and Jerry Yang at Yahoo did this immediately in 1995, by bringing in Tim Koogle from Motorola as their CEO and a professional manager as the CFO. I imagine they were nudged a bit by Sequoia Capital, which invested $2 million in the firm at that time.

Founders are usually convinced that only they have the knowledge and ability to lead their start-up to success. After all, they conceived the idea of the business, they possess most of the insights about the opportunity, and they know the product or service better than anyone else. They too want to create a unique organizational culture as an extension of their own personal style and personality. Many entrepreneurs do not understand when they celebrate the shipment of their first product, then, that moment is a milestone in the transition from being an entrepreneur to a manager. The venture now becomes more complex, more technical, and must be structured with formal processes include formal positions of production, marketing, and finance. This dramatic broadening of required skills needed to operate the venture often stretches the founder beyond his or her ability. So now, Mr. Entrepreneur, you know! You need to be highly sensitive to this known entrepreneur-management-conversion situation and make plans for someone else to run the show. This will free you up to go out and create other new ventures and become a serial entrepreneur.[91]

Now if you really insist on being the top dog and run the show, here is another piece of advice from Anthony Tjan, CEO, and founder of the venture capital firm, Cue Ball. Tjan's advice has credence in that he is a venture capitalist and is well-thought of to the extent that his comments are also published in the *Harvard Business Review.* He tells us entrepreneurs should be able to do three things in their sleep: *planning, selling,* and *execution*. Tjan says these are the three most important things entrepreneurs need to *get done* [note he implies others might help]. Anyway, regarding selling, Tjan says, "Great entrepreneurs need to be constantly selling the story of their vision, as well as researching how it should evolve." Further, he says the best entrepreneurs execute their visions by establishing the right metrics by which to measure their business progress; then they religiously monitor them as the business progresses. What Tjan is tell you is this: To be successful, G/Es must acquire these *three management skills* or get other professionals to operate the business, just as Richard Branson has done with his 240 business entities.[92]

One last bit of advice to G/Es if you choose to run your own high-growth venture. The Renaissance Leadership Model, discussed in chapter two, will help you achieve the highest possible performance from your associates and will provide you with the best possible relationships with people. The

Renaissance Model states that managers should be "Hard on Performance" and, simultaneously, "Soft on People." Being Hard on Performance means you design, expect and accept only a high level of continuous performance improvement from associates. Soft on People means you must continuously do a better job of meeting the needs, wants, rights and culture of your associates in a non-threatening manner. Work at achieving these two functions and you will accomplish greater managerial success in your venture.

Creating a successful global company is a product of hard work over a period of time (sometimes very short), with a lot of luck thrown in. Note that most of the great companies emerging today are not products of a solo entrepreneur, but are a team effort from the beginning, and they frequently include an international founder or co-founder. Also, ideas for great companies don't just fly out of thin air and land on a branch to be plucked by entrepreneurs. Original ideas are often nurtured, modified, and tailored to market conditions in order for a company to be successful. That is one reason why investors will choose an A-class entrepreneurial team with a B-Class product every day over a B-class entrepreneurial team with an A-class product. Products don't change entrepreneurs, but entrepreneurs can certainly change products. Obviously, your goal as a Global Entrepreneur is to build an A-class entrepreneurial team and create that A-class product. That is your winning combination.

8

Developing the Global Enterprise

"Whatever you can do, or dream you can, begin it.
Boldness has genius, power and magic in it."
Goethe

A New Structure for the Global Economic Era

One of the greatest shifts in business over the past 20 years has been the recognition that real wealth does not reside in natural resources, but resides in knowledge and technologies for exploiting them. Our new Information Era economy is about creating value through the use of knowledge as productive *inputs* and *outputs* in business enterprises. The New Global Economic Era clearly reveals a relative decline in the value of plants, equipment and tangibles, and the rise in relative importance of intellectual capital. Commodity-rich nations will discover that it's not their mines, but their minds that will be the source of future prosperity. The natural resources of nations will be greatly exploited by individuals with astute business acumen; their astuteness will enable them to convert resources into wealth.

Just look at the successful economies of Japan and Hong Kong. They have very few natural resources, but have created substantial personal and national wealth. By contrast, Russia and Africa, even with their abundance of natural resources, have some of the world's worst poverty. While commodity values decline in price, the value of technology and intellectual capital increases. So, the winner in the new global era will be intellectual capitalists—those who have the ability to conceive and develop knowledge products and market them on a global basis. Many people work with knowledge products daily, but have not discovered how to convert them into profit-making ventures. Many business people are exposed to knowledge-based products that can be marketed globally. Accenture Consulting catalogs its clients' "best practices" and then uses and resells that knowledge by subscription on the Internet.

The ability to continuously innovate and to adapt to an ever-changing environment is more important than ever. As technology and world markets constantly change, Global Entrepreneurs (G/Es) recognize they must have lean, flexible, and innovative enterprises. They must conceive radically new ideas, reconceptualize old products into new ones and explore new global distribution channels. Their management philosophy is radically different from earlier times when managers forced individuals to conform to company policies and practices. An overall challenge of G/Es will be to figure out how best to capture and leverage knowledge and experience that each organizational member brings to their venture.

Changing Nature of the Corporation

The large corporate organization has served business exceedingly well in the past and has helped create a worldwide productive capacity that currently exceeds consumption in developed countries. For the United States, this productive capacity has created the most advanced economy in world history. Such capabilities have aided Japan and Germany in rising from the ashes of World War II to become the third-and fourth-largest world economies. Other countries throughout the world have increasingly benefited from successes of large corporate organizations. Designed to produce long runs of standardized products, the corporate structure of the past was hierarchical and bureaucratic. New and improved products were introduced on a predictable basis, and there were fairly good relations with employees, somewhat guaranteed by labor unions. A certain amount of economic stability was created, especially, in the U.S., by a number of large, quasi-benevolent, oligopolistic companies, particularly, three automobile firms and five steel mills.

Now these major corporations are losing out around the world. They are being transformed by global competition that forces them to shift production from high-volume to high-value, from standardized to customized, and from large-scale to small-scale. Management hierarchies have been flatted to create more nimble and flexible organizations. Lifetime employment in Japan is gone, and job security in the U.S. does not exist anymore. One reason for a continuous rise in entrepreneurship in the U.S. is that individual employees realize they must provide their own job security. All types of entrepreneurs seek this through establishing their own businesses.

The Changing Organizational Environment

New structural innovations in large business organizations are not an option; they are a necessity. The traditional command and control organization is dysfunctional when it tries to take advantage of all opportunities presented by an emerging global economy and a strong emergence of knowledge workers. A new model of international companies is emerging, driven by networks, global linkage and adaptability. What we refer to here are established firms that are required to adjust to a new competitive world. However, this is good news for G/Es because this new organizational option is available for them on a small scale, which is more suitable for innovative start-up ventures.

As mentioned in chapter six, the G/Es 21st century organization is likely to be a "virtual organization" in the beginning, simply a product of the mind of the G/E. Such an organization will appear seamless, permeable and will frequently reflect a continuous, changing network of company associates, suppliers, manufacturers, customers, stockholders and outsourcing. Again, in the beginning, the virtual organization will be unlike the traditional hierarchical entity with line and staff positions, but will appear less as a discrete enterprise and more like a constantly changing cluster of networking-related activities. G/Es will create functions and add people only as needed, based on demand in the marketplace.

The New Corporate Structure

We see today an emergence of radical, new corporate structures. With the advent of the Information Age, one can instantly create a virtual business firm, whose domicile can be in any jurisdiction, depending on what the marketplace demands. Micro-technology allows firms to be small and very footloose regarding location. Knowledge-related businesses can be located anywhere on the planet since they are not confined to a specific location such as a port, physical plant, or a mine. Knowledge is the key. A key characteristic of G/Es is the creation of a knowledge-based venture - one that has the ability to create, assemble, integrate, transfer, and exploit knowledge as a revenue-generating asset. David Teese characterizes the G/E's organization this way: "The firm's capacity to secure and seize opportunities, to reconfigure its knowledge assets, competencies, complementary assets, to select an appropriate organization form, to allocate resources astutely, and to price them strategically – all of which constitute a dynamic capability."[93] That dynamic capability is a hallmark of the G/E.

An example of this emerging, and certainly more efficient, new corporate structure is the Monorail Corporation, located in Atlanta, Georgia. Monorail sells computers, but has neither factories, nor a warehouse, nor any other tangible assets. It leases its office space, and freelance workers design Monorail's computers. In placing orders, customers call a toll-free number connected to a Federal Express logistic service, which passes the order on to a contract manufacturer for assembly. FedEx ships the computer to customers and sends the invoice to Monorail's local bank, which performs the accounting function. Monorail's virtual business is a good illustration of radical changes taking place in modern firms.

Even the military has recognized attributes of virtual organizations for wartime activities. In the 1980s, retired Army General Paul Gorman wrote an interesting article entitled "A Command Post is Not a Place." Gorman felt that restricting a commander to a single communication center would encourage him to accumulate a cumbersome amount of equipment and personnel, forming an attractive target for the enemy. Furthermore, the commander would not have the mobility and flexibility of being in the field and sizing up the situation firsthand. Gorman's simple definition of a command post is relevant today— the "post" is located wherever the commander is at any given moment. Today military commanders carry a portable device, called a Battle Board, which is a combat-ready personal digital assistant with wireless communication including all code words and frequencies necessary to summon supporting forces to a location as needed.[66]

Developing the Virtual Global Team

Rarely are G/Es' businesses solo entities. They must have a networking team spanning the globe to assist them. It is a tough job to put together a cross-border team of individuals of different nationalities, with distinct cultures, who agree to work together in a multinational business operation. Having a good team of qualified business associates enables G/Es to co-ordinate complex ventures across a widely dispersed number of businesses. This is a real challenge for G/Es, since inherent in the use of virtual teams is a range of problems resulting from a dispersal of members and national differences. Tim Kayworth and Dorothy Leidner tell us that there are four major challenges that must be dealt with concerning a virtual global team. These challenges are communications, culture, technology, and team leadership.[94]

Regarding *communications,* the G/E will have to manage the team even without frequent face-to-face communications. This means G/Es will have to rely on e-mail, group Web pages, and other web-based communication tools such as Internet Relay Chat, PowWow, and various computer-mediated communications systems. As useful as these communication technologies are, Kayworth and Leidner's research indicates that such technology has notable limits and is not able to transfer the same rich social, emotional and nonverbal information usually present in face-to-face communication.

Culture is a second problem facing the G/E. Fortunately, this problem is minimized, but certainly not eliminated, when the G/E's virtual team is composed of associates who are native locals. Even so, the most common cultural problem will be language difficulty between G/Es and their associates from various countries. English is most likely to be the common business language, as it is currently most widely used. When sending e-mail instructions, i.e., quotes, prices, etc., G/Es must ask for confirmation to ensure messages are fully understood. Also, western G/Es must be aware that some cultures vary in sense of urgency, or timing to complete projects and meet deadlines. For example, in Africa there is real time, and there is "African time," a point in time later than originally agreed upon. Workers in the Latin culture tend to be slower in execution as compared to North Americans or Northern Europeans. Through study and experience, one learns to address these and similar issues. They can be anticipated and dealt with by well-informed G/Es.

Communication *technology* will be the primary enabling tool for G/Es. In the absence of face-to-face meetings, the second most important facilitating tool of the G/E will be the communication linkage among associates. The various Internet communication tools available to every G/E were mentioned earlier, with e-mail and cell phones being the primary linking devices. Most potential associates of G/Es are business people currently engaged in international trade. Therefore, G/Es can be reasonably assured that associates are relatively proficient in English and have a grasp of communicating via e-mail. The introduction of other Internet communication tools, such as Skype, Dimdim, Google Chat, and iPhone's video can serve as a substitute for face-to-face communications and will be helpful to G/Es.

Another pressing issue for every G/E is *team leadership*, which is clearly his or her responsibility. We can define *leadership as being the progressive pursuit of extraordinary, long-term profitable growth, through being among the first in anticipating, recognizing, and exploiting new market opportunities, while capturing the minds, hearts and energies of associates.* G/E's leadership role also includes global integration, or linking their associate business activities across nations in a manner that will minimize overall costs, avoid unnecessary taxes, and maximize income. Here, too, having direct and frequent communication is vital in providing leadership to the associate team scattered around the world. Building trust among team members is critical to the success of the global venture. Such trust will encourage more cooperation and will minimize unproductive conflicts.

Leadership is the aggressive pursuit of extraordinary, long-term profitable growth, through being among the first in anticipating, recognizing, and exploiting new market opportunities, while capturing the minds, hearts and energies of associates.

Each team member will bring unique abilities to the group. If these abilities are harnessed effectively, the resulting diversity can yield significant synergies to produce a whole greater than the sum of individual parts. On average, people will trust one another when they share similarities, when they communicate frequently, and when they operate in a common cultural context that imposes rigid sanctions on those who act in an untrustworthy manner. Trust building is a high priority for G/Es and must start early in negotiations with prospective global partners.

Many economists and management scholars are struggling to understand the emerging industrial trajectories that advanced economies must follow in attempting to remain competitive in a new global environment. Clearly, a search is underway for a new organizational model that will serve to gradually replace the restrictive pyramid organization of the Industrial Era. Many new organizational initiatives today have elements of a virtual corporation and characteristics of an elusive quantum organization. The quantum organization is a constantly-learning organization; it is culturally rooted in trust and requires individuals to share their expertise, ideas and information. The quantum organizational entity flows, bends, and molds its shape to fit the circumstances. It is a phantom entity at first and, thereafter, it becomes virtual whenever possible.

Initiating a global enterprise does not involve a formal corporate structure. Rather, establishing structure is the end of the process, not the beginning. A number of necessary preliminary steps have to be carried out by G/Es before designing and shaping the corporate entity. These steps include finding the product niche, achieving a focus, deciding on your customers and markets, determining the corporate structure selection criteria, and establishing measures of success.

Identifying Your Global Product

Exploring a virtual product concept opens many opportunities for cosmopolitan-thinking G/Es. For example, the company itself may be a "product." A young aspiring German entrepreneur is attempting to set up one company per month with the idea of selling them as different business entities. An American entrepreneur is selling newly-formed corporate shells in Japan. As you search for your potential global product, Al Ries has some useful advice. He suggests that you identify a very narrow product category and then market that product globally. To attempt to be "all things to all people" in a global marketplace is the wrong strategy for a small business, and even for large ones. Ries suggests that one should think about developing a unique product niche as the following firms have successfully done – Apple "innovation"; FedEx, "overnight delivery"; Jiffy Lube, "ten-minute oil change"; Phil Crosby, "quality"; Michael Porter, "competitiveness."; and Disney, "Magic." Once you have identified this narrow product niche, you can then be much stronger, wherever the market is located. Ries says having a single or narrow product position is better than trying to expand existing product lines and possibly being weak everywhere.[95]

G/Es can choose traditional product/market routes, which start with making or buying a tangible product, warehousing it, offering it for sale, and later delivering it to customers. Or the G/E can begin the business with a virtual product, one that does not physically exist at the time it is sold. With a virtual product, the concept, design, and production are in the mind of the G/E and can be instantly customized and delivered in response to unique needs of customers. The most high-profile application of a refined virtual product is used by Dell Computers. Michael Dell has become a multi-billionaire utilizing the virtual product concept. The heroes in this arena are going to be the G/Es who are able to combine a global outlook with imaginative knowledge in providing both new and already familiar products and services.

One creates substantial success by occupying a unique spot in the minds of customers and in a global marketplace. An ideal way to create a great business is by doing something others cannot easily replicate. But since this means creating something very close to a monopoly it is not very easy and can be illegal. However, Bill Gates has substantially accomplished this at Microsoft. Some 90 percent of worldwide PC software applications are run on Microsoft Windows software. Microsoft's competitors, the U.S. government and the E.U. are all attempting to end what they consider to be Microsoft's monopoly. Other firms like Amazon are actively trying to hold onto dominant market positions. This is why Amazon continues to expand its product offering and customer base—to stay ahead of its competition. It is desirable to have a near monopoly as Microsoft has in the computer world and as De Beers has in the diamond market. However, very few firms have been able to develop and sustain a monopoly over the years.

Product selection is critical for G/Es. They have two concurrent challenges: to be local and global at the same time. Localizing the global village is no easy task. But some things work in the G/Es' favor, in particular if they are selling in the developing world. Individuals in developing societies are very keen on products from the United States, European Union and Japan. Many Third World consumers believe products from more advanced regions are superior in quality to locally-produced goods. This is where the entrepreneur's honing talents can be utilized to identify alternative goods and experiences being sought by global consumers. The G/E may capitalize on products perceived as representing the "good life," which are highly desired in less-affluent societies. G/Es can energize local firms in developing markets by making these sought-after products available and by sharing proven marketing techniques. It will be difficult for G/Es to "out-globalize" larger transnational competitors, but they will be able to "out-localize" them within specific international markets.

What really opens G/Es' vista of opportunities is recognizing that "knowledge" is perhaps their most important product. Indeed, a major thrust of the new Global Economic World is concerned with creating value from knowledge and technology, both as business *inputs* and *outputs*. These two business components are frequently considered to be the most important ingredients bought and sold by businesses. Knowledge has many forms and faces. Knowledge is a value-creating component in business, i.e., in creating a product or service. Knowledge can also be used in the business functions of marketing, finance and administration of the organization. Knowledge has the potential to add value in all core functional areas of the enterprise. For example, it is possible for one to acquire a "best practice" business process, and then sell this knowledge product to others around the world. One example of this is the Six Sigma quality package being marketed by the Six Sigma Academy in the U.S.[69] The challenge to G/Es is to use their creativity for recognizing, developing, or acquiring a unique knowledge product that can be widely used in businesses, or sold to consumers in the global marketplace.

In the long run, G/Es should try to get their unique product category to be recognized simultaneously with their company name. Two outstanding corporate examples of an immediate connection of product and firm are Microsoft and Amazon. The G/E should strive to develop a product-company combination to be fused in the minds of consumers and, when developed, expand that competitive advantage on a global basis. All big businesses start small. One must remember that Bill Gates and Paul Allen began Microsoft as a two-person business, and Apple was a three-person start-up for a short period. In *Inc.'s* annual listing of the 500 fastest-growing private companies in America, more than 50 percent of these ventures were started in the home.

Discovering your tangible product or unique knowledge product, and finding the right words to describe it, are not easy. Again, a critical goal, according to Al Ries, is to own a word that will come to the mind of consumers everywhere when a product is mentioned. Fortunately, if the product is good enough, consumer consciousness will tend to join two names together – i.e., the product category and the company name. Certainly, on a worldwide basis, when one thinks of hamburgers or pizza, McDonald's and Pizza Hut come to mind. Ries says when you see a company experiencing explosive growth, in many instances it is because the company has a very strong, single-word product concept. Of course, even though it is very expensive and time-consuming to develop such a recognizable product-company combination, it is a noteworthy goal to pursue. Normally, it takes a business an extended period of time to capture a category in the minds of the consuming public. It happens first locally, and then gradually the mindset can be expanded into other regional and world markets. G/Es should not attempt to develop a product to please all consumers. The best route is to develop a narrow product niche, world-class quality that can be marketed on a global basis.

Develop a Unique Product Identification

The challenge for G/Es is not to find products, services or even new business ideas. The difficulty is selecting the most promising opportunity that provides primary focus for a global venture. This requires astute judgment of the G/E. Fortunately, this process is easier for a new venture than a well-established business. Managers in established firms must overcome the successes (and failures) of the past and the reluctance of fellow managers to take the risk of exploring new ideas. G/Es typically do not have this problem. When searching for a new business idea, G/Es intuitively narrow their attention to a few ideas with the greatest promise of success. Once the venture product or service is chosen, the question is this: What is the best way to say, "Look, world, I'm here! Come let me solve your problem." A powerful tool for the G/E in an overcommunicating world is to have an oversimplified message—that is, one to three words that crisply define the product and enterprise. Al Ries calls this a *"focus,"* which he says is a powerful concept for introducing your product and business to the marketplace.

Ries says "focus" is a simple idea that encompasses the essence of your business. It is not the product, per se, but it often embodies some aspect of the product. A focus is an *enticement* that attracts people to your product or service. The firm's focus must be expressed in simple words, which are immediately understandable by your employees, your customers and, most importantly, by the media. Your focus needs to be catchy, memorable and future-oriented. By definition, a focus is not designed to cover all products or services offered. It is more likely to be an attribute, or a point of concentration of a single product, rather than a range of products.

Ries does a great job of exploring this concept in his book, *Focus.* He mentions Subaru's advertising focus as an example of this concept: "Inexpensive and built to stay that way." Ries claims that size is not the determining factor in creating a profitable business. But a *focus* is.[96] BMW apparently lost its focus when it acquired the mid-price-range automobile producer Rover. Then, after selling Rover, BMW returned to its original focus of making high-quality automobiles. Its profit margin also jumped to the second highest in the auto industry.

It is easy to get confused at this point between having a narrow product niche and achieving a *focus*. By necessity, the G/E will start the enterprise with a narrow product range, maybe only one or two items. Doing so will enhance the G/E's ability to develop a clean, crisp focus for communication purposes. With a single focus, it is much easier for G/Es, with their limited resources, to concentrate efforts on their firm's primary growth goal. Finding the right word or phrase can also help influence the masses. Persuasion is very important in business. Focus can also be important in politics. In the U.S., James Carville developed a sharp focus for Bill Clinton in his first-term election when Clinton defeated the incumbent, George Bush, Sr. Carville's message was simple and straightforward - "It's the economy, stupid." It is important to avoid confusing a focus with a core competence. A focus is a very telling conceptual message, whereas, a core competence is a world-class attribute of the business—something it does better than others.

In shaping their global business, G/Es can develop their own *product niche* through buying or otherwise acquiring one from someone else. There is an abundance of business ideas lying around, which are either not being utilized or are underutilized. Someone else may be using a good business idea and may even be losing money with it. An astute G/E can acquire that idea, expand the business, and make it profitable. That is what Ray Kroc had in mind when he purchased his first restaurant from the McDonald brothers in California. Now is a particularly good time to acquire ongoing businesses as major firms restructure and divest many of their non-core business assets. Some of these spin-offs can make attractive businesses for the G/E. Why are large firms engaging in such transformations? Many corporate giants, too, are belatedly learning the power and importance of *focus*. Ries suggests the future of your company depends on this very simple, but powerful concept.

Global Customers, Business Partners and Markets

G/Es have a dual administrative imperative of *globally integrating* business operations and simultaneously *achieving local customer responsiveness*. Integration is a major concern of G/Es and a real test of their leadership. Integration deals with the coordination of the activities among the G/E's local associates, or business partners. These activities take place across the various countries in which associates operate. Integration is geared toward maximizing the collective advantage of these divergent associates. At the same time, local responsiveness is concerned with how associates deal with various needs of consumers in their native country. Local associates can be chosen for their ability to successfully negotiate through unique cultures, markets and business practices, all of which will contrast sharply with the G/E's native country.

Global integration is primarily achieved through the leadership of the G/E, whereas local responsiveness is influenced by the situational factors at the local associate level and through the associate's own leadership ability. The G/E must be in close contact and communication with business associates in order to be sensitive to contingencies arising from local customers and the market. Local associates are in a much better position than the G/E to screen and appraise local needs, wants and desires, as well as to identify various impediments to marketing products/services in their country. Having local associates in multiple countries allows the G/E to better adapt to cultural environments while maintaining a coordinated system of integration and location-specific advantages. The aim of the G/E is to create and maintain a high level of local responsiveness, which will help the firm to pursue the overall goals of the enterprise.

Having a business partner as an international subsidiary helps to establish a sustained relationship with local customers, suppliers, distributors, competitors and government authorities, all of whom can greatly assist in creating more competitive opportunities for the parent organization. This is particularly true when product differentiation and customer responsiveness are required to gain a local competitive advantage. In a dynamic, emerging market, component localization may also be an important factor because some governments require substantial local purchasing. In emerging markets such as China, conducting commerce is shaped by unique business and commercial practices, which have long historical and social dimensions uniquely known by locals. Also, by having a profit sharing, local business partner, the G/E can avoid the requirements, once present in China, for the business to be majority locally- owned.

Access to the Internet is intensifying an international desire in less-developed countries for products, services and experiences produced in highly-developed economies. The Internet provides greater transparency than ever before through product identification, 24-hour accessibility, immediate communication by customer and/or seller, greater product information in regard to availability, feature comparison, and pricing. Customers like having the opportunity to customize products and/or services according to their personal desire. The Internet is a powerful, enabling technology allowing firms like those of G/Es to promote networking, collaboration, loyalty, quicker time to market, and information flow. But most of all, the Internet gives the consumers individual control—unlike anything they have ever had before—over purchasing and delivery functions.

Simply striving to beat your competition with a high degree of customer satisfaction will not suffice today. Customer expectations will never be the same as they were in the old economy. Customer expectations are becoming exponentially more demanding everywhere. One must offer *Outrageous and Unforgettable Service,* according to Scott Gross, who has authored a book by this title. Both new and existing enterprises must strive to achieve an ever-increasing level of "customer excitement" by offering products and services in a way that attracts and keeps customers.

Today consumers are clearly smarter, better informed, and more demanding than ever. Obviously, they are still human, and they want to be treated as individuals. They will always have personal needs, wants, and desires, which now continue to change frequently. The G/E must be mindful of the factors deemed to be of great value to customers. In developed countries, a few of the factors important to consumers are recognition of the value of time, quality, sustaining value, high performance, transparency, convenience, simplification, customization, and quick delivery. These consumer-friendly attributes are important to upscale consumers in the developed world, but other factors are likely to be more important to consumers in less affluent economies.

One trap the G/E will avoid is getting locked in a fight for share in a highly competitive market. The G/E will not have the money or personnel to fight big firms early on in the life of his venture. Now Richard Branson may be the exception to this statement, as he will frequently take on well-established firms with his ventures. Branson's challenge to major businesses is not easily accomplished. On a recent TV show, Branson was asked how to become a millionaire. He replied, "Well, start with a billion and then buy an airline." The G/E understands these rules of war: never target more than one enemy (competitor) at a time; never wage warfare on two fronts (two competitors) simultaneously; never start a war with inadequate weapons (against competitors with vast resources); and always have a backup strategy (a planned exit strategy) in case something goes wrong. What G/Es must do is carefully choose a narrow product niche, select the most desired markets and then attack these markets with their unique focus. Fortunately, there is an abundance of opportunities to do so emerging from today's innovations, technology, globalization and corporate spin-offs.

In defining (and sometimes redefining) a market, G/Es must keep a couple of truisms in mind. First, there is no such thing as a mature company or industry. Ram Charan and Noel Tichy explain this in their book *Every Business Is a Growth Business.* These authors stress that any company in a so-called "mature" market can still grow. All it takes is the right leadership, one that will look outside the box and discard traditional definitions of their market and of the industry itself. Charon and Tichy say growth is a "mindset" championed by a leader of the enterprise. If a company is not growing, then a CEO must change the company's genetic code. Often the present code embodies the thinking of past leadership, who most likely accepted the premise of a mature marketplace. The new leader must introduce a new, growth-oriented genetic code that will bring about a rebirth of the business and, eventually, a transformation of the entire organization.[97] The G/E has this type of growth mentality; he or she envisions what can be, as opposed to what is, or what has been. The G/E thinks of potential customers, and then designs virtual products and a virtual organization to serve those markets with a minimum of expense. This is how G/Es will attempt to position a wealth-creating vehicle in the global marketplace.

The New Era Enterprise – A Virtual Entity

The Internet has been discussed with such frequency in this book that you may think that all G/E firms will be Internet-based. Well, that is true to a large extent, perhaps up to 80 percent. The architecture of most conventional corporations will evolve over time to accommodate networking and the virtual organization. Not all new-era enterprises will be Internet-based businesses to the extent of Amazon and eBay, which both continue to add products and services to their offering. But the Internet will frequently serve as a driving force, a facilitator, and a communication tool for all new enterprises.

The virtual organization represents a major management change in the Information Age. Someone described a virtual organization as one that, when you go to examine it, you find there is nobody at home. The virtual enterprise has many possibilities; it will appear endless, will be permeable, and will have continuously changing interfaces between the parent firm, its suppliers, customers, and other constituents. Each department will evolve and will reshape itself according to specific needs. The organization itself will appear less as a discrete enterprise and more as an ever-varying cluster of activities functioning together in a networked fashion for a common purpose. Such an organization will be based more on information and relationships and less on hard-core, capital-intensive factors, such as plants and buildings.

The Internet forces us to view the world through different lenses. It affords us the opportunity to achieve an ultimate goal - being able to buy, sell, and transact business over a *global network* in a variety of marketplaces.

An Internet business of this nature will offer individuals the opportunity to *interact with customers* in ways that were never possible before. When the G/E begins to conceptualize the new enterprise, he or she will first envision it as somewhat of a *phantom organization,* which will be *virtual, global,* and *uniquely customer-interaction.* These three attributes are very important foundational features of the 21st century enterprise.

A unique characteristic of the G/E's virtual enterprise is that it can be located anywhere in the world—a domicile in any jurisdiction. Headquarters location will ideally be in a tax-sheltered country, but the business will be able to serve many different markets across the world. We are no longer hostages to the farm, factory, or port as places to conduct business. This new-found freedom is further supported by the fact that a huge infrastructure is rarely needed anymore for many businesses. Technology now enables us to transcend locality and to avoid burdensome overhead. This means that *almost any business can be global.* Therefore, the G/E disregards tradition and does not take the historical route to internationalization. G/Es will ensure their *enterprise goes global at birth.* They will bypass formal time-consuming steps of starting locally, growing regionally, then nationally, and finally moving into international markets as the final stage of business development.

Technology now enables us to transcend locality and to avoid burdensome overhead. This means almost any business can be global.

Other great features of virtual organizations are their *flexibility* and *mobility.* The Information Age makes it possible to create a virtual enterprise anywhere in the world based on the immediate opportunities of particular markets. Business success in some countries will often attract attempts at extortion by local mafia and sometimes by local government itself. If such pressure becomes unbearable, the activities and the minimal assets of the virtual enterprise can quickly flee the jurisdiction. Microtechnology allows the firm to be small and footloose. Since most virtual enterprises deal with services, knowledge and network-related businesses, these activities can be conducted anywhere on the planet, as long as the commercial and political climate are reasonably favorable, the region is safe, and it's an enjoyable area to live and work.

Outsourcing in a Shrinking World

Outsourcing of various business activities will be a major attribute of virtual enterprises. Traditional Entrepreneurs are known for being poor administrators, for not tending to business details, such as taxes and other essential matters. Now these don't have to be dreaded or unattended chores. An increasing number of entrepreneurs are outsourcing non-core business functions while focusing on their primary revenue-earning activities. Outsourcing has become so prevalent in the U.S. that a number of new Internet-based, small business service providers have emerged to handle such tasks as raising funds, writing legal contracts, submitting bids for tender, handling credit and collection, and running the office in general. Astute G/Es are learning these new management practices. They also know the essence of management is getting work done through the efforts of others. It is much easier for entrepreneurs today to be good managers than it was in any previous business period because of all the expert assistance readily available.

Outsourcing allows G/Es to focus on core, revenue-generating functions by letting other business specialists outside the firm perform some or all of the administrative activities required to operate the business. Such outsourcing can take the strain and time of administration off the shoulders of entrepreneurs, particularly in areas in which they may not have such expertise. As the business grows, the G/E may want to use an Enterprise Resource Planning software package to connect major business functions and link them into a cohesive whole. Of course, this function can be outsourced as well, depending on the capabilities of the G/E.

Outsourcing has not escaped the attention of major international consulting firms. Accenture extensively advertises three major business functions — consulting, outsourcing and technology. It is obvious that Accenture is in the knowledge business. To illustrate the growth of outsourcing, in 2003 India was providing IT outsourcing solutions to more than 40 percent of U.S. *Fortune* 500 major corporations and today that figure has jumped to more than 75 percent.

Outsourcing has radically changed over the past few years. For one thing, new service outsourcing opportunities have emerged in Costa Rica and other Latin American nations. They also have plenty of English speaking individuals and a modest time zone difference from the U.S. Outsourcing a business service can sometimes cut costs in half, and successfully outsourcing manufacturing can save even more. Investors know this, and some venture capitalists won't look at your business unless you have an outsourcing plan. Outsourcing requires serious study due to changes in exchange rates and time required to manage an overseas relationship. U.S. production facilities are particularly important for firms with products with short life spans, which cannot afford to be in transit for weeks, or when custom orders require quick turnaround. Douglas Hall also point out that outsourcing is just as good for a small business as it is a large one.[98]

Routes to the Global Marketplace

The G/E must decide which countries he or she intends to operate in and what mode of entry is to be used. The selection, number and locations of specific countries will depend on the G/E's objectives and the resources available for establishing a network of global partners. Product characteristics – size, weight, perishability and composition - will often dictate where items are to be made and sold. Some countries have high tariffs on importing selected products produced by their local industries. The global marketplace is becoming more integrated as World Trade Organization memberships continue to expand. Consequently, many governments are removing and reducing international trade restrictions as required by the World Trade Organization.

Prior to entry in the global marketplace, resources need to be allocated to investigate international marketing opportunities, to select which countries to enter, and to determine what mode will be used to enter those markets. A number of factors influence the mode of entry into the global marketplace. These include unique country characteristics, trade restrictions, product characteristics, and strength of the G/E's motivation towards international expansion. Country size and economic growth potential are very important, as is the opportunity to serve neighboring countries. The three major modes of entry into the global marketplace are through wholly-owned subsidiaries, exporting, and contractual arrangements.

Wholly-Owned Subsidiaries: Many organizations prefer this route to international business since it allows complete control over all aspects of the venture to the extent allowed by the host country. The approach allows the firm to devote maximum effort to developing the market and to introduce and protect new production technology. All the profits accrue to the parent company. The decision to establish a wholly-owned subsidiary depends on available resources and will result in either acquiring an existing business or building the venture from the ground up. Most often this mode is too expensive for the G/E.

Exporting: Exporting is the most common mode for initial entry into the global marketplace. As sales volume increases through exporting, the business will evolve towards a more permanent type of international operation. Export management firms and their agents will perform a limited or a wide range of functions for their clients. Some specialize in clearing goods through customs, freight forwarding and billing. Others offer full-service wholesale functions. A firm engages in indirect exporting when it sells its products to a foreign sales organization located within its own country. The direct exporter then takes full responsibility for all exporting activities and contract with international customers. Some firms will align themselves with other local businesses that have distribution in foreign markets and thereby piggyback on their exporting expertise. A third method of exporting is utilized by businesses with their own sales organizations in their domestic market or in foreign markets. Many G/Es develop international exporting experience early in their careers while working for others.

Contractual Agreements: Various contractual agreements can be utilized for entry into international markets. Among the types of agreements are contract manufacturing, franchising, licensing, joint venturing and various partnerships. Contract manufacturing allows a firm to outsource production to other businesses, thus allowing the parent firm to control marketing and distribution of its products. The virtual micro-factory discussed in chapter six is a good example. Such an arrangement is attractive when sales volume does not justify an investment in a manufacturing facility or when the firm chooses to focus on its core competencies, which may not be manufacturing. Contract manufacturing may allow a firm to lower costs through renting production capacity from a local manufacturer, and it may allow one to bypass high local tariffs.

Licensing is another form of contractual agreement and is useful when a firm has proprietary asset on which it wishes to capitalize in a global marketplace. Such an asset may be a patented product, process technology, trademark, brand name or unique service. Using licensing agreements allows a firm to enjoy the benefits of international sales by utilizing unique proprietary assets with minimum expenditure and risk. The firm granting the licensing agreement (or franchise) must closely monitor the activities of a licensee to ensure adherence to quality standards and contract agreements. The licensor may receive payments or royalty fees based on a percent of sales or some other arrangement, such as a flat fee for representation. A licensing agreement is an appropriate means for a firm to enter a number of international markets very quickly with a minimum of financial commitment.

Franchising is also a formal licensing agreement in which the parent organization offers the franchisee the right to do business in a specific manner for a royalty payment, usually designated as a percentage of sales. Established firms like McDonald's, Pizza Hut, Hertz Rent-a-Car, and Manpower have expanded internationally primarily through franchising.

G/Es are often prevented from establishing themselves unilaterally in global markets due to a lack of internal resources, i.e., financial and managerial. G/Es may want to form some type of joint venture or partnership with international companies to take advantage of their existing warehousing, distribution and marketing systems. Joint ventures and partnering work best when each party brings value to the venture. Such partnering with a foreign firm will limit the domestic company's control; however, the agreement also reduces risk and limits expenditure of the firm's financial resources. The most important advantage for G/Es in international partnering consist of having a local partner who can help bridge the inevitable cultural divide of doing business in a different country. For example, by having one or more networking partners in a single country, G/Es will have an easier job of working through different customs, perceptions, and languages involved in business transactions. Americans, in particular, have a problem in this area, as they are often perceived as too persuasive, aggressive, superficial, and nonresponsive to cultural differences. Of the various modes of entry into the global marketplace, some form of joint venture or partnership will be the likely avenue taken by the G/E.

Of the modes of entry to the global marketplace, some form of joint venture or partnership will be the likely avenue for the G/E.

With today's open innovation, a G/E can tap into the creative genius of partners outside his or her company, and everyone involved benefits. All G/Es have to do is to recognize that not all smart people work for their company and to partner with anyone who will help create their product or service. Open source innovation is a new way of making and managing partnerships – that is, forming alliances with others to accelerate your own innovation. If you have an idea for a smokeless grill, but don't have a design staff to make the grill, then it is better to find a partner that is already making such grills. Contract with them to make the grill with a royalty payment, and you will probably save 80 percent on development cost and a year or so of research and development time.

Also keep in mind that the use of technology is a wealth creator. A recent study of 738 manufacturers by the Georgia Tech Program in Science, Technology and Innovation Policy in Atlanta found that companies pursuing *innovation technology* as their primary strategy nearly double the profit margins of those following a strategy of low cost (14.5 percent vs. 7.5 percent). They also realize nearly 50 percent higher profit margins than those who focus on quick delivery, high quality, or adapting to customers' needs.

Establishing a local partner in a foreign country may not be as hard today as many people claim it to be. Let me share with you one personal example. I live on the coast of Georgia, where we have year-round sunshine on the average of five hours a day. Germany, number one in the world in solar energy usage, has sun for an average of three hours a day. Consequently, the opportunities for solar manufacturing and certainly solar marketing are abundant on the U.S. East Coast. Since the Chinese are the leaders in solar panel manufacturing, I reached out via the Internet - to more than 65 firms, and 12 responded, inquiring what I had to offer. At one firm in Fujian Province, I established more than a business relationship with Mr. Beijng (pseudo name) after discovering his interest in America. It took a period of several months to get on a personal footing with him (developing "guanxi" is essential), but now Mr. Beijng has offered to assist me, during his personal time, in learning about the Chinese culture and to establish a small joint venture in China. This small venture will cost little money on my part, and the real value in it is learning how to do business with a Chinese partner.

From USA/China …

Katie Smith has conducted business in China for 25 years, mostly outsourcing handsewn ties for her last company, the $50-million Mulberry Neckwear. Now she is hunting down manufacturers for her firm, Rockflowerpaper, a four-person gift and home accessory store in San Rafael, California. On a recent order, the Chinese supplier in the southern China city of Shenzhen said her 5,000 coffee mug order did not meet their 12,000-unit minimum. She walked away and the manufacturer promptly did an about-face and took the order. China has been hit by the world recession too and contract manufacturers are more receptive than ever to small customers. For the near future, i.e., at least the next four to six years, China's big draw will be its manufacturing capabilities. Smith stresses how important it is to get to know the manufacturers personally; and she has made three trips to China in the past year and a half and makes frequent calls via Skype. The latter is also a must skill development for the G/E.

Developing the Global Enterprise

Typically, the G/E will enter a limited number of countries or geographic locations and then gradually expand as additional networking associates are identified. A limited expansion will minimize the risk for G/Es since they are able to examine whether their core competencies and competitive advantage, developed in the domestic market, will extend to international markets as they had envisioned. The G/E has to assess the firm's ability to leverage its competitive advantage internationally and must evaluate the expected return on the investment required.

Typically, small-to-medium-sized enterprises (SMEs) will take a traditional, incremental approach as their route towards internationalization.

The following are several distinct stages of development that a majority of SMEs take when entering the global marketplace:

Stage One: Passive exporting. Just filling international orders when received without actively seeking such business.

Stage Two: Seeking exportation. The firm recognizes it has an exportable product or service and it actively seeks export sales.

Stage Three: An export department. The firm establishes an organized management structure to seek increased revenues from exporting.

Stage Four: International sales offices. A foreign sales office is established with company and/or local personnel recruited to stimulate sales.

Stage Five: Production abroad. This stage usually begins with contract production in a foreign country while the parent company retains control of marketing.

Stage Six: Fully integrated international sales. The firm now possesses a fully integrated international sales network in the desired countries.

These progressive stages are mentioned here to show the normal historical path of international expansion by SMEs and large businesses. But G/Es are not the norm! They will deviate from the established path by skipping several of these stages; in fact, they may structure their business to go global at the birth of the venture.

Traditional Entrepreneurs can exponentially expand their chances of success by moving from the local to the global marketplace. However, in order to compete in a global market, G/Es need to be able to respond to a variety of emerging opportunities and combat different competitors as they move through a multicultural maze. There will be the challenge to bridge time and distance in a cost-effective manner. Staying on the cutting edge of communications technology will help a business maintain its competitive position. The size of the firm often becomes irrelevant as communications technology can bring customers and suppliers together around the world for business transactions. But even under the best of circumstances, it is not easy for the G/E to establish a fully functioning global network of business associates. Many different factors must be assessed simultaneously to arrive at entry markets and to acquire the networking partners required to serve those markets.

Traditional entrepreneurs can exponentially expand their chances of creating greater wealth by moving from a local to a global marketplace.

From USA & Vietnam ...

Arian Roefs of Santa Fe, New Mexico (USA), discovered that it was too costly to continue making products for her children's clothing company in the U.S. She did not have contacts south of the border in Mexico. After research with the U.S. Commercial Service (buyusa.gov/Vietnam/en) and U.S.-Vietnam Chamber of Commerce (usvnchamber.org/index. html), Roefs reached out to a small factory near Vietnam's Ho Chi Minh City. There she discovered they could make her trademark bibs for one-fifth of the $15 cost U.S. manufacturers charged. Now her two-employee company has sales in excess of $100,000 and is growing again. Vietnam is enjoying a relatively new reputation for outsourced manufacturing, prompting some to compare it with the China of 25 years ago. However, Vietnam is not without its challenges, which Arian tries to overcome with her regular contact with the factory owners, all of whom speak English, in her regular phone contacts and email communications.

For every mode of entry into the global marketplace, there are unique problems facing G/Es. Selecting the appropriate global market involves much more than a designation of a country choice. You must make a careful assessment of the country's potential, along with the risk involved in conducting business there. Locating networking partners requires lots of travel, assessment, and negotiation, as well as marketing skill. Joint venturing and partnerships provide access to the global marketplace on a variety of levels, but they are a challenge to establish and manage. No one says it is going to be easy. To establish a global entity is tough, a real challenge for anyone. But mastering this challenge will be the key to creating new wealth in the 21st century.

Incubators, Relationships, and Networks

Another way to develop and shape your emerging venture is to utilize an incubator facility to help kick-start the business. As a result of the 2007-09 recession, business incubators are expanding nationwide amid increased demand for resources, services and counseling activities. Driving this increased interest in incubators is high unemployment and a dearth of adequate financing in the current economy. Universities and research laboratories have been traditional sponsors of incubator facilities, helping with the flow of technologies and patents for the commercial sector. Incubators will normally provide minimum office and production space, advice, phone lines, and some office equipment; this assistance serves to minimize the cost of start-up of a venture.

Recently, in the United States, the private sector incubator market has exploded to more than 1200 entities, according to the National Business Incubator Association, is a great source for finding a local incubator in America. We notice that many newly-established incubator organizations are business-to-business Internet incubators, rather than university-sponsored entities. These new incubators provide a wide range of start-up accommodations, such as T-1 lines, access to venture capital markets, market research, review and enhancement of technology, and a detailed roadmap for helping entrepreneurs to take their ventures to the marketplace with great speed.

One of the oldest and most successful incubators in the U.S. is the Austin Technology Incubator in Texas. About 70 percent of start-ups that are accepted obtain investor funding during their residency, according to its director, Isaac Barchas. Over the past two years, its incubator occupants have raised more than $50 million, - about $750 million since its inception, says Barchas. The incubator is a division of the University of Texas at Austin and constitutes four programs that support young companies: information technology, wireless communications, clean energy, and healthcare-focused life sciences.[99]

Paul Graham has stormed Silicon Valley recently and pioneered a better way to build a company with his personal business incubator – the Y Combinator. Paul has helped some 200 technology start-up companies in the Valley since 2005, and he has chiseled a new paradigm for launching a technology company. Graham personally picks off the very best technology firms as soon as they leave the womb, funds them with small amounts - $11,000 to $18,000, and insists they go to the market quickly in search of customers and revenues. A key attribute of Graham's formula is to get the business up and running (bugs and all) quickly, gather customer feedback, tweak it, and go back to the marketplace. He also nurtures them by insisting on weekly reports on their progress and brainstorms how to solve nagging problems. He invites other investors to come to his-show-and-tells and has raised two pools of funding from outsiders - $2 million in 2009, and $8 million in 2010 - from the likes of Sequoia Capital and other prominent angel investors. His own wealth, of $45 million from the sale of his firm Viaweb to Yahoo in 1998, helps supplement his business operations.

G/Es are likely to be the new kid on the block when entering most foreign countries. How can the G/E compensate for being young (the average age is 34 in the U.S.), inexperienced in business, and yet determined to build a global venture? Being cheaper, better, and faster than the competition is desirable, but not good enough. Those attributes alone will not suffice today.

There must be more pizzazz in terms of creative products, services and unique experiences for customers to enjoy. Fortunately, the world of knowledge and technology has become so sophisticated, broad, and extensive that even the largest of companies doesn't have all the answers. Then how does one propose to start a new business, striving to offer world-class products, services and experiences, while at the same time developing a global enterprise?

The Trillion-Dollar Business

Well, here is a good suggestion to consider. Cyrus Friedheim, of Booz Allen Hamilton consulting, explains a route for developing a trillion-dollar enterprise. Freidheim says that becoming extremely large is very possible with a network of "relationship enterprises." In the model he recommends, the entrepreneur and business leader become "the captain of his ship and the leader of a flotilla of independent vessels [business firms] from several countries, each with missions and objectives of their own that are quite separate from their mission as a member of the flotilla."[100]Sounds familiar doesn't it? This "flotilla" business model is what we are suggesting for the G/E's venture. International business alliances are the key for G/Es if they are to develop a global enterprise.

Is a trillion-dollar enterprise a possibility? Well, Friedheim certainly thinks so. In his book, *The Trillion Dollar Enterprise*, he challenges entrepreneurs and corporate CEOs with a road map leading to such an enterprise. His message is clear: Those who plan to "win big" in the new global economy need to understand the requirements for success of a "relationship enterprise," as well as how to prepare themselves for a new route to wealth accumulation. An important point for the G/E is that the architectural framework for developing a trillion-dollar enterprise is the same for the founder of a small venture as it is for the executive of a large corporate organization.

Just how many new billion-dollar firms would it take to permanently increase the U.S. GDP by one percentage point? A new Kauffman Foundation study estimates the answer is most likely between 30 and 60. According to their study, "*Inventive Billion-Dollar Firms – 2010,*" the collective impact from high-growth firms that are able to realize $1 billion in revenue could significantly accelerate the U.S. economic recovery, and over time increase the income and wealth of the average American household.

At a firm's conception, the G/E will craft a business structure based on the attributes of a virtual organization. Such a structure will be a network of relationship enterprises sharing a common business purpose. *So, from the beginning, many G/Es will start with a world model.* Then they engage in outsourcing production. Finally, they develop a global marketing plan.

Their global networking system will be designed to span many countries at the same time. "Connectivity" is the key—having a diversity of small multinational businesses networking under the umbrella of a single parent firm. Globalization serves as an advantage to the enterprise because the G/E can select his or her niche products and markets on a worldwide basis. With a networking group of like-minded firms around the world, the G/E can indeed create a multimillion-dollar enterprise and, perhaps, someday be one of those trillion-dollar businesses Friedheim talks about.

We live in an age of smart people, smart products, and smart organizations. G/Es are very intelligent people, and they require an equally intelligent organization as a vehicle to enable them to achieve their global vision. The G/E will obviously collaborate with many other knowledge workers who are equally (or more) intelligent than himself or herself. The effectiveness of knowledge workers will be amplified when they are part of the G/E's networking organizational enterprise. Today's smart organizations are quite different from Industrial Era organizations, which were designed to quickly train uneducated people to do simple, highly repetitive tasks on assembly lines, thus facilitating mass production. The system worked well for many years, but it is becoming obsolete in a business environment dominated by knowledge workers in developed countries. Industrial Era management and organizational technology will still be useful in less-developed countries as they progress through that developmental stage.

The G/E's venture is quite different from an ordinary small business. It is characterized by four basic factors: it is dynamic, evolving, and constantly changing in scope and design; the business will demonstrate an innovative use of knowledge and technology; it will have a strong focus on global growth; and will reflect the G/E's desire to create significant personal wealth. The traditional small business is somewhat different. It, too, is a venture that is independently owned and operated, but it is neither a business that dominates its field, nor does it offer innovative products or engage advanced marketing techniques. The traditional small business owner operates his or her business to achieve a personal goal of independence and provide a primary source of individual or family income. Clearly, the small business is not the long-term aspiration of G/Es.

Building the Successful Enterprise

Several basic criteria will indicate the success of a business. First, there is *survival.* A majority of new businesses do not survive the first five years of life. Therefore, staying in business is one clear sign of success. The second criterion has to do with the owner's definition of success. Success can be defined as *the progressive realization of one's goal.* You are successful if you are on track to accomplish what you personally planned for your business. A third criterion is *business growth.* To what extent is the business developing in terms of sales, profits, productivity and shareholder value? With sales being the single most important growth factor, one must ask what level of annual sales growth will be acceptable to the entrepreneur? Is a 20-percent or 30-percent growth acceptable? Absolutely not, and let me tell you why. Each year, *Inc.* magazine lists the top fast-growing private companies in the U.S. Every year, we find that the *bottom* 10 percent (not the top) of these companies have growth rates that exceed 500 percent (yes, 500) per year. In addition to sales growth, profits must be high enough to pay all expenses, provide attractive salaries, offer fringe benefits, and render a return on invested capital greater than the prevailing market interest rate, plus some percentage factor based on the risk of the venture. That is a bare minimum. You can be certain that *extraordinary business growth* is an important goal for G/Es.

Forbes magazine uses different success measures in developing its list of the world's top 400 companies. The *Forbes* list includes companies that have risen to a significant economic leadership position in their respective industries over a four-year period. The five criteria *Forbes* uses to evaluate companies are these: average annual return on capital for the past four years; sales growth over the same period; change in stock prices over the past year; net profits per employee; and a consensus forecast by security analysts of the company's prospective annual earnings-per-share growth. *Forbes* says that, of the five measures, the return on capital and expected profits growth carry the most weight.[101]

Everyone is interested in success, especially when starting a new enterprise. To learn more about success, look at the fast-growing companies and analyze the factors they have in common. For several years, *Fortune* magazine has looked at the factors and developed a timeless list that seem to be shared by all these successful firms: "These firms are never late" - they are very serious and determined to deliver on time; "They don't overpromise" - they deliver just what they promise and avoid seeking the one-time gain; "They sweat the small stuff " - all cost items are closely scrutinized; "They build a fortress" - they identify their market niche and spend lavishly building a wall around it for protection; "They create a culture" - everyone knows, understands and accepts the company's philosophy; "They learn from their mistakes" - it is OK to make mistakes, but can the company do better as a result of them?; and "They shape their story " - they carefully fashion their messages and time them to maximize positive public impact, i.e., they have a *focus.* These fastest-growth companies, using the strategies listed above, have succeeded in posting staggering gains in profits and revenues for their stockholders.

These are *timeless attributes* important to every business. Certainly, there are good lessons to be learned from these practices of such extraordinary growth companies.

Robert Stuart and Pier Abetti reveal that successful and less-successful enterprises devote close to the same amount of time to pre-venture activities, such as starting the firm. The real difference is that the more successful establishments devote a considerable amount of time to the next step—setting up ongoing business operations. In contrast, the less-successful entrepreneur is not very good at establishing operational activities. It is well accepted that entrepreneurs tend to be great at starting ventures, but not so adept at managing them. Successful entrepreneurs also perceive opportunities differently than do less-successful entrepreneurs. Thriving entrepreneurs seem to have more skills and abilities that match the particular opportunity they are developing. Successful entrepreneurs also tend to be more global in orientation and better prepared from their previous work experiences to start an international enterprise, according to Stuart and Abetti.[102]

An Energized Organization Entity

The G/E's virtual enterprise will have many features that modern-day organizational experts exhort. Its virtual dimension offers economy, flexibility, and scalability. It is a learning organization, which will grow organically with each enterprise, creating its own shape and configuration. The organizational design will be quite different than in the past. Even though today's organizational design may resemble a shamrock, a spider web, an octopus, or a pot of boiling spaghetti, it will still have clarity of meaning to the G/E and his or her associates around the world.

The virtual enterprise will be constantly evolving, taking a new shape as the need arises, and when its members expand their individual capacities. The virtual entities, shaped by emerging G/Es, will embody, by necessity, the total quality movement in the quest for world-class products and services necessary to win in global markets. G/Es understand clearly that they will have to meet and exceed the highest-quality operational standards everywhere in order to attract resources and to successfully operate across national borders.

The G/E's interest in the virtual enterprise parallels the recognition by many top business leaders that firms have to be *transformed* today in order to successfully compete in the New Global Economic World. Proactive business leaders carry out that transformation. The G/E is acutely aware of the emphasis that top industrial organizations are placing on the following factors: achieving excellence in performance, developing world-class quality, operating a lean organization, being a continuous-learning organization, achieving global competitiveness, implementing transformational change, and accepting and responding to increasing expectations of customers in every market. All these initiatives are aimed at revamping products and services, as well as revitalizing the total organizational entity. These factors include the recognition that intellectual capital and technologies are the major sources of creating wealth today. All of these factors are combined in the present paradigm shift from the Industrial Era to the Information Age. G/E and proactive business leaders recognize this.

Old economies die slowly. For more than a hundred years, we have been taught to think in terms of economies of scale and the scarcity principle. Now we must think in terms of economies of scope and the plentitude principle. We have been trained to see, hold, feel, touch, and count the things of value, such as hard assets. Now that has changed to a significant degree. To make the shift is difficult for millions of traditional managers around the globe who suffer from "hardening of the categories," or a fixation with an Industrial Era paradigm. To bring about such change, we need proactive business leaders who can energize their employees and spark a rebirth of learning in their large organizations. On a smaller scale, it will be the Global Entrepreneurs emerging in the New Global Economic Era that will develop innovative-knowledge-based enterprises around the world that create new jobs and generate new wealth.

Chapter Endnotes

Ten Ways to Measure a Start-up's Progress

You have worked your butt off 20 hours a day for months on your new global venture, have spent your last dollar and still have few results to show. Now the real question is this: Does your dream vehicle have wheels that might appeal to investors? After all, that is your most critical problem in starting a venture – funding. Well, here are ten things investors will be looking for when you share your venture with them, according to Mark Zwilling, founder and chief executive officer of Startup Professionals.

1. A Well-Documented Business Plan. It is difficult to build a growth business without a formal business plan since it is the blueprint of your business. An executive summary is important to attract individuals to the venture, but thereafter the formal plan is important.
2. Realistic Objectives and Milestones. You must have written measurable, achievable, anticipated results that can be used as a yardstick to measure the progress of the company in various stages.
3. A Well-Rounded Entrepreneurial/Management Team. At some point the entrepreneur must rise to the occasion of being a manager and/or bring on board other professional managers to help run the business. Investors will expect this.
4. A Qualified Advisory Board. In addition to your formal board, you must attract at least a couple of experts in your industry to be part of your extended management team.
5. A Working Prototype. For growing businesses, product development never stops. The earlier you can test something – a beta product – in the market, the better. Investors insist on seeing a product and some showing of customer interest.
6. A Honest-to-Goodness Sale. It is OK to give away something as long as it links directly to other revenue coming in. Having customers shows the market is willing to pay, and you can get additional feedback for further product improvement.
7. Registered Intellectual Property. Investors are impressed even with a provisional patent, a registered trademark, and your company Internet domain name being registered for five years (shows long-

term commitment). IT is a large element of most early-stage company valuations.

8. Letters of Intent or Endorsement from Major Clients. It is better to have a letter of intent or written endorsement from Federal Express than John's Trucking Company. Of course, a real contract or purchase order is even better.
9. Personal Investment. Investors want you to have "skin in the game," beyond your sweat equity. They want to see that you have invested your own savings; otherwise, why should they?
10. Expert Status. Your visible expertise in public and among industry organizations impresses clients and investors. You can raise your profile by writing articles, speaking to trade associations and issuing press releases on the market in general rather than on your future product.[103]

9

Developing the Personal and Business Wealth Plan

"You gotta have a dream, if you don't have a dream,
then how are you gonna have your dream come true?"
Rodgers & Hammerstein

Personal Wealth Planning

Dreams can be turned into reality when one systematically plans and makes a dedicated effort to achieve them. For the Global Entrepreneur (G/E), the business plan is the core of the personal wealth planning process. However, the business plan itself is only one of a number of things which the G/E must be set in motion to achieve a position of personal wealth. Some behavioral academic types may be upset by our emphasis on wealth creation by the G/E. But let's be realistic. If a firm stops paying its regular employees today, just how many will show up for work tomorrow? Not very many. Likewise, if the ultimate incentive of creating wealth by entrepreneurs is removed, just how many would risk their time, effort and resources to start new ventures? None!

In the past, having a job was considered the primary route for creating one's personal wealth, but that is no longer true today. The stable workplace of gainful employment of the past is gone and will never return, whether in the U.S., Japan or elsewhere. In times of layoffs and corporate restructuring, individuals must prepare themselves for a radically changing world of work by developing and honing skills that can be quickly adapted to many new situations, whether working for others or for one's own business. Now, if you desire to create substantial personal wealth, you must create your own employment. Starting and operating your own business is a viable way to create that self-employment.

A small percentage of people inherit wealth to the extent that they do not have to be concerned about working for others. But waiting around for rich old Aunt Mary to die can also be risky. Today we find that some 96 percent of the people in the world have to work to earn a living. There are others who do not have to work but do so for personal enjoyment. When you have to work, you have two choices—to work for someone else or to work for yourself. Here, too, some 95 percent of people choose to work for others for various reasons. Only an elite number of people become wealthy by working for others. When working for others, who makes the most money? Obviously, it is the people who own the business and those high up in the company. Businesses don't pay people what they are worth; instead, they base salaries on labor replacement cost in the local market. Just remember this point—rarely does anyone become wealthy working for someone else. Becoming wealthy means you must own a successful business that provides you with an unlimited source of income - or you finally inherited money from Aunt Mary.

A major tenet of this book is that knowledge and technology are the keys to power and wealth creation. Knowledge teaches us how to use the fewest resources to achieve our wealth goals; for example, the use of a virtual enterprise. G/Es use knowledge to transform their dreams into the ultimate reality of a wealth-creating vehicle. With knowledge being the ultimate amplifier of human potential, the G/E uses this understanding as a key to unlock the vast potential of the global marketplace. The G/E is among the few people today who recognizes and capitalizes on this new system of wealth creation.

Just to have knowledge is not enough. You must do something productive with that knowledge. That's the job of the G/E, as both a "knower" and a "doer." We have discussed the G/E as being the highest order of entrepreneurship—more educated and more cosmopolitan than other entrepreneurs. Most often, the G/E has been dreaming and rethinking his or her future for some time while witnessing a sea change in the global business world. They have made and are still making extensive preparation for an onset of their new global enterprise. They understand that the new operating terrain will be tough, entirely different, but wildly exciting. They will design their business to be flexible, mobile, virtual and global. But they need much more than just a new vehicle and the traditional business plan of the past. Let's look at a few other requirements that the G/E will need to be successful.

Developmental Entrepreneurial Requirements

How can a young, aspiring person prepare to become a Global Entrepreneur? For starters, acquire a good formal education such as an MBA in international business from a well-known university. Fortunately, most MBA programs today will include several courses in entrepreneurship. Other basic requirements include employment in a major multinational organization and living in a country other than one's national origin. Major corporations today are seeking executives for global expansion. General Electric says the types of individuals they are looking for to fill management positions are "two by two by two people." You will need to serve in two top positions, in two separate divisions, located in two different countries to be considered for a key management slot at G.E. Another absolute requirement is to get involved in international networking and global alliances as part of your regular job, or through something you develop outside your regular employment.

Prospective G/Es take charge of their own personal development and, at an early stage, begin to design their future. It is well established that firms no longer offer individual job security, particularly in the United States, which has less-restrictive social legislation than Europe. Instead, many progressive firms are intensifying their training and development activities so employees can enhance their promotability and employability. G/Es will actively participate in all internal development activities offered by their employer in addition to initiating many opportunities on their own. In addition, they will have their own personal growth plan that includes reading intercultural books and international magazines, as well as studying general information about the countries they seek to enter. The G/E will get involved, internally and externally, by volunteering for assignments, which may be critical to the company's growth in international markets and with those alliances crossing cultural boundaries. Knowing what the firm is doing with its Internet, Extranet, and Intranet communication systems is very useful. Emerging corporate entrepreneurship activities are also an important activity in which the prospective G/E should get involved. All of these exposures will help provide critical experiences and serve to broaden the knowledge and skills of potential G/Es.

In addition to the developmental activities mentioned above, one or more foreign languages will be a strong asset for the G/E. Someone said that if you know three languages, you are trilingual; if you know two languages, you are bilingual; and if you know one language, you're an American. Unfortunately, that is true. For a global venture, English is essential and it is becoming more and more the universal language of the business world. Even the European Union, with its current 20 official languages, uses English as its primary working language. One can land a corporate jet anywhere in the world and communicate in English with air control towers. However, it is certainly a show of courtesy and respect if you speak the language of the country in which you live and operate your enterprise.

Another critical requirement for the G/E is to identify the product or service they propose to market on a global basis. A likely scenario is that a G/E is from the U.S., E.U. or the Far East. Many will elect to sell existing and perhaps branded products in totally new market areas. Others will choose to make and distribute a product or service with which they are familiar through their work or avocation. Eddy Merckx from Belgium produces and sells his high-quality bicycle frames at $3,600 each in a number of countries. He won the Tour de France five times as well as many other international races. His wife, daughter and sister-in law work with him in his multi-million-dollar-a-year business.[104] It was real easy for Eddy to be in a business dear to his heart when he retired from racing. Living in the heart of Europe with close proximity to other countries, it was easy for him to become a G/E

Normally it takes G/Es longer to prepare for their global enterprise than Traditional Entrepreneur. G/Es' education is more advanced, and they will have accumulated a variety of work experience, including various international assignments. Another major requirement for the G/E is the identification and development of a contractual relationship with associates in their target market countries. To do this requires lots of travel, market analysis and time spent in screening prospective associates. However, such work experience and travel just may come as part of one's life, as it did for David Ji and Ancle Hsu—two Chinese-born American G/Es. These two hustling immigrants developed a partnership with a scrap metal business in California in the early 1990s. They struck it big time early in 2000 when Apex Digital started producing inexpensive DVDs that could play MP3 files, the format used to swap music over the Internet. Located in Canada with no factories, no engineers, and production outsourced to China, these two G/E are making the cheapest DVD players on the planet. Today they have over a billion dollars in revenue with only 100 employees. There are many routes to becoming a G/E.

Developing the Entrepreneurial Team

A well-known trait of Traditional Entrepreneurs is that they are not good managers. These entrepreneurs are good at making things and starting ventures, but not so good at developing and growing businesses. Investors have long recognized the importance of the management team and, consequently, they often place more emphasis – lots more – on the team than the product, market or finances. If an entrepreneur plans to develop and grow an international organization, one additional factor is essential – managerial leadership. In this regard, the Global Entrepreneur is typically different. In most instances, G/Es already have leadership training. They will have honed their leadership skills during the developmental process and will be astute enough to continuously develop an ongoing network of potential associates for their venture—be it their first, second or tenth. The G/E will learn from other leaders like Edson Mitchell, an American now with the Deutsche Bank AG. When Mr. Mitchell left Merrill Lynch to join Deutsche Bank, he brought along about 60 of his banking associates (yes 60) and others followed him later. Some say that Mitchell's disciples will follow him almost to the end of the earth.[105] It is a real measure of one's leadership to have such dedicated followers. Company loyalty has declined sharply, particularly in the U.S. due to its massive downsizing, but it seems that personal loyalty to coworkers, colleagues and mentors remains very strong.

There is evidence of leadership ability in the G/E's strategic intent and global vision. G/Es are fully cognizant of the present-day leading-edge management concepts, such as re-engineering, benchmarking, continuous improvement, just-in-time production, total quality management, outsourcing, and Six Sigma—all of which assist in improving the efficiency required in today's highly competitive marketplace. But G/Es will move beyond these popular efficiency techniques, for they are trailblazers in developing creative techniques to grow their business. Most of all, G/Es dream of new markets that do not exist and think of ways to make them a reality. The G/E will keep foremost in their mind the importance of a focused-product concept that can be produced and exported to a global market.

G/Es understand the importance of developing the management team, which will help them to make their dream a reality. They may not have the desire, or patience, to be good managers themselves, but as strong leaders, they will ensure early development of a competent management team for their ventures. According to academic research, a management team is far more likely to lead a successful venture than a solo entrepreneur. Also, management tends to be more important than the product, according to investors. Private equity investors strongly emphasize this point. In the funding of new ventures, investors have long maintained that they prefer an A-class management team with a B-class product over a B-class team with an A-class product. So team development is uppermost in the mind of G/Es; for some time before they commence the operation of their enterprise, G/Es will be giving careful thought to the composition and ultimate development of the management team.

Private investors prefer an A-class management team with B-class products over a B-class management team with A-class Products

Products and Markets Define the Plan

Marketing is not a major strength for most entrepreneurs. Their strong suit is typically production—the ability to make their unique product or service. This, too, is a contributing factor influencing Traditional Entrepreneurs toward being more local than cosmopolitan. It is a necessity for the G/E to possess, develop or acquire a high level of marketing expertise. The successful G/E will be one who will have the ability to operate in many different environments, in different countries, in a variety of cultures and in the Third World with the same ease as the First World. Fortunately for the G/E, the operational model we have suggested includes having key associates in various markets who have business experience and are attuned to their local markets. Finding such associates is a major task for the G/E, but it is certainly a key to marketing and business success in the global marketplace.

Several markets are available to G/Es. One is an existing market where known products are sold to a known customer base. A second market is one where known products are successfully sold to new customers in new geographical areas. Note the phrase "successfully sold." Remember that a market exists only when individuals *have a desire to purchase* and *have the money* to make that purchase. A third market exists when someone invents a previously non-existing product or service and then creates a willing customer base to purchase that product. To create both a new product and a new market is costly and time-consuming. Traditional Entrepreneurs are more likely to be found selling existing products in an existing market. They will find a marketing niche where a product or service is being overlooked or customers are being underserved by others. The Traditional Entrepreneur will capitalize on the situation by fulfilling that niche and/or by making the product cheaper, better and faster than current suppliers. Global Entrepreneurs are more likely to be found in the second and third markets mentioned above; that is, offering an existing and sometimes a new product for sale in an entirely new geographical area.

Creating a business plan for selling existing products in an existing market is relatively easy. One starts with competitive product comparisons; i.e., product features, price, and quality that can then be presented to your present customers and their reactions can be determined in a fairly reliable manner. Such information can be incorporated into a business plan with a reasonable degree of confidence. This is why college textbooks on entrepreneurship always include a chapter devoted to the preparation of the business plan. Such plans are based on the assumption that if the entrepreneur has created a "better mousetrap," then the world will beat a path to their door. Each assumption in the business plan regarding a new venture must always be questioned. Even if one can accept the assumption that this new product is "better" in various ways, then one must ask: Do customers really want a better product, do they really need it, and most important, is the proposed extra value worth the increased cost? However, this can be complicated. Some people will say one product is better than another, yet, as consumers, they will then purchase the other product, especially when it is a more recognized name brand. In some markets, Coca-Cola outsells Pepsi for this reason. Regardless, we can place more confidence in researching known products in existing markets than in researching unknown products in previously non-existing markets. Again, the known product in a known marketplace is a more typical domain for Traditional Entrepreneurs than it is for Global Entrepreneurs.

Discovering and building new markets for existing and new products will be the route taken by most G/Es. Certainly the previously nonexistent marketplace is far more elusive than the known-product market. That makes the unknown market an exciting challenge for the G/E. Of course, G/Es do not discard the notion of finding an existing need and filling it with cheaper, better, or faster products or services. However, they are much more likely to look for un-tapped markets and then find or create new products for those markets; rather than finding an existing need and filling it with cheaper, better, or faster products or services. However, G/Es are much more likely to look for potential markets and then find or create new products for those markets. Not only do we live in a world where consumer appetites seem insatiable for greater quantities of existing products, but consumers are also very anxious to seek new and untried products and services of all kinds, whether they are toys, tools, or toupees. We noted earlier that Third World consumers have healthy appetites for First World products and services. The challenge for the G/E is to figure out the way to use their knowledge, technology and First World resources for tapping into Third World markets with desired products and services. This requires an overall business plan that will appeal to a number of associates in various countries around the world.

When assessing an unknown virtual product or a new market area in the global arena, it is *not* possible to ascertain the size, volume and magnitude of this market in advance. So G/Es have no choice but to take their product idea to the market without first proving its viability, sustainability, or profitability. They will use customers and the emerging market itself as an *experiment* to see just what direction the business will take. Clayton Christensen of Harvard University says, "Markets that do not exist cannot be analyzed. They are not only unknown, but unknowable."[106] The key factor upon entering an unknown market is to identify an overall *strategic direction* for the business. As G/Es learn more about the environment of their unknown emerging marketplace, they can then adjust resources and efforts in light of competitive conditions as they emerge. But trying to preplan for such a marketplace is just not possible.

Again, the "unknown" is the toughest of all markets. Some individuals cannot handle such high uncertainty and will wait until others have defined this market before they enter. Of course, those who do that lose the powerful first-movers advantage (time monopoly). Discovery-driven planning is often substituted for formal business planning when entering markets with an unknown product and when entering new market areas. In the beginning, the unknown marketplace may best be described in a narrative story-based business plan. The 3M Company in the U.S. still tells the classic story about one of their scientists who, while singing in a choir, wished for a bookmark that wouldn't fall out of the hymnal. Later he created Post-it Notes. In unknown markets, if an action plan exists, it should be used for learning and discovery rather than as a detailed plan of execution. The market for new products or services can be created and will evolve based on strong marketing efforts of various entrants.

For a new potential market, you must first find customers, educate them as to the benefits of your products and services, encourage them to buy, and then keep them coming back for more. For the G/E, this is the primary role of local associates with guidance and direction from him or her. Associates will assist in finding customers, determining who they are, where they are and how best to reach them. In educating customers, you must inform them of the product and service, teach them how they will benefit, but, most of all, get them involved in using the product. To keep them coming back for more, you must quickly respond to customers, asking them how they like the product and services and how they can possibly be improved. Then it is necessary to discover any way the company can further assist them in the future with other products. Americans in particular understand and put into practice a very high level of *customer service,* which is not present to such an extent in the developing world, and certainly not in Third World countries. Knowledgeable G/Es can use this business attribute as a strategic advantage in entering world markets.

Building a new market where one did not exist is difficult, time-consuming and expensive in comparison to marketing to known customers in existing markets. This is why many new Internet companies give their products away, hoping to quickly attract a mass market of customers, then later determining some way of developing a stream of revenue - from online advertising, by charging for product improvements, and through other creative means. This strategy of offering a free service or product, which delays the receipt of income and substantially increases expenditure, is indeed a risky Internet business model. Some have succeeded, but many have not, as evidenced by the failure of many dot.com firms. Certain parts of this model are valid today and can be used to market-test unknown products. Having potential customers where one can pre-test products can be very practical and useful in many ways. It is just a question of the scale and magnitude of the market test and the difference between spending thousands and millions.

With a good understanding of the ultimate market, one is in a much better position to develop a useful business plan. The plan can serve as a vital tool for the G/E. It offers strategic direction, can be used to promote the business to investors, can attract associates and is evidence of the knowledge and strength of the G/E. The most important use of the business plan is that it is a vital story that helps G/Es attract funds for growth and expansion of the venture. It is rare that an entrepreneur has enough internally-generated funding to finance a rapidly-growing enterprise.

The World Marketplace is Insatiable

The insatiable appetite of an increasing number of individual consumers is just part of the global equation. Businesses, too, have needs for new products and technology for their global operations. Business firms everywhere are now awakening to the fact that knowledge and technology are the major drivers in achieving efficiencies and economies in their organizations. As a result, massive changes are underway in major organizations worldwide. Many large business firms have discovered that *corporate entrepreneurship* can be used to their advantage in creating new growth opportunities and directly improving bottom line profits. These organizations now realize that they can have the benefits of being a large-scale business, i.e., size, scale and resources, and simultaneously have the entrepreneurial spirit, heart, mind and behaviors of a small firm.

There is good reason to believe that every marketplace is *insatiable.* This means that, regardless of what people presently have, they will always want more, and, furthermore, they want more of those things they do not currently have. Take the United States as an example. It has the highest standard of living in the world for the largest number of people, with an average income of $47,970 per capita in 2008 for 305 million people. This compares to $59,250 per capita for Norway for 4.6 million people; Luxembourg, at $52,770 per capita for 4.6 million people; and $47,970 per capita for Singapore for 4.6 million people. Some say America's high standard of living has its origin in the concept of the "Golden American Dream," something which has fuelled economic growth in the United States for more than 50 years. A minimum base point for the "dream" was the desire for a well-equipped, ranch-type house in the suburbs with two cars in the garage. That minimum has now been realized for a majority of U.S. citizens. However, the American dream is being expanded with U.S. consumers wanting more and more—bigger houses, more furnishing, and more expensive automobiles. Now, the two-car garage is too small for the average family with two children who also want their own automobiles. The prime residence has been supplemented with a condo on the beach, and sometimes a pleasure boat docked in Barcelona. However, this exuberance in spending in America is being restrained now as a result of the 2007-09 recession.

There is good reason to believe that every market is insatiable. People everywhere want more and more goods and services.

This pattern of continuous spending will develop in all parts of the world as individual income levels increase. Most consumers will not be satisfied with just the basic necessities of life once their primary needs have been met. They will move up Maslow's hierarchy of needs and wants and continue to spend in accordance with Veblen's notion of conspicuous consumption. Now consumers everywhere want more of everything for themselves and their families, and this will create an ever expanding global marketplace. For all practical purposes, there is no end to the expansion of economic growth of the world's population due to this insatiability of human needs, wants and desires.

Resources for New Enterprises

Resources are required for the start-up of every business venture. We are living in a unique period of unlimited resources for those individuals who can think clearly and understand how to tap into advanced knowledge and technology. Earlier, we mentioned Paul Pilzer's suggestion that, when we combine physical resources with technology, we can create an abundance (he even says an unlimited amount) of additional resources needed for our enterprises. Technology is nothing more than applied knowledge—something created through one's intellect. Entrepreneurs use their minds, bodies and spirits in shaping their ventures. Some have additional resources to contribute, i.e., capital, but others do not. In the final analysis, entrepreneurs bring to the table a range of tangible and intangible resources for starting and operating their enterprises.

The individual entrepreneur as a person is a tangible asset, meaning he/

she should be considered as human capital and potentially represents an ongoing financial resource for the business. A strong entrepreneur enables the firm to secure the necessary financial backing for starting and operating the business, in another sense, he or she can actually be a partial *substitute* for start-up capital. The personal attributes of entrepreneurs, their *competence* and *commitment,* have long been recognized by investors and venture capitalists as being the two most important ingredients for a successful venture. Angel investors have gained this insight regarding an entrepreneur's competence and commitment by assessing past successes and/or failures of individuals having and not having these qualities among those they previously financed. Their common sense tells them not to invest in a new venture unless they can detect a satisfactory level of competence and commitment in the individual entrepreneur and/or the management team.

There is strong academic evidence that supports the combined importance of these two personal entrepreneurial attributes - competence and commitment. The notion of entrepreneurial competence has to do with one's ability to identify good opportunities and then to acquire the necessary resources to pursue those opportunities. We see the second attribute of commitment as a reflection of the entrepreneur's capacity, spirit and perseverance to see the venture through to a successful enterprise. In research conducted by Truls Erikson, he strongly recommends the presence of both competence and commitment and not just one or the other. He says that both attributes are absolutely necessary for the successful operation of new ventures. In discussing the importance of these attributes, Erikson says entrepreneurial commitment proved to be the strongest variable in his research.[107] Note again, both of these are *learned attributes* (or acquirable with effort) that significantly affect the success or failure of a business. If you personally do not have a needed competence, acquire it by hiring someone who does, or outsource these operations. Regarding commitment, the G/E and the management team should be very open about their commitment; they should also demonstrate high enthusiasm for the venture.

It is essential that G/Es demonstrate their personal competence and commitment for the venture toward potential stakeholders. The sole entrepreneur must strongly show both attributes to potential investors. If the start-up venture is a team effort, then the presence of these two should be evident among team members. Keep these two entrepreneurial attributes in mind, as they are very important assets to the G/E and represent a unique competitive advantage in seeking venture funds. They must be flaunted. They can possibly mean the difference between getting your funding and not getting it. If competence and commitment are sufficiently strong, then the entrepreneur (as a person) can be considered a substitute for monetary capital in the eyes of investors.

Sources of Enterprise Funding

The most important limiting factor for every entrepreneur in starting a venture is the availability of tangible capital, i.e., money. There are four legal ways of acquiring money: personal savings from money earned; borrowing from friends, relatives, financial groups, or government organizations; earnings from a business or investment; and inheriting money from others. Potential entrepreneurs in developing countries such as Russia and China are severely limited in securing funds from all four of these sources. Again, we cannot overstate the importance of being in a country that allows for the *ownership of private property.* Such ownership of private property will offer an incentive to entrepreneurs by providing a means to borrow money that can be used to start a business. Even the availability of financing for a new venture in the developed countries of Europe has been rather sparse historically. Entrepreneurship has not been highly regarded as a profession throughout Europe. Fortunately, in the European Union, this situation is rapidly changing. The E.U. is now actively promoting entrepreneurship, and many European business schools are offering courses and degrees on the subject.

But there is a serious financial question here which entrepreneurs should consider. Is it wise for an entrepreneur to invest his or her own money in the business when capital is available from other sources? Perhaps not! Let's examine this proposition. Of course, entrepreneurs are expected to invest their capital in the business for a number of reasons, but few of these reasons are to the entrepreneur's advantage. Entrepreneurs are expected to put their personal funding into the venture because investors and bankers see this as evidence of their commitment (it's called your "skin") in the venture. This is important, but there can be other ways for the entrepreneur to evidence commitment rather than by the equity they are willing to put into the venture. A *suggestion to entrepreneurs is to keep your money out of the venture to the extent possible and use other people's money to finance the enterprise.* There are several reasons why this may be a smart decision by the entrepreneur.

Is it a wise decision for an entrepreneur to invest his or her own money in a venture when capital is available from other sources? Perhaps not!

First, new ventures have insatiable appetites for money. Entrepreneurs generally have a limited amount of money to invest for the start-up venture. Once you put your money into a start-up venture, it is quickly consumed. Then where do you turn for additional funds that will inevitably be needed by the business? A better strategy would be to use available money as collateral; use it to borrow the money needed for the start-up of the business. Many Americans use their home equity or other personal properties as collateral when borrowing. A problem now is that the recent financial crisis has substantially reduced household values in the U.S. By borrowing against collateral, you can gain access to two to three times the original amount you originally planned to put in the business. Then, assuming success of the venture, this process will build a good credit record for the entrepreneur with the borrowing institution. A second reason for not putting your own money in the venture is that the funds are after-tax dollars, representing only 50 to 60 percent for each dollar previously earned. Once that money is put in the business, the only way it can be taken it out again is to pay taxes on it a second time as income, and sometimes a third time as a dividend. That is not very smart. Third, if the business is sold, the purchaser will assume the business debt, but will not give much consideration to the equity investment by the entrepreneur. A fourth reason is that entrepreneurs can hold onto their non-cash assets, e.g., real estate, autos, antiques and other family valuables, which otherwise would have to be sold to generate money for starting the business.

A last reason for not putting your own money in the business is financial accountability. Strange as it may seem, people tend to be better custodians of other peoples' money than their own. Why? They are forced to do so. The entrepreneur is directly accountable to their investors (who often are now members of their Board of Directors) and/or to bankers who want to scrutinize their expenditures. Therefore, when using other people's money, the entrepreneur is frequently required to justify and provide detailed documentation for major expenditures. When an entrepreneur invests his or her money in the business and then makes a bad decision resulting in a loss, he is likely to say, "Well, so what, it was my money anyway." Entrepreneurs will often rationalize the loss of their own money without worry because they are not accountable to others for the funds.

Securing Bank Start-up Funds

Keeping your own money out of the business is worthy of consideration whenever possible. Sometimes it is difficult to find others to lend you money, but if you own property or have certificates of deposit, these can be used as collateral for loans. Having this guaranteed collateral may be the only way entrepreneurs can get a bank to lend them money, since banks are risk-averse. However, after the entrepreneur exhausts his/her own funds and those of friends and family, banks are normally the first source of outside finance for most ventures. Some claim banks will lend you money only when you don't need it; that is, when you have plenty and when you possess good collateral. Even when you have a well-established small business and request a bank loan, it is normal for banks to require you to personally guarantee the loan (meaning that you are personally liable for the loan and not your company). You have to have a major, well-financed corporation to secure a bank line of credit where you just sign the loan agreement as a corporate officer rather than personally guaranteeing the loan.

Banks are normally the first source of external funding for a start-up venture.

As with every generalization, there is a caveat. Banks do have money—as the famous bank robber Willie Sutton cogently reminded us. It is well-know that banks are reluctant to lend their money to entrepreneurs for start-up ventures. A simple solution is to not ask a banker for money to start a new enterprise. An aspiring entrepreneur in Georgia wanted to start a prestige, used-car business; he had some personal cash, but, as always, not enough. He went to the bank, put up his cash as collateral (a certificate of deposit from that bank) and borrowed several times his CD amount in order to *renovate the leasehold property* where he was going to start his business. The money was lent to him personally (being partially collateralized) on an interest-only basis for the first six months, and then he was expected to reduce the principal by some amount at the end of the second six months. He used two-thirds of the borrowed funds to renovate the building and the rest to kick-start his new venture. His initial inventory of automobiles was acquired on a consignment basis. So do not overlook your friendly banker as a source of funds.

As an entrepreneur you will invariably need to borrow from a bank at some point. There are reasons why you would favor borrowing from a community bank. One, it is a cultural fit; it is nearby; and it may be your current bank. One study I saw stated that 68 percent of small-bank customers plan to borrow from their primary bank in the next year. Therefore, get to know the branch manager and build a relationship with her. You may want to ask her what kind of experience she has had with a business like yours. The manager should have some expertise in your industry so that she understands the business and can help bring solutions to your firm beyond just money. Make sure the bank is capable of handling your special needs, like a letter of credit or other tools for international transactions. Pledging too much collateral may limit your options to borrow again when you need it for growth or for other reasons. Terms and interest rates are often negotiable, especially at smaller banks, where the chain of command to the ultimate decision maker is shorter. One successful entrepreneur told me, "Always borrow more than you need and for a longer period than needed." In doing so, you won't run out of money, and you will impress the bank by paying it back early.

When applying for a bank loan, you will often be surprised that a banker can look at your company financial statement and know, in a matter of minutes, whether you will get the loan. Is he or she really that smart? Not likely. Here's is the secret: bankers don't actually read financial statements – well, not at first. They typically give you the eyeball test and determine rather quickly three things: Can you pay the loan (knowing and considering your cash flow)? Will you repay the loan (good indicator here is how you handled your past debt with him)? What if you don't pay (what is the value of your collateral)? So the final loan decision will take into a number of factors up front and lastly your financial statement.

One type of equity input is obvious to every entrepreneur. That is "sweat equity." You will be required to work long hours in getting your business underway, and initially much of that time and effort will be without compensation. In spite of your hard work and perhaps that of other family members, banks and private investors just don't give much credence to your sweat equity. That is just an inherent part of being an entrepreneur; they want to see the real thing - your personal assets in the business, i.e., your money. At this point, there are two universal truths you must remember. In order to have a viable expanding venture, you will, without exception, need outside funding during early-stage growth and development of the firm. Rarely, if ever, does a business generate enough internal profit to fund rapid growth and expansion. If you try and fail to get your start-up funds from your community bank, don't give up, there are a number of other sources to pursue.

Alternative Sources of Start-up Funding

Several sources indicate that entrepreneurs spend from $5K up to $25K to start their ventures, with many of these expenses being incurred during the start-up phase - creating the corporation, license, rent, brochures, business cards and the like. The cost for an Internet business will be higher, as it will include the cost of creating a quality Website. In order to generate this $5K to $25K, in the past, entrepreneurs have relied on their credit cards and equity in their homes as sources of funding their ventures. That abundance of credit has been reduced for many Americans, and they must seek alternative funding sources such as the following.

Small Business Grants. There are federal and state funds being made available to foster new alternative-energy sources and other technological breakthroughs. Team up with a professor at your local university and seek a grant associated with commercializing a product.

Incubators. A start-up incubator is a company, university or other community organization that ponies up resources - labs, office space, consulting, marketing advice and sometimes a small amount of money. Some incubators will even exchange their services for equity in your venture.

Bartering. Exchanging goods or services as a substitute for cash can be a great way to run on a small wallet. Example: trade free office space by agreeing to be the property manager for the owner. This technique can also work with legal, accounting and engineering services.

Commit to a Major Customer. Some customers are willing to cover your development cost in order to be able to buy your product before it's available to the rest of the world. It gives them control over your product and for you, the promise of dedicated support.

Accounts Receivable Financing. This is commonly referred to as "factoring" and allows the small business firm to sell its receivables at a discount; this results in receiving immediate cash and allows others to handle the collections.

Credit Unions. Local credit unions now see the small business arena as a fertile place to make loans because of the surging demand resulting from limited bank funding.

Peer-to-Peer Lending Networks. Entrepreneurs can also tap into peer-to-peer lending networks such as LendingClub.com, Zopa.com and Peer-Lend.com., which allow lending directly between individuals. Requirements for such loans are listed on their Websites.

Micro-Lending Organizations. Most major cities have micro-lending organizations as well as your state. Georgia has its Georgia Micro-Enterprise Network listed on the Internet. ACCION USA operates internationally and lends from $500 up to $25,000, with applications taken over the Internet. Kiva.org from East Africa is currently expanding into the American market as well. With micro-lenders, just be careful to check the amount of interest you are required to pay; some lenders are being investigated for charging excessive rates.

Community Development Financial Institutions. If you don't qualify for a traditional bank loan and you have a venture that will benefit the community, then contact your local CDFI. This is an often overlooked source and some CDFIs make direct loans ranging from $1K to $500K.

Small Corporate Offering Registration (SCOR). Regulators in 47 states have been allowing start-up businesses to raise up to $1 million a year through selling shares prices as low as $1 through SCOR. Once the offering is registered, firms can engage in a public solicitation to potential investors, placing it on the Internet, take orders, and give such investors a subscription agreement and take in money in exchange for securities.

Securing money is going to be the most critical activity in starting and growing your business as previously mentioned. A great idea and a good business plan are two prerequisites for convincing others to lend you money. Still, keep in mind that *you* are more important than the idea or the plan, so prepare for the occasion and show lots of enthusiasm for starting and operating the business. If you have a super idea for a high-growth, technologically-oriented venture and need big money, then you need the help of "angels" - well, angel investors, that is.

Money from Private Equity Investors

Historically, angel investors provide from $200 thousand up to $3 million in funds while venture capitalist provide funding of $4 million and up. You are in deep trouble if you are seeking $3 to $4 million, for that is a gap that neither angels nor VCs tend to serve. VCs are declining in number today, due to poor earnings over the past 10 years. In a recent 2010 Angel Capital Conference, there was much discussion of VCs moving downstream to the funding range of angel investors. This offers opportunities and competition for angel investors. Angel funding is somewhat a mirror of funding by VCs as they follow the same basic process. Some say angel investing is just "venture lite" since the two differ primarily in the amounts provided to entrepreneurs. Another difference in the two is that angels tend to specialize in early-stage ventures, whereas VCs seek to invest in growth ventures that are several years old and have a track record of customers and revenue.

G/Es will have a greater interest in angel investors since they focus on seed, early revenue, and pre-revenue ventures. According to the Angel Capital Association, in 2009 more than 400 angel capital groups in North America invested $28.1 billion in 40,000 plus early-stage ventures. The same year, 425 VC firms invested $30 billion in *only* 3,226 firms, according to the National Venture Capital Association. G/Es should note two points here. It is extremely difficult, almost impossible, for you to attract the attention of a VC firm with your early-stage company. Even if you are able to do so, these firm invest in a very small number of the total investor-funded companies (8 percent) compared to the larger number funded by angel investors. Consequently, for several reasons, angel investors are a much better choice for funding your global start-up than VCs.

Getting funding from angel investors or VCs is a dream of many entrepreneurs. How realistic is that dream? The Kauffman Foundation looked at the *Inc.* 500 list of fastest-growing private companies in the U.S. and found only 16 percent of these 900 unique companies from 1997-2007 had received venture funding. This research shows that only a tiny percentage (less than .05 percent) of the estimated annual 600,000 new employer ventures in the U.S. were financed by angel investors or venture capitalist. Furthermore, getting money from these high-profile investors is no assurance of success of your venture. In fact, only two out of ten ventures that are investor funded are successful. On average, six out of ten funded ventures typically fail, two break even, one provides a very nice return, and number ten is considered a "homerun." The proceeds from the homerun pay for the total investment in the ten ventures and provide a nice return to the investors. Google, Genentech, Home Depot, Microsoft and Starbucks are all firms that were started with venture funding.[108]

A Venture Assessment Model

Now, can *you* beat the odds mentioned above, that is, attracting funds from angel investors? If so, then you must have a really great idea with lots of growth potential. How can you tell if you have a venture that *may* be attractive to angel investors? One way is to evaluate your venture using our Venture Assessment Model, which will generate an overall quantitative venture score. This composite venture score can then be used to assess the attractiveness of your proposed business. I mention angel investors above, for I am assuming you will be a seed or start-up stage venture, and not an operating venture that is several years old with customers and revenue, which *might* be attractive to a VC. The six venture characteristics in the Assessment Model are scope, scale, technology, risk, significance, and management. A brief summary of each characteristic is listed below.

Scope. One can assess and quantify scope with a low to high (1-10) scale as to whether it is local, regional, national or international. Obviously, an international venture offers the greatest scope opportunity for G/Es and investors.

Scale. This is a measure of how quickly the venture is likely to grow into a multimillion dollar business. They key factor here is the potential size of the market for the product or service.

Technology. Technology is quantifiable as low, moderate, medium, or high for its use in the product itself and or in the business operation that makes the product or service.

Risk. An assessment of the venture's key risks, how big they are, at what stage of the business development they are most likely to occur, and their potential threat to the firm's assets/resources.

Significance. This factor is more tangible to measure. For example, an outdoor grill will have a low significance measure as compared with an improved heart stent device.

Management. To what extent can the founder-entrepreneur run a multimillion dollar business and how receptive is he or she to plans for bringing professional management in to run the venture?

Every venture characteristic can be individually assessed quantitatively and then a composite score can be determined for the entire venture. Angel groups will establish their own venture funding breakpoints; for example, an angel group may determine that a venture must have a composite score of 70 points before it is to be referred to due diligence. Other ventures that score from 50 to 70 could be put on a "watch list" to be evaluated based on a change in status of the venture, such as landing major revenue-generating customers.

Let me caution entrepreneurs in making a quantitative assessment of your own venture – *you* are not objective! Have members of your board, an accountant, and other business associates evaluate your venture based on these six characteristics. If you have a venture with a score of less than 50 points on these characteristics, it is doubtful that angel investors will have an interest in funding the enterprise. If you cannot correct weaknesses in your venture, you may have to abort and find a new venture idea to pursue. The Venture Assessment Model is a proprietary product of the author. If you have a venture that you desire an independent assessment on the six factors, feel free to contact the author at the website address listed in the rear of the book.

The above six characteristics will help you to be considered by angel investors for potential funding. Your next job is to get on the radar screen of your local angel investor as well as other angel groups in your region. An important point here is that you will be expected to receive positive attention from your local angel group before other distant groups will seriously consider your venture. Most angel groups have Websites specifying how you can apply to them for funding. Typically, you have to upload an executive summary and a business plan in order for their initial screening committee to consider your venture. Many U.S. angel groups use a software program on their Website called AngelSoft. This software provides entrepreneurs with tools that help you find angel investors and private equity start up funds. AngelSoft operate a global collaborative infrastructure for early-stage equity investments in more than 45 countries.

If interested in private equity, your first step is to get on their radar screen for consideration. Then their formal evaluation process will begin, which involves a series of sequential steps. These steps are as follows:

1. *Deal Origination.* Many venture deals are referred to angel groups by

other angels, accountants and bankers as being a potential investment prospect. Entrepreneurs can also find local angels on the Internet.

2. *Deal Screening.* Entrepreneurs are asked to upload their executive summaries and business plans. The screening committee looks at this information with predetermined criteria to determine if this venture should be considered for a "show-and-tell" in front of the full angel investment group.
3. *Deal Presentation.* A twenty-minute show and tell presentation is made by the venture team to the investment group. One of three decisions is made: Yes – we like it and it now goes to our due-diligence team for review; No – it is not a venture in which we have an interest; Maybe – we need to see more information at a later date.
4. *Deal Evaluation.* For the "Yes" venture, due diligence begins. A detailed "go-no-go" assessment of the venture is made by members of the group based on a weighted evaluation of risk and expected return.
5. *Deal Structuring.* A "term sheet" of angel requirements is developed, determining the investment amount, the equity to be given up by the entrepreneur and other restrictive covenants limiting the risk to be assumed by the investment group. This term sheet is presented, discussed and agreed upon by the entrepreneur and the investment team. Normally it includes an investment member on the board of directors of the entrepreneur's firm.
6. *Post-Investment Activities.* Investors will provide assistance to the entrepreneur in strategic planning, management recruiting, additional funding and opportunities for selling the venture (an exit) at the earliest date.

Angel investors seek a very high rate of return on their invested funds due to the high risk involved with start-up ventures. Risk is so high that returns must also be higher – such as 5, 10, 20 times or more than the original investment. A very high rate is necessary for every ten investments by angels, as they will lose money on six, break even on two, make a nice return on one, and number ten is the homerun – the big money maker. Securing large sums of money is not the forte of most entrepreneurs, so it is prudent to constantly seek professional advice in this area. Astute entrepreneurs will often seek an advisory board member with investment banking or private equity experience. The Internet is a useful source of term sheet development information and names of attorneys who specialize in working with start-up ventures.

Preparing For Private Equity Funding

According to the latest data from AngelSoft, fewer than 1 out of 100 companies that make a formal request to angels for funding ever manage to secure such capital. Among the axed, three-quarters never make it past the initial screening process; of those that do, more than half are eliminated during live presentations and discussions, and another 10 percent during the following due-diligence process. It is a brutal process. Martin Zwilling, a former entrepreneur who previously sought angel money, and now is a member of the selection committee for the Arizona Angels Investment Network in Phoenix, provides a list of 10 action steps for those looking to land angel funding.

1. *Incorporate your business.* You will need a C-Corporation rather than a LLC, partnership or proprietorship. Corporate entities make it easy to carve out slices of equity to be shared with investors.
2. *Line up an experienced team.* This adage is true: "Investors fund people, not ideas." Poorly assembled teams are probably the biggest stumbling blocks in the initial screening. If you as the founder-entrepreneur, find a couple of advisors who are experts in your industry for your advisory board.
3. *Launch a Website.* In today's world, you need a cleanly designed, easy-to-use Website. You will not be recognized as a real company without the Website. Investors troll sites looking for companies with good ideas in order to get a feel for their tone, scope and other characteristics described above. Also, protect your virtual real estate by reserving the company name on social-networking sites.
4. *If you have intellectual property, show how it is defended.* Be sure to file your trademarks and patents. They may not be true barriers to entry, but first-mover advantage can be more powerful than any patent and are often perceived as such. Start the process early, as it is truly time-consuming.
5. *Build a prototype product.* Most entrepreneurs need capital to build a prototype product, yet most angels expect to see a prototype before they invest. Do what you can to demonstrate early progress.
6. *Hit the high notes.* A two-page summary is a must. Be specific regarding your financial model – how you intend to make money. Limit your PowerPoint presentation to 10 overheads aimed directly at investors.
7. *Prepare an investment-grade business plan.* Even though many investors don't have the time to read your business plan, you absolutely must have

one that clearly explains your vision and detailed plans about how you are going to achieve it. It should address every question investors may ask.

8. *Finalize your financial model.* This is the most important aspect of the plan and must impress the investors. Use an interactive Microsoft Excel spreadsheet with projections, assumptions, revenue, expenses and cash flow for the next three to five years.
9. *Close at least one customer.* This must be someone who is willing to pay real money for your product or service. All the conviction and market research in the work is no substitute for a customer.
10. *Network – ahead of time.* This last item should be your first. Build relationships with investors and friends of investors *before* you need their money. Start by taking an active role in relevant technology groups, trade associations, and university functions.

This is great advice from Martin Zwilling, who is also founder and chief executive officer of Startup Professionals, a company that provides products and services to start-up founders and small business owners. The author can testify as to the soundness of his recommendations as a result of being a member of the Ariel Savannah Angel Partners, LLC, in Georgia.[109]

From what we have discussed in this chapter, it is easy to see that most entrepreneurs face serious financial difficulty when they attempt to start their new enterprise. Banks consider start-up ventures too risky, angels invest in less than .05 percent of new ventures, venture capitalists provide only 3 to 5 percent of their capital for start-ups, and entrepreneurs have a number of reasons for not putting their own money in their venture. Consequently, it is difficult to provide definitive advice to aspiring G/Es regarding funding their enterprises. Each situation is different and each G/E's resource availability will vary widely. Many G/Es are already in business as Traditional Entrepreneurs and now seek to expand their business to the global arena. Fortunately for them, they have moved beyond seeking start-up funds and are faced with a second or third-stage financing, which is more available than start-up funds. This is where professional assistance from a financial advisor will be most valuable to G/Es as they begin to borrow money from banks, angel investors and other financial institutions. Strategic business planning becomes more essential as the G/E's firm grows in size, complexity and geographical scope.

The Business Plan Process

Nearly all of the 1600 colleges and universities in the U.S. that teach entrepreneurship have a business plan at the core of the subject matter on the discipline. I, too, have professed this in my teaching of entrepreneurship for more than 20 years in seven countries. In no way am I attempting to change this momentum in favor of the business plan. But I have revised my thinking in that the business plan should not be the beginning, but it should be the end product for the aspiring entrepreneur. There are a couple of steps and subsequent documents that should be developed, refined and proven prior to the formal development of a business plan. First, the G/E should start with a one-page concept document simply to test the initial viability of the idea. Once the G/E has sufficient proof of the soundness of the venture idea, then he or she should develop a two-page executive summary showing the full business concept including the financial viability of the business.

However, there are both naysayers and proponents of the merits of business plans. Some say business plans are of little value, they are a waste of time, most are not used, they are an oxymoron created by college professors, they are rarely accurate, half of successful businesses do not have them and angel investors make deals with people and not plans. Others have more positive comments about business plans: they are the starting point for creating a venture; they force one to consider all aspects of the business; they provide an opportunity for others to critically evaluate the venture; they are a major tool in guiding the initial formation of the venture; they assist one in getting the big picture across to bankers and other investors; and they can be used as an information tool in teaching associates about the venture. There is no question that developing a formal business plan is a good idea for every entrepreneur. However, there is not a single all-purpose plan; rather there is a range of planning options open to the entrepreneur.

During a brief period in the late 1990s, angels and VCs threw millions of dollars at a few Internet entrepreneurs based on proposals only two pages in length. That period is certainly gone forever. Those were really special cases during the U.S. period of "irrational exuberance." Don't waste your time today trying to approach private investors with a two-page business proposal, unless you are just testing your business concept. Some form of formal planning will be expected from entrepreneurs in starting a business, even though the nature of the plan will be quite different, depending on the particular situation and stage of business development.

Personal development planning includes a number of business plan *options*. The first option may be just to describe the business in *story form*—a narrative descriptive plan. Make the plan simple, so that anybody can pick up the plan, read it, and understand the business. A second option is a *developmental business plan*—one that is not tied down in great detail, but will evolve as the business flourishes in the marketplace. A third option is the more *formal plan* that is based on substantial market research of known products and existing markets. Then, of course, there is the "*madness*" business plan that flourished in the frenzy of the Internet rush of the late 1990s. It, too, has some redeeming features that should not be overlooked.

Today entrepreneurs have wide choices among three or four types of business plans.

The folks at 3M are strong advocates of the *narrative-story type business plan,* according to Gordon Shaw and his associates. Instead of illustrating the business from a list of bullet points, Shaw says a better way is to use a story to tell the goals of the venture and how the entrepreneur plan to reach them. Shaw suggests that "presenting a plan in the narrative creates a richer picture of strategy not only for the plan's author but also for its intended audience." The narrative story lays out the vision, not just a generic platitude, but in a fully enunciated statement of how the business will create value. According to Shaw, the narrative plan has three parts: (1) Setting the stage – the current situation is defined in an insightful, coherent manner; (2) Introduction of the dramatic conflicts – specifically illustrating the challenges the firm currently faces and its obstacles to success, and (3) Reaching a conclusion—telling how the firm can overcome the obstacles and become successful. The authors feel the narrative plan is more likely to generate excitement and commitment than the traditional bullet-laden plan.[110]

A second approach to business planning is the *developmental plan*—a process that starts with a concept proposal and is continuously modified based on changing market conditions. The developmental business plan evolves over a period of time during the start-up, rather than being formally constructed prior to the start-up of the business venture. For example, Honda initially came to the U.S. hoping to sell its large motorcycles in competition with Harley-Davidson. After Honda set up shop in California, it accidentally discovered there was an unknown market for the small 50cc motorcycles that some of its staff used for local transportation. A failed foray into one market opened up an entirely new market for Honda and served as a starting point for its motorcycle success in the United States.

Regarding the developmental business plan, a number of ongoing business activities often precede the preparation of a formal business plan. If a business is started without a formal business plan, a logical step is to develop an overall strategic intent—a statement of overall direction for the venture. However, in the preparation of the developmental business plan, it is important to understand that no one really knows how large the demand will be for products in new markets. It was impossible for Amazon to know in advance if people would buy books on the Internet and in what quantities. Some risks are obvious before the startup of the venture. But many other uncertainties occur only after the venture commences operation. For many people, both pre and post risks are too great. Consequently, they never start their business or they wait until others have more clearly defined the market before they enter. Second and third movers to a new market also have their advantages. Someone else has already spent lots of time and money in making customers aware of the product or service, and creating in consumers a desire to purchase it. That is called a market.

The content suggested for a traditional *formal business plan* can be found in every college textbook on entrepreneurship. In most instances, it is recommended as a one-size-fits-all plan. The average length of such a document is from 25 to 40 pages. Typical topics include the product concept, marketing, manufacturing or operation, finance, management, and then an appendix for further details. The preparation of a formal business plan can be useful in many ways. It forces the entrepreneur to seriously think through all the functional requirements of the business. Entrepreneurs generally start their ventures based on their dominant strength, which is their unique ability to create a product or service. From a business function perspective, that dominant strength is called production when the firm has a tangible product, or operations management when providing a service product. Since other business functions, such as marketing, finance and management, are not typical strengths of entrepreneurs, the preparation of the formal business plan will force them to give careful thought to these core business functions and to indicate how they propose to manage the venture.

Another major reason for a formal business plan is that it can help secure financing from banks, business angels and venture investors. Otherwise, the development of a business plan would not be high on the entrepreneur's order of priorities. Additionally, the plan can be a useful document in attracting managers and other key employees to join the business venture. It can also be used as an indoctrination document for new employees, e.g., providing a central focal point for performance and a blueprint for action. A comprehensive document not only demonstrates to interested parties that you've thoroughly researched your venture idea, but it also shows them that you've critically examined ways to implement it. Therefore, some form of formal business planning is a prerequisite for the G/E.

The good news is that preparation of a business plan has become easier.

There are various software packages available that are very useful in the preparation of the document. It's easy to go to www.vfinance.com and download a 5,000-word template for the development of a formal business plan. The site also provides a well-organized list of venture capital firms, investment banks, and accountants that specialize in providing assistance to start-up ventures. Be sure to check out the free business plan template on the SCORE website. Additionally, *Inc.* magazine offers its Pro-Business Plan for a reasonable fee, and it can be downloaded from *Inc.'s* Web site. After you enter all the data for the Pro-Business Plan, just press the button and it compiles the data and prints your completed business plan—cover page, a table of contents, tables, text and charts. This is a salvation for many entrepreneurs. College courses in entrepreneurship will never be the same now that students have access to ready-made business plan templates.

Business plans templates are free and easily available. Just go to the Internet and download one.

Tom Peters ask, "If you don't intend to raise hell, then why bother getting up in the morning." This must be what William Gurley had in mind when he developed what we call his "madness" business plan. It is Gurley's belief that, if you have it, then you should flaunt it. His four-stage business plan below was a standard for launching a business in Silicon Valley in the 1990s.

1. Define your service product, start your company and commence with production.
2. Declare your product does not fit any existing market, but rather it is the first entry into a soon-to-be-hot and huge market. Legitimize your product category by giving it an arbitrary but prestigious-sounding three-letter acronym like ERP (enterprise resource planning).
3. Declare yourself and your firm the leader of this new emerging market.
4. Shout from the highest mountain top that you are truly a Muhammad Ali, "the greatest." Get others to testify on your behalf that you are indeed the "greatest," and show how they are going to assist your endeavor by adopting your product.[111]

We are not suggesting you use Gurley's so-called madness plan, but don't completely dismiss it; it definitely shows commitment. The *Red Herring* magazine contends that today is the greatest time ever to be an entrepreneur because most of the innovations associated with the Internet are still being invented. They report that, in 2002, a half-billion people and virtually all significant commercial business in the world were dependent on the Internet. Now a host of a new generation of proven applications and services are getting faster and cheaper every day. IBM's advanced, new supercomputer, Blue Gene, is scheduled to have the processing capability to theoretically be able to download every page on the Web in less than a second. Now, a scrappy entrepreneur can build a fully functioning Website for less than $10,000; that is 25 times less than what a consultant group would have charged just four years ago. This is a good time to start your company because many of the dot.com loonies are off the street, rent is cheap and legions of highly skilled people are available to assist you.[88] And just remember, every G/E is "mad" to some degree!

How to Get in the Door

It is obvious that the G/E must have some type of business plan, whether a narrative story plan, a developmental plan, a more formal plan or even the madness plan. The next step is to get someone important, like a moneylender, to read it. A few angel investor groups advertise for clients; however, most work on a referral system from other angel investors, banks, individual investors and other professional contacts. G/Es challenge is to get their plan noticed and read. Guy Kawasaki, author of *Rules for Revolutionaries,* suggests these 10 steps for improving the odds of getting your business plan read and hopefully funded.

1. Remember that less is more.
2. Do not make the plan excessively long. The potential investor will ask for more if they are interested.
3. Make your numbers reasonable. If you have invested $1,000 and are working only part-time on the venture, do not ask for $20 million.
4. Ensure that your business concept is unique, different and has something special to offer.
5. If there are strong competitors, how will you differentiate your venture from theirs?
6. Indicate with enthusiasm what you propose to do, without unduly overstating that you are going to revolutionize the world.
7. Avoid using "Chinese math," i.e., all you need is just one percent of the world's population to buy your product and you will make zillions.

8. Make your proposal very neat and professional in appearance. Do not send your plan as a file attachment.
9. List your management team, starting with the most important person down to the least important person. If you state that you have revolutionary technology, then you must also demonstrate that you can deliver that technology and that your team has convincing experience in the area.
10. Just remember rule one.[112]

Unfortunately, there isn't a template or a Web site available to assist the G/E with a personal development plan. Each personal development plan is an individual endeavor and one which will constantly evolve, change, and be reshaped as the G/E continues to discover new opportunities while they are searching the globe. The personal development plan is a composite of ever-changing formal and informal development activities. One activity includes a written business plan as required by potential sponsors, but most activities are personal growth and development endeavors. The age-old question of nature or nurture is clearly answered. Aggressive development through constant nurturing is the clear winner. The Global Entrepreneur is a product of an ever-changing environment, and G/Es are constantly reshaping their personal development activities in response to a multitude of unfolding business opportunities.

Rethinking and Reshaping Your Future

One purpose of this book is to encourage you to rethink your present situation and design a future with new entrepreneurial strategies, hopefully, some you have not seriously considered before. Many individuals, businesses and nations are attempting to address their futures by developing and redesigning a closer alignment with a turbulent, new world environment. We must keep in mind that the things that got us to our present position are not the things that will keep us there in the future. Entrepreneurs invent their own future by recognizing and exploiting new opportunities. This is your moment for action - for we are at a "strategic reflection point," particularly for a global business venture. The business landscape has fundamentally changed at the core. It will never be the same again. Neither should you!

Hopefully, there is a reason why this book appealed to you in the first place, and now you have read it. Perhaps you are approaching that defining moment in your own career, when you are ready to make a *fast-forward* move towards starting your own enterprise or accelerating the growth of your existing business. You may have played the game previously, but may not have understood all the rules. Now, you know some fundamentals. The most significant - k*nowledge and technology* are the principal drivers for *creating substantial wealth*! This fact has triggered a fresh burst of opportunities for entrepreneurs on a global basis as never witnessed before.

It is clear that power and wealth are shifting to those who have access to the most knowledge and technology. But power and wealth also gravitate to those who are best connected. Clearly G/Es will be the most powerful entrepreneurs; they are the individuals who have the most links to others around the world. Many G/Es are already taking advantage of these opportunities. The question for you is this: Are you prepared and ready to be included in the sea change of present opportunities in the New Global Economic Era, as well as in the newly emerging Creative Era? Are you committed to be part of this dynamic growth as a G/E? As the world's center of economic gravity shifts in many global directions, this can be your defining moment for action—the time when you *reinvent yourself* as a G/E. The fences are down, the boundaries are gone. The *world* is your market, your domain. Think seriously about your desired venture and then channel your knowledge, technology and commitment towards becoming a Global Entrepreneur.

10

An Emerging New Global Economy: Creativity, Innovation, Growth, Sustainability

"Progress is inexorable, cumulative and collective if humans beings exchange and specialize; then globalization and the Internet are bound to ensure furious s economic progress in the coming century."

Matt Ridley

The Emergence of a New Global Economy

Economic growth has provided America and the rest of the world with remarkable increases in per-capita income and increasing standards of living for the past two centuries. Economic growth is not inevitable or a natural process; it must be intentionally developed by individuals, organizations, and government itself. Also, growth and wealth creation is not confined to middle and upper income countries; it also occurs in countries at the bottom of the economic pyramid. Thirty years ago, poverty was mostly an Asian phenomenon with over 80 percent of the world's poor living in East and South Asia, including China and India. Today, poverty is more of a problem in Africa, where about two-thirds of the world's poor live, compared with only 18 percent in Asia.

Today the Far East is growing three times as fast as America. China, with its estimated 1.6-plus billion people, started its economic reform in 1978, led by Deng Xiaoping, and the country has been growing by leaps and bounds ever since. In a mere 30 years, China's annual 9 percent growth (some years even larger) in GDP has led to a six-fold increase in real per-capita income. It is now the second-largest economy in the world and the place of choice for most American firms to manufacture tangible goods.

India also had an impressive growth record over the past decade, and the next decade is not likely to be any different. At the end of 2007, India became the latest member of the trillion dollar club, a country with an annual GDP in excess of one trillion U.S. dollars. This reflects India's latest step in its rise to becoming one of the most significant economic powers of the 21st century. With its 1.1 billion people, the country is enjoying an 8.5 percent growth in GDP, and this figure has been rather constant for the past few years. India's traditional IT service sector, recognized as the country's major economic driver, is now being supported by manufacturing, which is growing at an annual rate in excess of 10 percent. A good example is the Tate Group, the giant Indian steel company that is leading the way in many areas including global manufacturing a $2000 four-passenger automobile.

The Asian-style 8 to 10 percent annual growth rate will further generate substantial improvements in industrial capacity in China, India, and other Asian countries and increase per capita GDP. This does not bode well for the U.S. since the American economy was expected to grow only about three percent in 2010, after shrinking by 2.4 percent in 2009. There is also evidence that the U.S. is lagging in innovation. In the 2010 *Bloomberg BusinessWeek* annual rating of the Most Innovative Companies, 15 of the top 50 are Asian, up from five in 2006. In fact, for the first time since the ranking began in 2005, the majority of corporations in the Top 25 are based outside the U.S.

Move over America - the battle is on. "We're starting to see the beginning of a new world order," says James Andres, a senior partner at the Boston Consulting Group who heads their global innovative practice. "The developed world's hammerlock on innovation leadership is starting to break a little bit." We see a clear pattern developing in that innovative leadership is going to be more dispersed around the world. Some 95 percent of Chinese business leaders today say innovation is the key to their growth, whereas only 72 percent of American businessmen rank it as being important.

Wake up, America! Generating new business growth is critical to our future, and now it appears to be on the wane. China, India, South Korea, and Taiwan are moving up the global value chain, from sneakers, toys, and T-shirts produced in the past to personal computers, consumer electronic gear, household appliances, and now big-ticket items, such as automobiles. Previously the saving grace for the West was that Asia's high-tech products were generally knockoffs of the items designed in U.S. and other developed countries. It now appears that the Asian countries are succeeding in designing their own cutting-edge products comparable to those developed in the West.

The Global Entrepreneur (G/E) should be engaged in facilitating economic growth in the fast-growing developing world in addition to developed countries. When 80 percent of the world is living on $1 a day, it is a great time for entrepreneurs to search for new product and service ideas to help millions in developing countries create a better life for themselves. For these individuals, it is not the revolutionary big idea that will be meaningful, but one or two small things that will make an individual's daily toil easier, quicker, safer, and more economically rewarding.

Also, Jordan Baruch tells us that by exploiting knowledge and technology, a central theme of this book, developing countries can vault over, shrink, and even avoid many of the heavy-industry investments required for developing a business. Baruch says, "By concentrating on intellectual and services trade (domestic and international), individual innovators, corporations, and societies can leverage the value of their resources much more extensively than traditional [business] models have allowed." Such companies focus on core competencies, strategic outsourcing, and alliances to develop an organization that leverages their intellectual capabilities more effectively.[113]

As the world's biggest economy, the U.S. is facing a much-needed transition in order to cope with two simultaneous occurrences: the wave of intensified global competition and a sluggish domestic recovery from the 2007-09 recession. For decades America has relied on its consumers' willingness to spend, which has in most years produced some 70 percent of national GDP. Now Americans are saving more and borrowing less, due to deflated value of their real estate holdings and job losses. Scarce credit and job losses are not the only reason for an economic slowdown. Energy, although not as expensive as in 2008, is still not cheap, and individuals and businesses are increasingly seeking ways to conserve and use more renewable fuel.

The question now is just *who* will lead this transition? A massive economic transformation generated by a host of *new growth trajectories* will be required. This must be done while taking into consideration a multitude of problems facing the U.S. and the world. This question has been answered several times in this book – *extraordinary new growth is the primary objective of entrepreneurs.* Why is new growth so important? It's simple; the fastest growing organizations generate the highest profits and yield the highest returns to stockholders. Growth provides funds for investment in new technology, which builds greater expansion capacity for the firm. Growth also creates upward mobility for present employees, which in turn attracts creative talent. All of these factors contribute to generating new growth.

A Solution for World Growth: Entrepreneurship

America truly has a unique challenge. It should seek to maintain its technological, economic and moral leadership in the world, while at the same time creating a more habitable planet for people. Clearly, a resurgence of entrepreneurship is needed. America has a unique role in the world as the leading and most productive economic country on the planet. This is a great time for U.S. to take its entrepreneurial knowhow and reach out to the developing world – Africa, Northern Asia and Western Asia - and to *assist* economic growth in these 100-plus developing countries.

The four billion people of the underdeveloped world are most likely eager to participate in a positive initiative that promotes their personal economic prosperity. They want to eat better, own a motorcycle or a car, dress better, be entertained, and savor the good life, which most U.S. citizens enjoy and take for granted. All this can be accomplished in these countries when new businesses are created and existing businesses accelerate their growth.

Business growth comes primarily from new start-ups and young established businesses. Between 1977 and 2005, large firms in the U.S. lost some 1 million jobs and new firms added an average of 3 million jobs. Kauffman's analysis of U.S. Census data shows existing firms, less than five years old, created nearly two-thirds of new jobs in 2007. Therefore, it is the new and young established firms, not their older counterparts that are driving growth and creating jobs in the American economy. This is a strong message for state and local governments, as well as academic institutions. New start-ups and young enterprises operated primarily by entrepreneurs need lots of extra support in their formative years so they can grow into viable job creators.[114]

Simply put, America's major economic challenge today is to *accelerate economic growth* domestically and worldwide. This is clearly the domain of entrepreneurs. We can rely on entrepreneurs everywhere to be *creative*, discovers of big *ideas*, and the generators of *inventions*, all of which ultimately results in value-creating *innovations* in the marketplace. These factors are the fundamental elements in developing and releasing one of the most powerful economic forces known to man – *the dynamic energy of entrepreneurship*. Let's look at these four elements more closely because they are the dominant drivers of entrepreneurship everywhere.

Creativity. Creativity is thinking about what others are not thinking about; it is observing and seeing what others do not observe or see. Anyone can be creative when faced with a problem to be solved. Keep in mind that creativity and intelligence are not the same. One can be far more creative than he or she is intelligent. To a large extent, it is how broadly you frame the problem you face. Instead, creative people ask themselves how many different ways can I look at a problem? How many different ways it can be solved? Do you approach problems from a narrow perspective by asking yourself, how have I been taught to solve this problem in the past?

Creativity is bringing something into existence, producing something new or original, or developing something of potential value using one's imaginative skill. The beauty of this creative process is that it can occur in a similar fashion by an uneducated farmer in China just as it does with a Ph.D. scientist in his university laboratory. Additionally, creativity can be incorporated in every aspect of life, whether you are a Chinese farmer, a scientist, or an entrepreneur.

Research shows entrepreneurs as a class are more creative than non-entrepreneurs. Actually, one measure of entrepreneurship is how many ideas you have created and are percolating at any one time. The more new ventures you have created and are pursuing at any given time, the more likely you are to start a new venture. In addition to the various methods of generating ideas discussed in chapter five, check out an emerging entity: the ***i»Create*** Foundation, Inc., located on a small island off the coast of Georgia, USA.

Ideas. Creativity is a thought process that results in a flow of ideas primarily for solving the problem one is thinking about. Einstein's thoughts about the universe resulted in his revolutionary new ideas: the Theory of Relativity and later a General Theory of Relativity. For ideas to have an impact, they must be encapsulated in an appropriate medium to capture attention. That can be a picture, a phrase, a video, a business plan or even a simply-stated mathematical formula ($E=mc^2$). Today's dominant medium for sharing your idea with the world is the Internet. Don't worry about someone stealing your idea; the quicker you get it out there, the quicker you can claim it was your original idea and act upon it. Ask yourself to what extent is my dominant business idea being appropriately expressed in a creative medium to a world audience? Sounds crazy, but read further and you will understand why this is a great idea.

Matt Ridley poses a novel idea about ideas. He says, "… the human race will prosper mightily in the years ahead, because *ideas* are having sex with each other as never before." He cites Darwin's evolutionary process in which creatures change depending on their sexual reproduction, bringing together various mutations from different lineages. With diverse sexual activity, the best mutations will defeat the second best, which are then pushed aside and lost forever. Consequently, the rate of cultural and economic progress depends on the rate at which good ideas are having sex with a wider collective. The lesson here: don't hide your idea; get it out in public where others can add to it and expand your original thought.[115]

The significance of Ridley's thesis is that the modern-day world is not shaped by the idea of a solo entrepreneur's venture. Lots of collaborative assistance is needed to bring a product idea or service to the marketplace. The American economy, as the largest and most productive in the world, is a product of *cumulative collaboration* of literally hundreds, thousands, and even millions of people from all over the world. Leonard Read succinctly illustrates this point in his classical essay – "I, Pencil" – in which he says producing a simple wooden pencil involves a collaborative process of hundreds of people and many business entities. For the most part, our economy is made up of thousands of "collaborative enterprises," where creativity, discovery, invention, and innovation tend to flow as a result of many people working together. Just "Google" the essay "I Pencil" on the Internet and you will find a great story of the collaborative efforts required to produce the pencil, a basic tool in our society.

New ideas are unlimited in number; however, business today are seeking *great ideas*, and you will find them to be less numerous. Taking this a step further, the developed world is actively searching for big ideas, or market-disruptive ideas. Clayton Christensen says there are three tests to determine if your idea is a market-disruptive idea. First, does the idea have a positive impact significant enough to creating a new-market situation? Second, can customers at the low end, or low-income level, in the market purchase this product at a cheaper price than what is currently available? Third, does this disruption affect *all*, not just a few, of the present manufacturers in the industry? Christensen says when a company is able to establish such a disruptive strategy; it increases the odds of that firm creating significant new business growth. Another critical point he makes is this: the best time to invest in disruptive growth is when your company is growing.[116]

Invention. America's present day *inventive environment* is at its all-time peak and is poised for an unparalleled explosion. The human mind *invented invention* some 45,000 years ago when man started developing elementary hand tools. Thereafter, human progress emerged dramatically as man invented agriculture, manufacturing, and more recently the elements of the Information Age. Matt Ridley tells us that it wasn't just the invention of tools that contributed to the development and prosperity of mankind. In some areas of Africa, the Neanderthals had the same monotonous tool design for hundreds of thousands of years, but made no real progress in their way of life and culture. Such tools helped provide better subsistence-level living, but two other factors were required before man made real progress and advancement. They are collaboration and trade. These two factors later occurred with the invention of small-scale business with merchants along the Silk Road in China around 100 A.D.

We have long recognized the importance of collaboration and trade. The merchant travelers along the historic Silk Road were some of the first Global

Entrepreneurs, engaging in trade among vastly different cultures of ancient China, Rome, and all points in between. Our modern-day collaboration and trade centers are "hotbeds" like Silicon Valley and other Centers of Excellence around the world. These areas are epicenters that generate a high level of creativity, ideas, inventions, and all kinds of product innovations.

Invention is the process by which new ideas are discovered. It is a product of the imagination when a product, contrivance, or process originates after thoughtful study and experimentation. Quite frequently, when an opportunity emerges, it arises at the same time from several inventors who are not aware of each other's existence, sometimes even separated by oceans. Coca Cola and Pepsi Cola were separately developed during the same period after Prohibition. Ironically, each beverage has similar ingredients, and both were initially marketed as a remedy for headaches. At about the same time that Newton developed differential mathematics, Leibnitz did as well. Although the light bulb and telephone were ascribed to Edison and Bell, they were previously invented almost at the same time, by others who were slow to commercialize the products.

In giving some credence to the adage, "There is nothing new under the sun," G/Es should also be interested in the "re-invention" process. Re-invention is the degree to which an innovation is changed or modified by users during the process of adoption and implementation. In today's environment, adopters are no longer passive acceptors of products or services offered to the marketplace, but active modifiers. Everett Rogers cites three reasons why products are re-invented: the products are difficult and complex to use, adopters lack awareness and knowledge of the product, and/or the product has many possible applications.[117] You can be assured that if a product is broken, an entrepreneur can and will fix it.

Who funds inventions? "No one," says Nathan Myhrvold. He has a great article in the *Harvard Business Review,* in which he explains how he is attempting to create a capital market for inventions, much like the existing venture capital market for start-up companies. He cites the major difficulty: very few organizations - or anyone else - are investing in inventions. Therefore, he is striving to make a successful company out of doing just that. Being a former Microsoft executive, with a few million dollars has helped develop a business of investing in other people's inventions. G/Es should contact Myhrvold's Invention Factory and see if he has inventions of interest for a global venture.[118]

Wendy Kennedy has written a very practical book about inventions directed to scientists, researchers, engineers and technological entrepreneurs. She describes her book as an inventor's commercialization toolkit, and it is chuck full of ideas for taking your invention past the "polite nod" you get when people don't understand what you are talking about and don't want to admit it. Her book helps one through funding the invention to final commercialization. You will find this a very practical guide for getting that invention to market.[119]

From United States …

As a child, John Atanasoff memorized the manual for his Father's Model T Ford and wired his own family home for electricity in Brewster, Florida. Atanasoff, the son of Bulgarian immigrants, was a precocious mathematician and often got into fist fights. In college he was known as the Mad Russian. He earned a Ph.D. at the University of Wisconsin and landed a teaching job at Iowa State. He toyed with the Monroe calculator and tinkered with IBM calculators, trying to make them faster. One evening he went for a ride on the back roads of Iowa, stopped at a roadside tavern, ordered bourbon and soda, took a sip, and had a *Eureka* moment – one he had been searching for his entire adult life. He jotted down on a napkin the design of the world's first digital computer. That was in 1937. Then, in 1940, with Clifford Berry a graduate student, he built the first prototype of his computer, which he named the ABC. Atanasoff's computer is probably the most important invention of the 20th century, for, without it, the Internet would not be possible today. Few people know John Atanasoff – the inventor.

Innovation. Innovation is using new technology and marketing knowledge for offering new products and services to the marketplace that consumers really want. In simple terms, innovation occurs when a new product creates economic value. As we mentioned in chapter six, innovation is more the normal domain of entrepreneurs and small business owners than large companies. Knowing this fact, innovation pundits have flooded the market with books to spur innovation in large corporations. Gary Hamel's *Leading the Revolution,* and two other books, *The Innovator's Dilemma* and *The Innovator's Solution,* by Clayton Christensen are among the best. The message is getting through to corporations; large firms like Clorox, Kraft Foods, Staples, Proctor & Gamble and GlaxoSmithKline are openly searching for business ideas with their Websites.

There are two broad types of business innovation. We have defined them according to the impact they have on the market and the extent they improve a firm's economic position.

Sustaining Innovation. This can be considered as the traditional method of innovation practiced by most companies. It is a form of incremental innovation that is part of the firm's normal processes of making product improvements, increasing product reliability, enhancing user-friendliness of products, and searching for ancillary products that will compliment its present product offering. These methods of innovation are designed to contribute to economic growth of the business through sustaining what is presently offered, and by making a sufficient number of improvements so customers will keep purchasing these products and services.

Disruptive Innovation. This is the core message of Hamel's entire book mentioned above. He suggests that most businesses are using out-of-date business models developed in a world that is gone forever; resulting in CEOs having a belief that incremental innovation is sufficient in today's environment. Hamel strongly suggests CEOs take the lead in reinventing the corporate organization with a new business model of continuous, radical innovation to be practiced by every employee. Hamel says, "Now such dis-continuous improvement, radical non-linear innovation is a must for every company."[120] Clayton Christensen, in his two books, tells more specifically what disruptive innovation is and just how hard it is for CEOs to develop a new business model for introducing such radical innovation in a large corporate organization. This difficulty in big firms is why entrepreneurs continue to take the lead over large organization in developing new products and services for the business world.

Another form of *indigenous innovation* has moved to the forefront in China. That country has decided to use indigenous innovation as its blueprint to world supremacy in science and technology. China has revealed a "Road to Renaissance"; a political and economic campaign under the banner of "indigenous innovation." It is an all hands on-deck call to action for the nation to turn China's economy into a science and technology powerhouse by 2020 and a global leader by 2050. The financial meltdown the West -along with China's deep financial pocket - has encouraged Chinese party officials to be less humble and more assertive about the country's future economic role in the world. China's roadmap to that future, which focuses on indigenous innovation, is indeed the correct path. That roadmap is based on scientific knowledge and technology (the principal theme of this book) as key processes for business development and wealth creation. This is perhaps the most significant discovery China has made in several hundred years. America should take careful notice.[121]

Two factors contribute to China's drive for more growth through its indigenous innovation process. When China faces a vital natural resources shortage, such as polycrystalline silicon used to make solar panels, it *can* nationalize its extraction and production, as was done recently with this critical raw material. When nationalization occurs, the product becomes a national priority, with banks pouring unlimited amounts of money into state-owned manufacturing facilities, and local governments expediting approvals for such new plant construction. This means crystal silicon is limited in supply, exports are restricted, and prices are increased – all for the benefit of the state-controlled China.

A second component of China's indigenous innovation is that of "nurturing home-grown technologies," which Norihiko Shirouzu says means "appropriating technologies from other countries." When the Japanese and European companies that pioneered high-speed rail agreed to build trains for China, they thought they would be getting access to a booming new market. What they did not count on having to compete with Chinese firms at their own game just a few years later. From the U.S. to Saudi Arabia to Brazil, Chinese companies are selling trains that in most cases are now faster than those offered by their foreign rivals. The progression of the Chinese rail business is part of a national economic strategy of boosting state-owned firms and obtaining advance technology, even at the expense of foreign partners, says Norihiko Shirouzu.[122]

China's New Innovative Growth Surge – A Road to Renaissance

In China, new growth is present everywhere. It is not just trains; it is also planes, ships, green technology (electric cars, wind turbines, photovoltaic panels) and a manned spacecraft in 2011, with which they aspire to achieve world dominance. Western defense officials and experts were surprised to see more than 25 different Chinese models of unmanned aircraft in the 2010 Zhuhai, China, air show. One was a jet-propelled model that is faster than the U.S. Predator. In 2006, China unveiled its first, non-working UAV concept at the same air show. China is catching up fast in UAVs and other areas of aviation technology, thanks in large part to technology transferred by foreign aerospace companies involved with Chinese joint ventures. China has been helped by Israel (U.S. and Israel lead the world in pilotless drones), which sold China anti-radar drones in the 1990s, much to the fury of the Pentagon. The Israelis no longer provide upgrades for these drones. In 1992, Russia licensed China to assemble its prized Sukhoi-27 fighter jet – along with imported Russian parts, avionics and radar. China cloned the jet through reverse-engineering, however, they claim it to be the result of their own indigenous innovation. Now they are selling the jet to the world at prices lower than all competitors.[123]

China's appropriating technology is a challenge to the U.S. and other developed countries, and it should be fueling angst among multinational firms doing business there. However, it doesn't seem to be doing so. The major reason is that China is a huge market, and firms are afraid they will miss out on that growth. American companies are super-eager to do business in the country by sending their technology-embedded products there in large number. Their new membership in the World Trade Organization has opened the doors to Western giants like Caterpillar and Boeing; China is now their largest customer outside the U.S. Not to be left out, Microsoft and Motorola have set up R&D facilities and are helping train a generation of Chinese scientists, engineers and managers. General Electric says it plans to invest more than $2 billion in China, creating 1,000 jobs. Another $1.5 billion from G.E. will be directed to joint ventures with Chinese state-owned technology companies, and $500 million will be spent for product development and development of innovation centers. It certainly seems that America and other developed countries are "selling" China vital business assets – imbedded creative ideas and innovation. In doing this, we should insist on simultaneous reciprocal trade agreements allowing free access to Chinese markets in exchange for sharing, using and appropriating such technology.

China's product cloning is no surprise. This has been done for years from designer clothing to weaponry. Countries such as Japan, Germany, Israel, Russia and America are well-aware of China's trade practices. Likewise, Caterpillar, Boeing and General Electric understand the risk involved. Then why do countries and companies unload years of research and billions of dollars of imbedded research and technology to China? There are two reasons. This is due to two "rules" that are not taught in our business colleges: Golden Rule # two – *"He who has the gold rules."* In 1992, Russia needed money after the collapse of the Soviet Union and it sold 24 of its prized jet fighter aircraft – the Sukhoi-27 – to China for $1 billon dollars. China not only has the jets, but also a Su-27 production template. The second rule is The Market Rule – "*He who has an unlimited market rules."* Companies throughout the world are racing to gain a foothold in China's vast commercial, industrial and consumer market which is growing at 10 percent a year, three times that of the West. Now these marketers will be facing four legal issues – censorship, corruption, information technology, and contracts – all with problem-solving remedies under Chinese laws that is quite different from those in the West. In the future, American companies will have to learn the skill of reverse-engineering when buying products from Japan to find the latest innovations from around the world. Truly, a new-global-business environment exist today.

Now American companies will have to learn the skills of reverse-engineering when buying products from China to find the last innovation from around the world.

Ian Bremmer has sounded the alarm for America in his book, *The End of the Free Market.* Bremmer says, "... a rising tide of 'state capitalism' led by China threatens to erode the competitive edge of the U.S." Therefore, the race is on! The future will tell us, just within the next five years, which economic system will be the *innovative* leader of the world – a Chinese state-controlled system or an American free-enterprise system.[124] Bremmer is not alone with his warning. The famed historian Niall Ferguson, in his new book, *Civilization,* says, "After 500 years of Western predominance, the world is tilting back to the East." Under state-guided economic reform over the past 30 years, China had become the fastest and biggest industrialization revolution of all time. It has plans for world dominance as a "Middle Kingdom," being the dominant state in the Asian-Pacific region and, in the long run, the world.[125]

A question to ponder is, just how long will the Chinese rapid growth continue? It is not possible for a central-state government comprised of a small group of people to make all the right economic decisions for a vast country the size of China. For example, a completely new city, Ordos, was designed and constructed for 1.5 million residents in Inner Mongolia. Today, the city is totally empty. This is not a very efficient utilization of capital. An additional one hundred cities of this size are scheduled to be built over the next ten years. Jam Chanos, CEO of the Manhattan-based investment firm Kynikos Associates, says, "China is on an economic treadmill to hell." Some credence should be given to Chanos' analysis for he was one of the few financial executives that predicted that Enron was a house of cards without a foundation. Chanos says more than 60 percent of China's rapidly growing GDP is in fixed-asset investments, which tend to drive demand for nearly every basic material. Throughout the country, one can see block after block of residential villas completed, and most are empty. Another 30 million new apartments, villas, and houses are due to come on the market in 2011. Some 2.6 billion square meters of office space have been constructed – that amounts to a five-by-five-foot cubicle for every man, woman, and child in the country. Prices continue to rise and the Chinese people continue to buy real estate (very few other investment opportunities are available) by paying 30 percent down, some 40 percent of buyers have long-term mortgages. Chanos says China is a "capital-destruction machine" much like Japan was in the 1980-90s, and a downturn is coming. Such a downturn in China will have serious ripple effects throughout the world. Consequently, Chanos has placed a substantial portion of his $1 billion investment portfolio in a short position on individual Chinese stocks, including Poly HK, a state-owned real estate developer.[126] Will such a downturn happen? Very likely, for China currently has a real serious estate bubble, but rising consumer income could forestall a downturn and overall decline in GDP for five years of longer.

China's massive infrastructure program should help that country, much like President Eisenhower's Federal-Aid Highway Act of 1956 helped the U.S. with the constructing the interstate highway system. Eisenhower saw the advantages the Germans enjoyed because of the autobahn network and acted upon this when he became President. For China, this new transportation system is designed to help the government's shift from a rural to an urban economy. If such a shift is to be successful, the rural population must be able to find jobs when they move into the one hundred newly-planned cities of one-million-plus people being developed throughout China. Having these millions of new jobs is predicated on today's thinking that China will continue to grow at the 10 percent level, as it has over the past 10 years. The country will be in serious trouble if and when a downturn occurs, for there are no safety nets for the unemployed as we have in the U.S. This could lead to serious social unrest among individuals who moved with great hope from the countryside to urban environments.

The point to remember on innovation is the U.S. has lost its leadership position in innovation over the past ten years, moving from number one position in 1998 to number eight in 2009. We discussed this 110-country innovation research project in more detail in chapter four. Small countries such as Singapore, South Korea and Switzerland top the list as the most innovative countries in this comprehensive study. These countries are a lesser threat to the U.S. due to their smaller size, but now the sleeping giant is no longer sleeping. China's Road to Renaissance includes a massive effort to improve science and technology, which are pre-cursors of innovation. Again, entrepreneurs, business organizations and our government must be made aware of this situation; otherwise, America will continue on a *declining* path of economic dominance in the world. America is on the verge of losing one of our greatest competitive advantages – leading innovation. As a G/E, you can help mitigate this threat through your creativity, ideas, and inventions, all which result in innovation.[127]

Embracing the New Global World Order

The U.S. is still the world's dominant force in technology, innovation (dominant in size), productivity and profits. But Americans don't quite realize how fast the rest of the world is catching up. In the 2010 *Bloomberg BusinessWeek* annual ranking of Most Innovative Companies, 15 of the Top 50 are Asian – up from 5 in 2006. In fact, a majority of the corporations in the Top 25 are based outside the U.S. for the first time. The extended Top

50 list is dominated by companies from Europe and Asia, with one South American company. China is the biggest gainer. The age of Asian innovation has begun, according to the article, and America's long-held hammerlock on innovation leadership is beginning to slide.[128]

Innovation seems to be the key to economic growth and this is where America has been strong in the past. In a 2010 global survey report, 400 top CEOs were asked their views on the key factors that drive manufacturing competitiveness. A most surprising finding is that it's *innovation*, and not cheap labor, that determines whether a company or country will be successful in manufacturing. Contrary to conventional wisdom, Rana Foroohar says manufacturing has not become a race to the top. That's perhaps why the U.S. still ranks as the fourth most competitive nation, after China, India, and South Korea, despite our higher labor costs.[129]

Unfortunately, the U.S. economy is in danger of losing what has always been our greatest competitive advantage - our genius for innovation. A recent innovation study ranked the U.S. sixth among the top 40 industrialized nations in *innovative competitiveness;* however, we ranked 40th (yes 40) out of 40 in the "rate of change in innovation capacity" over the past decade. This certainly means we are at serious risk of falling behind. We have to renew our innovative strength as a nation. Fortunately, we can take the best features of our free-enterprise system – our openness, creativity, innovation and entrepreneurship – and enhance these unique attributes to respond to the new challenges facing America. Again, what we really need is a resurgence of entrepreneurship, one in which all American entrepreneurs can assist in the renaissance.[130]

A Powerful New Cultural Movement – Social Media

Harvard's Clayton Christensen and his co-authors in their book, *Seeing What's Next*, asked this question: "Where will the next, big creative idea come from?" I think it is already here in the form of a new type of organization; this new idea comes from yet another Harvard student dropout. It is a radical new *social organizational model* - Facebook. This social media site and its digital cousins, Twitter, LinkedIn, and MySpace, represent a new digital social phenomenon that is America's newest form of business-model innovation.

In today's Information Age, we have witnessed the emergence of massive, collaborative, social media organizations. These social media organizations are developing, growing and mutating faster than the general public's ability to comprehend even their presence and purpose. This new *invention* of the Information Age – the collaborative enterprise - has the potential of reshaping mankind in ways never before envisioned.

Clearly there is a social-cultural movement underway being fueled by masses of online users who have an incredible willingness to share, cooperate, and collaborate freely with people they don't know throughout the universe. This Internet phenomenon allows millions of random people around the world to quench their thirst for personal contact with others in various forms: socializing, friendship, love, music, entertainment, politics (Egypt, etc.), and business.

Facebook is the largest of the world's social networks, but there are many other global sites: MySpace concentrates on music and entertainment; Linkedin targets career minded professionals; and Twitter, a networking service, lets members send out short, 140-character messages called "tweets." These sites are the world's most popular networks, ranked by total monthly Web visits. One finds such sites today in India, China, Brazil, France, Russia and South Korea, and their popularity continues to expand.

Why such growth? It is in part man's primal instinct to be in contact with others, but there are other reasons as well. The sites are amplified through the global reach of the Internet. They can grow quickly without one having to spend lots of money on marketing. The cost of hardware needed to store and process data has fallen drastically. The sites offer much that engages people and perhaps the biggest reason of all is the "network effect," meaning the phenomenon becomes more valuable as more people use it, encouraging an ever-increasing number of adopters.

Social media appears to be one of the most powerful emerging forces in the Information Age. Websites like Wikipedia, Flicker, and Twitter aren't just revolutions in online media; they are the vanguard of this cultural movement, according to Kevin Kelly. A true global collectivist society is underway, and it is making lots of business people very nervous. Even Bill Gates originally derided open source advocates with this comment: "They are a new modern-day sort of communists, or a malevolent group bent on destroying the incentives that help build America." Others disagree with Gates, claiming this digital collaboration is perhaps the newest and most creative American *innovation* in recent history.[131]

What bothers Gates and a few other capitalists is this new, share-friendly creative commons is substantially *free;* a few sites have shunned capitalistic investors and kept ownership in the hands of the founders, and to some extent the consuming masses. Some ask this question: "Isn't it anti-capitalistic and anti-corporate America when a user doesn't pay for the collaborative experience?" The traditional Industrial Age business model is based on customers paying up front for a product so the firm can be profitable. Web-based businesses are different. A Web user experience may or may not involve an initial monetary transaction. Most social media transactions are free; all you have to have is a PC or cell phone and a broadband connection. What is overlooked here is the user's economic "time-value" paid by each individual in terms of his/her personal log-in time, their searching for various sites of special interest, and their determining what personal and private information they will share. This personal data from users has utility value to the social media organization; for example, consumer marketing organizations may be willing to pay millions to tap into such information for market research on product/services usages and for identification of potential new products.

Why Social Media is so Powerful

People around the world are spending an enormous and increasing amount of time on social media sites. Another reason people are flocking to these sites, according to Tyler Cowan, an economist at George Mason University, is that individuals feel they can shape their own future through "Creating Their Own Economy." This certainly appeals to entrepreneurs. Each day brings more enjoyment, more social connection, lots of voyeuristic pleasure, business opportunities, and all this is substantially free. Cowen says, "Billions of people are rapidly becoming more knowledgeable and better connected to one another. Self-education has never been more fun, and that is because we are in control of that process like never before." For individual users, their compensating utility value is accepted as a pleasurable enrichment of their human capital.[132]

The challenge for the G/E is to learn how to tap into Facebook and other social media sites and use that collective engagement activity in your global company. Facebook, with its 550 million world users (165 million in the U.S. alone) has developed a potentially powerful kind of collaboration, larger than ever known before. Regular Facebook users average about six hours a month on the site, far more than on Google, Yahoo and AOL. Many consumer marketers would love to tap into these casual conversations between friends, colleagues, and family members as they discuss a wide range of topics and products.

The "hive mind" of Facebook could be used as a great creative milieu to search for innovative solutions to some of the world's greatest problems. When one mentions the word "*inventor*," most people think of a solitary genius toiling in his laboratory or garage, but that is not the case in the real world. Steven Johnson and Kevin Kelly argue that great discoveries typically spring, not from an individual's mind, but from the "hive mind." The authors draw on seven centuries of scientific and technical progress, from Gutenberg to the GPS, to show what type of environment nurtures ingenuity. Their findings show that teaming and diverse colonies of creators who interact with one another are the ones with the greatest creative discoveries. They also explode the myth that innovation is derived solely from the profit motive. History shows that innovation comes from a creative environment where ideas can connect, as is happening on a social level on Facebook. As a reader of this book, join with me in asking Mark Zuckerberg to create a societal division of Facebook dedicated to creating inventions and for solving critical problems facing mankind. He just donated $100 million to education; let's get him to make a like donation for curing cancer.[133]

A More Sustainable World

Innovative opportunities for sustainability are more abundant in a changing world than in a static one. In spite of the fact that, at current gasoline prices, replacing the family sedan with a hybrid or fully, electric car doesn't make a lot of economic sense for most people. However, it seems that the age of the electric car is approaching. Firms like Tesla Motors are making cars with zero emissions, which are fast, flashy, and totally fun. Elon Musk, the 39-year-old CEO of Tesla, looked like a kid in a toy store as he toured the equipment in his 5.5 million square foot New United Motor Manufacturing (NUMMI) plant in Fremont, California. He just bought the plant from Toyota and General Motors. After earning $180 million as a cofounder of PayPal, he got Tesla off the ground in 2004, with an initial personal investment of $6.3 million. Now he hopes to make his mark on the automobile industry and society with the Tesla Model S, a stylish four-door sedan powered by more than 7,000 lithium-ion batteries. The future looks promising for Tesla, for it has formed partnerships with Daimler and Toyota and just raised $10 million in an IPO to help start production of cars in its new plant.

Others are following Tesla's lead into the electric automobile business. By the end of 2010, there will be at least three and possibly four totally electric automobiles (EVs) arriving in U.S. dealer showrooms. Yes, EVs are expensive, even with the $7,500 federal tax credit; cars with cords are far pricier than equivalent gasoline burners. The Chevy Volt has a $41,000 sticker price, and Nissan's Leaf is a bit cheaper at $32,780. A host of other EVs are scheduled for the showrooms over the next couple of years, including Ford, Mitsubishi, Fiat, Honda, Toyota, Mercedes, and Volkswagen models. Other start-up companies from the U.S. and abroad have announced their planned entries of EVs in the near future.

Sure, I understand that very few G/Es have Elon Musk's available capital for starting an EV venture. I share his story with you because sustainability is another emerging major economic movement and G/Es will be scouring the earth for less expensive product and service ideas to support this new growth area. There will be expensive product like the EVs, but there will be even larger projects, such as the entire city of Masdar, Dhabi. Masdar will become the world's first zero-carbon, zero-waste city, powered almost entirely by the plentiful desert. Ground was broken in 2007 for the $22-billion project, financed by the government of Abu Dhabi and outside investors, and it is slated for completion in 2016. I am sure the United Arab Emirates will discover lots of sustainable ideas in the course of Dhabi's development of an entire sustainable city.

China has just announced the equivalent of an Apollo moon shot. The Communist government decreed that five million electric cars will be on the roads by 2020 – up from basically none at present. A recent study by Ernst & Young found 60 percent of the respondents showed a strong interest in purchasing an EV; that is five times the number in the U.S., Britain, Germany, and Japan. The hand writing is on the wall America. China zipped by the U.S. last year as the world's largest market for new-auto sales, and now has set an obvious goal to become the *innovator* in sustainable automobile production. It is not just EVs; Beijing's long-range plan calls for expanding all phases of electric transportation - bullet trains, subways, and buses - to improve traffic flow and reduce congestion. Shai Agassi, an EV innovator and CEO of Better Place in Israel and Denmark, says, "In 10 years China will be a 100% electric vehicle market." The real question is whether in 10 years the U.S. will be a world leader in EV technology and production.

The green movement has been an emerging trend for about 25 years, but it has only recently become mainstream. In a longitudinal study of 30 large corporations, Nidumolu, Prahalad and Rangaswami have made a significant discovery about sustainability that is counter-intuitive to the traditional thinking on the subject. Their research "shows that sustainability is a mother lode [an abundant store] of organizational and technological innovations that will yield both bottom-line and top-line returns." Becoming environmentally friendly lowers the cost of operational inputs and generates additional revenues from better products, thus enabling the firm to be more profitable, as well as creating new businesses. The authors conclude that "smart companies now treat [investments in] sustainability as innovation's new frontier." It can also be a new frontier for G/Es as they search for new venture ideas.[134]

A Pathway to a More Sustainable World

America has the opportunity to do something for the world that no other nation can possibly do. We can take the lead in creating a more sustainable world and, at the same time, accomplish this in an economically feasible manner. This means we can do good for the environment and make money doing it. I believe that Thomas Friedman has given us one answer as to how this can be achieved. If implemented, his recommendations will have a positive worldwide impact. In his book, *Hot, Flat, and Crowded*, Friedman says the U.S. seems to have a "loss of focus and national purpose," but we are the only country with the leadership potential to respond to the energy crisis, which so seriously affects the population of the entire world. He says America should take the lead in a worldwide effort to replace wasteful, inefficient energy practices with a proactive strategy for clean energy, energy efficiency, and conservation of energy. In doing this, the U.S. can demonstrate moral, economic, and technical leadership in creating a more habitable planet.[135]

Actually, Tom Friedman points us in a broader direction than energy alone. Developing a new national cause and universal purpose can be an inclusive effort under the label of "sustainable capitalism." We can define sustainability as the capacity to endure, the potential for long-term maintenance of people's well-being, which in turn depends on the well-being of the natural world and the responsible use of natural resources. Sustainability has become a wide-ranging term that can be applied to almost every facet of life on earth, from a local to a global scale and covering various time periods.

There is abundant scientific evidence that humanity is living unsustainably in both the developing and the developed world. Humans are using natural resources from the ground and the ocean in an unsustainable manner and simultaneously polluting the air. To change this will require a major, global collective effort, and some countries are not ready to assist in this endeavor. Ways of living more sustainably can take many forms, from reorganizing living conditions (eco-villages, eco-communities, sustainable cities) and reappraising economic sectors (perma-culture, green buildings, sustainable agriculture) or work practices (sustainable architecture), to using science to develop new technology (green technology, renewable energy) for adjustments in individual life styles that conserve national resources.

A Defining Moment in American History – Greening the Economy

This can be our defining moment, the chance to restore the American brand in the world through *sustainable capitalism.* We can do this by designing, building and exporting technology for developing *clean energy, clean water, clean air,* and *an abundance of food.* Friedman says "the green economy is poised to be the mother of all markets," for it is fundamentally needed on a worldwide basis. He even claims it will be an economic transformation that will be greater than the first Industrial Revolution. What we can offer is a more compassionate form of capitalism that helps solve our own critical problems and the world's as well? Alternatively, the consequence of not doing this is that America will have to be even more aggressive in *fighting others* for a declining share of the world's natural resources. It is very clear why we have American troops in the Middle East.

Friedman's suggested world-saving scenario offers great opportunities for G/Es. Our country and the world are ready for a nation to take the lead in energy efficiency and conservation. It is a very compelling model, and American G/Es can assist in making it happen. You will recall Pilzer's comment in chapter four that there is no shortage of natural resources that technology can't remedy. Technological innovation and energy conservation can begin at the individual level -- even include our children. For example, your author is publishing a children's book on conservation of electricity: what it is, how it is produced, its CO2 by-product, its cost, how it is wasted, and what can be done in the home to reduce its usage. As adults, we have done a lousy job of addressing the energy crisis. Perhaps our children can be a viable source of help creating energy efficiencies, reducing wasted energy and decreasing electrical energy consumption.

What is refreshing about Friedman's is the idea that America can lead by example, with concern, and helpful assistance, not by force or compulsion as in the past. We should first start solving own energy problem, and then we can contribute to providing an abundance of clean energy to the rest of the world, along with ideas and technology for using fewer natural resources. People everywhere may begin to appreciate the American brand again, particularly when we show a real concern for the environment and help bring about a reduction in the usage of precious, limited natural resources. In the new Global Economic World, millions of people obviously want to improve their quality of life. Yes, we can show the world how to do this. So, Mr./Ms. Global Entrepreneur, apply your creative thinking in search of innovative solutions that will contribute to developing a new Green American Economy.[136]

A New Green Industrial Revolution

Will a sustainability renaissance happen in America? Well, history tells us it is possible. David Rothkopf, an energy scholar and visiting professor at the Carnegie Endowment says this: "We reinvented ourselves as an industrial power in the 19th century, and we reinvented ourselves as a global industrial power in the 20th century, and more recently, we have created a global information society in the 21st century." Now America must reinvent itself again by taking the leadership role in a worldwide sustainability effort to replace wasteful, inefficient energy practices with a strategy for clean energy, energy efficiency, and conservation. We and the world need an increasing amount of clean, reliable, cheap energy that doesn't deplete our remaining natural resources.

Again, the handwriting is on the wall for everyone to see. If we don't, the Chinese will! One area of hot pursuit for Chinese entrepreneurs is green technology. China has a fast-track program called "Torch." It's a program for entrepreneurs who want to open green-technology companies; they get offers of cheap land for factories, export tax breaks and even free apartments for the family for three years. These companies will serve the Chinese market, as well U.S. and Europe. In addition, these state-supported firms get direct, long-term loans from the China Development Bank; the bank also lends money to foreign buyers to finance their purchases. Consequently, G/Es must research their future global markets carefully to determine if a U.S. produced product can be cost-competitive with those produced by a state-owned and state-funded competitor. We indeed live in a new globalized world, and the playbook has changed.

Hopefully, the 2007-09 recession had a positive benefit in leading Americans to consider reducing their personal consumption and wasteful ways. The U.S. per-capita oil consumption is twice that of Western Europe. Also, personal consumption of goods and services is 32 times higher in North America than in the developing world. The people in the Third World are aware of this difference, and many are frustrated and angry; as a result, some become terrorists, or tolerate or support terrorist movements. Recent terrorist events here have made it clear that the oceans that once protected the U.S. no longer do so. Therefore, establishing an entrepreneurial agenda for helping to create a more sustainable and prosperous world environment beyond our shores can be an appealing challenge and opportunity for America.[137]

A Need for National Conservation Goals

Now, just how is it possible to start a consumption reduction movement? First, we should start with national goals for a reduction in wasteful and excessive consumption. Perhaps the recession has already started the reduction in personal consumption of goods and services, for many American are becoming more frugal and are spending less. Next we should focus on reducing oil consumption and electricity. What is needed is a 10 to 20-year Presidential or Congressional national-priority goal to reduce U.S. 2009 level of foreign oil dependence from 69.62 percent down to 41.78 percent level by 2020 (a 40-percent reduction), and a further overall reduction down to a 30.0 percent level by 2030 (an overall reduction of 57 percent from 2009). Additionally, we need a related 10 to 20-year, national-priority, electricity-consumption goal: to reduce the 2008 average U.S. residential electric-power consumption from

1460 watts down to 1168 watts per capita by 2020 (a 20- percent reduction) and a further reduction to 1022 watts per capita by 2030 (an overall reduction of 30 percent reduction from 2008).

America needs a national-priority goal to reduce both oil consumption and use of electricity

The above national goals are needed, but are far removed from the everyday lives of most Americans. Getting presidential and congressional leadership to take action on these goals is no small achievement. It should, but may never happen. However, the Friedman approach can ignite a bottom-up movement in America. This can happen with the power of the people behind it. Each *individual* can become a part of a green revolution, which will in turn support national conservation interest, regardless of the action or non-action at the national level. The above national goals are hard to quantify on an individual basis, but personal consumption of electricity is not. Every electrical utility has the capacity to tell you your average monthly usage of electricity. Currently, in my home I use on the average 9,500 kWh (kilowatt hours) per month, based on a flat-rate billing that evens out my electricity bills throughout the year. Every household has some control over its consumption of electricity, both its usage and waste. I plan to cut my electricity consumption by 15 percent within one year, with a gradual 5-percent reduction per year over the next four years thereafter. That is my personal goal to help reduce carbon emissions from coal-fired electric generating plants. What is your goal?

A national-sustainability goal can be used to summon the intelligence, creativity, and entrepreneurial spirit of every man, woman, and child in the country, thus encouraging them to join the green energy revolution. Such an effort will ensure a more promising future for all of us. We can become less foreign-oil-dependent with or without Presidential goals. You can help *now* in achieving an energy conservation and savings goal in your home or business. Enlist your children or grandchildren and set a household and business reduction goal. Set your personal goal to reduce your home electricity consumption by 2 percent a month below your present average monthly rate over the next 12 months, and then another goal to reduce electricity consumption by 5 percent a year over the next 5 years. Get the children in your household involved by assigning them responsibility for electricity reduction activities and letting them conduct monthly measurement activities. Children will respond to this challenge and will adopt a life-time conservation habit. Accomplishing this goal has several benefits; a saving in your cost of electricity, a reduction in coal-burning power generation that produces environmentally destructive CO2 emissions, and teaching a new generation how to be active participants in the sustainability movement, which is critical to our nation's long-run success.

Every man, woman and child in the country can join the bottom-up green energy revolution.

This proposed national engagement is where G/Es fit into the picture. Here is your chance to join the sustainability revolution if you agree that reducing foreign oil dependence would be beneficial to our nation. One can envision the impact this would have on our present $692 billion annual U.S. military spending and 820 installations operating in 135 countries. It is obvious that a considerable part of this military funding is used to protect the continuous flow of foreign oil to America. Such reduction in military funding is needed to help rebuild America as a dynamic, caring, economic superpower; one like the world has never known before.

Join the sustainability revolution. Write your representatives and members of congress encouraging the President to establish and implement a national goal of reducing foreign oil dependence. Then, as a G/E, apply your creative thinking towards designing energy-saving ventures with both local and global appeal. Hopefully, this book will help stimulate your desire to join the green revolution. Fortunately, a collaborative-sustainable process seems to be emerging, which should encourage many to join the energy-conservation revolution.

Enhancing the American Brand

Yes, it is time for America to renew its face to the world. All too many individuals around the world have felt imposed upon by America's past forceful global intrusions; they have also been put off by our arrogance regarding foreign policy under a previous governmental administration. It has only been in the last few decades that America seems to have lost its way as a highly respected country throughout the world. Twenty to thirty years ago, American were liked abroad, welcomed and respected almost everywhere. This changed dramatically in recent years, and anti-American sentiment became evident even among our allies, but more so among non-allied countries. This decline in the American brand can be attributed in part to an aggressive foreign policy: the requirement to have troops in and around the Middle East to protect the flow of oil to our ports, and the plan of both President Bushes to build a New World Order through imposing American values and democratic system on other nations.

In spite of having the most productive economic system in the world, there is always room for improvement in our free-enterprise democracy. I believe we should seek to *revive* the American brand around the world by developing a kinder, gentler, more compassionate, sustainable form of capitalism, one that renders greater consideration towards the world's less fortunate people and shows a greater concern for our limited natural resources.

We should seek to *revive* the American brand around the world by developing a kinder, gentler, more compassionate from of capitalism, one that renders greater consideration to the world's less fortunate people and shows a greater concern for our limited natural resources.

There is no question that the American brand needs a makeover. For that matter, it needs a new stylist as well. Instead of imposing our military might on the world, a new form of national leadership may be evident. At the beginning of President Obama administration, he offered a new leadership approach in reaching out to other countries of the world, both friend and foe. He expressed a new approach of reaching with an out-stretched hand, or "soft power," but also with "hard power," if and when it is required. His outreach may have some impact, as he received a Nobel Peace Prize very early in his administration. The Nobel committee cited the President's outreach for creating a new [positive] change in global politics. This new form of leadership may also have something to do with the U.S. being elevated from seventh place to the number one position as the most admired country in the world, according to the 2009 National Brand Index. However, the 2010 midterm elections in the U.S. reflected a rebuke of President Obama's leadership in America and that will impact his leadership standing throughout the world.

William Parker, a political advisor to the U.S. Strategic Command, said, "We cannot fight ideology with force." He is right! First, let's not attempt to *impose* our brand of democracy and values on the rest of the world. There is a better way. What the world admires most about the U.S. is our American free-enterprise culture. Consequently, let's *engage* others with a powerful economic force – the positive energy of entrepreneurship – which can help each person improve their standard of living, regardless of where they live. There is no question, people do appreciate lots of things about America: our music, film, creativity, business acumen, and the resulting creation of economic wealth for the largest number of people in the world. Let's use these factors to reach out in a more positive way to the rest of the world and help them develop and enjoy a better quality of life.

As a G/E, you can help rebuild and restore the American brand. America is in an economic transformation, and we will have to rely more on selling abroad (the domain of the G/E) than on domestic consumption for future growth. Most everyone says the days of easy money and exuberant U.S. consumers are gone forever; consequently, the primary G/E's activity will be marketing to the developing world. In those markets you will have to discover and create innovative new products and services really *wanted* and *needed* by individuals who have the *ability to purchase* them.

Where to start? Each G/E will have to make a choice based on their knowledge, technology, and a product or service they believe will best serve as the core of their venture. A positive step for entrepreneurs is to consider a product for your venture representing one of the greatest need today – *energy* - in its development, usages, conservation, and supporting products and services. At least, we encourage all entrepreneurs to add some form of energy efficiency or energy savings activity to their portfolio of new ventures.

Social Entrepreneurship

In John Elkington and Pamela Hartigan's book, *The Power of Unreasonable People: How Social Entrepreneurs Create Markets That Change the World,* they explain how capitalism can be successfully applied to Third World problems. Their book is filled with stories of "unreasonable people" who have successfully applied their drive and imagination to nontraditional markets at the "bottom of the pyramid," a sector having a whopping $5-trillion value in purchasing power. The authors suggest this underserved sector will be "a new [growth] phase in the evolution of business, markets, and capitalism itself."[138]

Today's entrepreneurs can clearly have a hand in reshaping capitalism and a more sustainable world. This is called social entrepreneurship by many. Martin Varsavsky (Spanish) of Jazztel and EINSTEINet donated $11 million to launch Educ.ar, an educational Internet portal in Argentina, and another $500,000 to start a similar project in Chile. The Entrepreneurs' Foundation, in Menlo Park, California, has 61 members, each of whom has donated roughly $100,000 of stock to address the needs of people in their community. The Triangle Community Foundation in Research Triangle Park, North Carolina, has agreements from 43 entrepreneurs to commit $10,000 or more in stock to address community needs. Hopefully, this trend of getting individuals to donate a portion of their future wealth, or a percentage of their pre-IPO stock, will become a world movement in *social entrepreneurship.* Below is what several other small firms are doing to earn a profit and simultaneously help others in need.

TOMS Shoes. Blake Mycoskie owns a shoe company, and for every pair of his rubber sole "alpargatas" shoes sold to the affluent, he gives away a pair to someone in the world who needs them, but cannot afford to buy a pair.

Sram, Inc. Frederick Day is the owner of Sram, located in Chicago, the second largest maker of bicycle component parts in the world. He gives away a number of special heavy-duty bikes made for the rugged roads of developing countries. The bikes are designed to carry a 200-pound cargo.

Ears to Our World. Thomas Witherspoon, an Afro-American originally from Hickory, North Carolina, distributes wind-up shortwave radio to isolated villages across South Africa, Belize, and Romania, thus providing listeners with vital local information. He also provided radios to Haiti when local stations and cell phones were not operating during the 2010 earthquake.

PeaceWorks. Daniel Lubetzky has what he calls a "not-only-for-profit" company. He deliberately mixes and blends food products from two warring factions, such as Arabs and Israelis. Through this process, he encourages these countries to engage in trading together. For example, he markets an Indonesian food product line produced in a women-owned factory in Bali, bringing together Muslims, Buddhists, and Christians.

Other opportunities are abundant. As an entrepreneur, you can consider building an elementary school in rural Cambodia. It will only cost $14,000, and you can even name the school and dedicate it to a family member or a favorite teacher. Your $14,000 will be matched by an equal amount from the World Bank, and $2,000 of this sum is put aside for teachers' salaries. For the above amount, a three-to-five room school building can be built. Throw in an extra $1,700, and the school gets a solar roof panel that provides power to computers, which Apple and others have agreed to donate to this cause.

An increasing number of entrepreneurs are getting involved in addressing the problems of society while making money. There is even greater opportunity when there is collaboration between large corporations and social entrepreneurs, for together they can create and penetrate markets on a scale not seen in any previous time period.

A New Face of Capitalism

America produces 25 percent of the world's gross domestic product ($14.2 trillion) with only 5 percent of the world's population. A major reason for such prosperity is the American entrepreneurial-based capitalistic system, which has created the highest economic standard of living for the largest number of people in the world. This is a blessing for most Americans, but it creates problems for us elsewhere in the world. In some developing countries, there are those who are resentful of our western culture and our prosperity. The result is the creation of radical extremists who seek to undermine our system and desire to bring harm to Americans at home and abroad. This has become an increasing domestic problem for the U.S., and these extremists will intensify their efforts in the future to initiate terrorist attacks in major cities and at critical water, electrical, and transportation sites.

We discussed the free-enterprise, capitalistic system in chapter one. We acknowledged the 2007-09 recession was caused by an unbridled financial system that triggered the world recession. Such widespread financial speculation had a root cause in the U.S. government's decision to allow Fanny May and Freddy Mac to finance mortgages by non-financially-qualified low-income homeowners. Now, new rules regulating the banking and financial system have been put in place, Wall Street should never again have the power to impact transnational affairs to the extent of affecting borrowers and lenders worldwide. Keep in mind that it was "greed," or a dollar-driven Wall Street Regime, that brought about the world economic crisis. It was not capitalism or globalization that caused the recessions, as some have claimed.

We can say without reservation that free-enterprise capitalism is still the world's economic ideology of choice. This is true because it is the only system that unlocks the highest degree of human potential and rewards people based on their hard work, creativity, and innovation. Obviously the 2007-09 economic crisis has shaken the world's confidence in the way capitalism has functioned in the U.S. over the past few years. Our high level of unemployment, sluggish growth, excessive health-care costs, public and private indebtedness, underinvestment in education, excessive energy consumption, and a worsening climate crisis – all are factors leading many to ask: What type of capitalism will maximize sustainable economic growth and set a good example for the world to follow? Our suggestion is a new and improved form of *sustainable capitalism.*

Perhaps it is time to see if we can use our capitalistic system to do "good" in the world, to "help" others, and to "improve the quality of life" for millions of people who have far less than we have. Take another look at the U.S. productive output and its population. This country consumes 22 percent of the world's gross domestic product and uses 25 percent of the world's energy, but has only 5 percent of the world's population. U.S. consumption is 32 times that of people living in developing countries of the world. Again, the likelihood of more terrorist attacks against America and other Western countries persists as long as this 32 times difference in consumption rates exists. Our challenge is not necessarily reducing our consumption as much as helping millions of others in developing nations to increase their consumption and the quality of lives of their citizens. Entrepreneurs can show the world how this can be done!!

A More Sustainable Capitalistic System

The U.S. is in a unique position to do even more for the developing world with two major positive initiatives. Now, in addition to providing entrepreneurship support, let's also "share" with the world a kinder, gentler, sustainable form of capitalism. Keep in mind the operative word "sharing," certainly not imposing our system on others by force or other punitive measures, as has occurred over the past 20 years. But this begs another question: Can our present entrepreneurial-based capitalistic system be improved? Sure, it can be done. There seems to be a clear call for a change in the system by key thought-provoking Americans. Bill Gates has suggested a new form of "creative capitalism," using innovation, entrepreneurship, and market creation to respond to the millions in Third World countries "who have been left out." Neville Isdell, Former Chairman of Coca-Cola, proposes "connected capitalism," which has the same environmental theme as "conscious capitalism," being promoted by John Mackey, CEO of Whole Foods in Texas. Even the 2010 BP ocean oil spill will bring a flood of calls from politicians and environmentalists to force businesses to be more mindful of their environmental responsibilities. It is apparent that a movement towards sustainable capitalism is needed and is partially underway in America and -- you won't believe this, also in China.

It is of interest how inventions and major thoughts occur simultaneously in the world, but quite often arise from some societal need. The ruling Communist Party in China just concluded, in October 2010, a gathering of party leaders to define the direction of the country for the next five years and beyond. The major task facing the government is how to keep the vast country stable while pushing ahead with painful reforms and economic development. The country faces many shortages, particularly in generation of electricity. Since 1990, China's electric power needs have risen by the equivalent of a power station a month. Some 178,000 people are estimated to die prematurely each year due to pollution from coal-fired power plants. In identifying the future direction for China, the ruling party coined a phrase – "inclusive growth" – to describe the twin goals of achieving economic development while being sensitive to the environment. In America, we call this sustainability.

Surprisingly, sustainability was highlighted in the 2010 Shanghai World Expo attended by 60 million people from 155 countries. The theme of the Expo – "Better City / Better Life" – was no surprise, for China plans to build a hundred new cities over the next 10 years, with each to support a population of over a million people. The Expo gave China an opportunity to have an in-depth intellectual exchange with urban developers from across the world, thus allowing a sharing of their creative ideas with China for its rapid urban development.

The Expo ended with an outreach to the world on these key propositions: establish an ecological civilization oriented towards a respect for nature and an accelerated transition toward sustainable development; pursue inclusive and balanced growth with an optimum relationship between social equity and economic efficiency; promote science, technology and innovation as a path to development; build a smart information society where innovation in communication and information technology is increasingly shared with residents; foster an open and shared multicultural society where cultural heritage is protected and intercultural exchange is promoted; and To pursue a balanced-urban-rural development with respect to the integration of rural population into cities. These are truly bold statements coming from China. It is interesting to see they desire to pursue sustainable growth and development. It seems China is beginning to recognize that continued growth cannot be at the expense of its vast population, its rich culture, and the environment. This new sustainability path is a recent recognition by China, announced to the world for the first time in late 2010. Sustainability and inclusive growth will take decades to implement in the country.

Is the door open wide today for entrepreneurs to *visit* China and offer their products and services for sale? Doubtful! But if so, this is quite a contrast to a China that closed its doors completely in 1793 with a letter from Emperor Qianlong to Britain's King George, III, stating, "We possess all things. We see no value on objects strange or ingenious, and have no use for your country's manufacturers." Some of the traces of China's closed door policy still remain today, in the view of many corporate leaders who complain that the business game is stacked against them, according to Michael Elliott. Elliott says, "… everything from standards to government procurement policies to intellectual property laws is being manipulated to benefit domestic Chinese producers over international companies. The door is open, but China will continue *to use the rest of the world's technology to build its own industrial* base [emphasis added]. As mentioned earlier, the central government is committed to build a broad-based scientific and technological platform of *indigenous innovation*, one which they expect to be on par with, or ahead of any nation and any industry they choose in the near future as they have achieved in solar energy. Next it's electric automobiles, unmanned space vehicles, and the list gets longer daily.[139]

A Reshaped Global Business World

The new Global Economic Era of the 21st century will reshape the business world even more than the 20th-century Renaissance period, which resulted in the Industrial Revolution. This is an exciting time, for it allows many people to use their knowledge, technology, creativity, and entrepreneurial talents as never before. This decade gives rise to the emergence of G/Es on a worldwide basis. A global economy has grown and will continue to develop in spite of anti-globalization sentiments. Today, many things in the business world seem to be in a state of upheaval and turmoil. A major reason for this upheaval is the arrival of a New Global Economic Order, one coupled with a revolutionary system of creating wealth through applying knowledge and technology. It is unlike anything that we have seen in the past, and it promises many new wealth-creating opportunities unequaled in human history. This new actual and potential wealth-creating process is raising individual expectations everywhere. It is facilitating the flowering of creativity and entrepreneurship in every field of endeavor, not just in business.

Fast-growth eras have one major characteristic in common; as new industries emerge, they produce huge discontinuities. Unfortunately, at the same time old businesses are destroyed, there is major job displacement. Some workers cannot adjust to late career changes, and their standards of living often suffer. On the other hand, rapid progress will bring major opportunities for those people with the ability to cope with change, those who can master discontinuities, and those who recognize the growth potential that lies within such change. Knowing the source of change is important in order to generate new ventures. Growth today is based more on knowledge and technology than on brick-and-mortar assets; therefore, it offers unprecedented ease of entry into business for the well-qualified G/E. And, if their business is Internet-related, they can instantaneously reach out to millions of global consumers, an impossible feat for solo entrepreneurs and small firms just a few years ago.

The world is certainly at a crossroads, a new turning point in history, as a result of this dynamic new system of creating wealth. The organizational paradigm and management models of the Industrial Era are quickly giving way to a fresh appreciation of outsourcing, collaboration, minimization of scale, maximization of scope, working with competitors, forming strategic alliances, utilizing networking, developing virtual organizations, emphasizing the empowerment of the individual, and with an understanding that *plentitude increases value.* This moment is indeed a turning point in economic history; we are experiencing great bursts of creative thinking in all disciplines. Such creative thinking brings about breakthrough innovations beneficial to all mankind. Now we have to ensure that all these benefits are known and used on a worldwide basis with a more engaging form of sustainable capitalism. This is the future job of the G/E and other enterprising entrepreneurs.

Global Entrepreneurs have at their disposal remarkable inventions and tools, never before available, for seizing the initiative, beating big businesses to the punch, harnessing emerging technology, and using new knowledge to build their global ventures. For the G/E, the beauty of starting a new venture today is that *you can design your own world* as you desire it to be. That is a powerful motivational force known uniquely to entrepreneurs. Traditional Entrepreneurs who aspire to move into the global arena can also be assisted by knowing and understanding the *six-step G/E process,* as well as the *thought patterns* and *behavioral* characteristics of the Global Entrepreneur. There is no other time in the history of mankind that has offered all entrepreneurs such great opportunities for creating *wealth,* while simultaneously preserving our natural resources and making a contribution to mankind.

Go forward, growth-oriented engenderers of the world – choose your route and pathway to wealth as a Global Entrepreneur.

Endnotes

Chapter 1 – A New Global Economic Era

1. Jamie Diamon, "America's Traditional Strengths Will Win Out," *Fortune,* May 4, 2009, p. 66.
2. Steve Forbes, "Capitalism: A True Love Story," *Forbes,* October 9, 2009, p. 24.
3. Harold Price, William J. Baumol, Robert Litan and Carl Schramm, *Good Capitalism, Bad Capitalism, and the Economies of Growth, (New Haven CT: Yale University Press, 2007).*
4. Carl Schramm, *The Entrepreneurial Imperative: How America' Economic Miracle Will Reshape the World,* (New York: Harper Collins Press, 2006).
5. Albert Keidel, "China's Economic Rise – Fact or Fiction," (Washington, D.C., Carnegie Endowment for International Peace, Research Repot, July 2008).
6. Richard Karlgaard, "Digital Rule," *Forbes,* April 12, 2010, p. 23.
7. John Mauldin, "The Threat to Muddling Through," Frontline Weekly Newsletter, March 20,2010.
8. David Futrell, "Now for the Real Problem: It's Structural, not Cyclical," *Money*, December 2010, p. 64.
9. Geoff Colvin, "It's the Ultimate Economic Experiment: Europe's Cutting vs. America's Spending. Who's Right, *Fortune,* November 15, 2010, p. 72.
10. "The World's Most Admired Countries," (New York, GFK Roper Public Affairs and Media Research Report, 2008).

Chapter 2 – Emergence of the Global Entrepreneur

11. Richard Branson, *Screw It. Let's Do It,* (New York: Virgin Books, 2008).
12. Ben Oviatt, Patricia McDougall, Mark Simon and Rodney Shrader, "A New Venture Without Geographical Limits," *Frontiers of Entrepreneurial*

Research, (Babson Park, Mass.: Center for Entrepreneurial Studies at Babson College, 1991).

13. Ruhul Bajaj, "The New Face of Emerging Market Competition," From: *Straight From The CEO,* by William Dauphinais and Colin Price, (London: Nichols Brealey Publishers, 1998), p. 68.
14. David Mercer, *Future Revolutions,* (London: Burler & Tanner, Ltd, 1998), p. 11
15. Ervin Williams, "A New Organizational Meta-Model: The Convergence of Entrepreneurship, Management and Leadership," Presented to the International Conference on Research in Entrepreneurship and Small Business, Helsinki, Finland, 1994.
16. Alvin Toffler, *Powershift,* (New York: Bantam Books Publishers, 1991), p. 13
17. Paul Pilzer, *Unlimited Wealth,* (New York: Crown Publishing Company, 1990), p. 12
18. James Gwartney, Robert Lawson and Joshau Hall, *Economic Freedom of the World,* Vancouver, B.C.; The Frazer Institute, 2010).
19. The Editors, "The Index of Economic Freedom: The Heritage Foundation, *The Wall Street Journal, 2008.*
20. Lester Thurow, *The Frontiers of Capitalism,* (London: Nicholas Brealey Publishes, 1999).
21. John Kotter, *The New Rules,* (New York: Simon & Schuster Publishers, 1995), p. 215
22. Annette de Klerk, *Variables Distinguishing Entrepreneurs and Non-Entrepreneurs from Different Ethnic Groups in the South African Environment,* A Doctoral Dissertation, The University of South Africa, Pretoria, 1998.
23. David McClelland and David Winters, *The Achieving Society,* (New York: Free Press 1961).
24. David McClelland and David Winters, *Motivating Economic Achievement,* (New York: Free Press, 19690.
25. Niels Bosma and Jonathan Levie, *The Global Entrepreneurship Monitor: 2009 Executive Report,* (Babson, Mass.: Babson College, 2009
26. Reven Brenner, "Land of Opportunity," *Forbes Global Business and Finance,* October 12, 1998, pp. 16.
27. Susan Bradley, Kids Money Camps, Inc., Sudden Money Institute, Florida, USA.

Chapter 4 – A New Wealth Creating Paradigm

28. Tom Stanley and William Kanko, *The Millionaire Next Door,* (New York: Simon & Schuster Publishers, 1999).
29. Luisa Kroll, Mathhew Miller and Tatiana Serafin, "2009 Forbes Billionaires," *Forbes,* March 30, 2009.
30. David Warsh, "What Drives Wealth of Nations," *Harvard Business Review,* July-August, 1998, pp. 171-183.
31. Patti Walmeir and John Reed, "China's Can-Do Carmaker, " *Financial Times,* March 3, 2010, p. 9
32. Ian Bremmer, "China Knows the Time for Lying Low Has Ended," *Financial Times,* March 2010, p. 11
33. Carl Schramm, op.cit., *The Entrepreneurial Imperative.*
34. Robert Buderi, "In Search of Innovation," *MIT Technology Review,* November-December 1999, pp. 43-51.
35. Eric Gregore and Laura Narvaiz, "America Ranks Eight in New Global Innovation Index, Behind Singapore, South Korea and Switzerland," Boston Consulting Group Research Report, Boston Mass., March 9, 2009
36. Lester Thurow, op.cit.
37. Hernando de Soto, *The Mystery of Capital: Why Capitalism Triumphs in the West and Nowhere Else,* (New York: Basic Books, 2000).
38. William Halan, *The New Management,* (San Francisco: Berett-Koehler Publishers, 1996), p. 69.
39. Alvin Toffler, op.cit.
40. Paul Pilzer, op. cit.
41. Clayton Christensen, *The Innovator's Dilemma,* (Boston, Mass.: Harvard Business School Press, 2003).
42. Clayton Christensen and Michael Raynor, *The Innovator's Solution,* (Boston Mass., Harvard Business School Press, 2003).
43. Ervin Williams, op. cit.
44. Ram Charan and Noel Tichey, *Every Business Is a Growth Business,* (New York: Random House, 1998).
45. Media Release, "General Electric Launches Ecomagination to Develop Environmental Technologies: Company-Wide Focus Addressing Diversity Challenge," May 9, 2005.
46. Alvin Toffler and Heidi Toffler, *Creating a New Civilization,* (New York: Turner Publishing Company, 1996).
47. Tom Friedman, *The World is Flat,* (New York: Farr, Straus & Giroux, 2005).
48. David Mercer, op cit.

49. Keith M. Bloomfield and Auss Alan Prince, "So You Want to Be a Millionaire," *Forbes,* August 30, 2010, p. 64.
50. Anne Kadet, "Reaching the $5 Million Club Takes an Open Mind," *Smart Money,* May 8, 2007, p.47.

Chapter 5 – Capitalizing on Opportunities

51. Michale Macrone, *Eureka!,* (New York: Barnes & Noble Books, 1994).
52. Shira White and Patton Wright, *New Ideas About New Ideas,* (Cambridge, MA: Perseus Publishing Company, 2002).
53. Karl Vesper, *New Venture Creation,* (Seattle WA: Vector Publishing Company, 1996).
54. Leigh Buchanan, "The 2009 500 Fastest-Growing Companies," *Inc.,* November 2009.
55. Dale Buss, "Twenty Million Dollar Businesses You've Never Heard Of." *Forbes,* November 5, 2010.
56. Jill Rosenfield, "Here's an Idea, *Fast Company,* April 2000, p. 97.
57. Anna Muoio, "Great Ideas in Aisle Nine," *Fast Company,* April 2000, pp. 46-47
58. Tom Kelley, *The Art of Innovation,* (New York: Doubleday-Random House Publishing, 2001).
59. D. F. Durako and R.M.S. Hoggets, *Entrepreneurship: A Contemporary Approach,* (New York: Dryden Press 1998).
60. Robert Sutton, *Weird Ideas That Work,* (New York: The Free Press, 2002).
61. Clayton Christensen, Scott Anthony and Erik Roth, *Seeing What's Next,* (Boston MA: Harvard Business School Press, 2004),
62. Williams Bygraves, *The Portable MBA in Entrepreneurship,* (New York: John Wiley Publishers, 2004).
63. Chris Anderson, "The New-New Economy," *Wired,* June 2009, p. 97.
64. Adam Penenberg, "Ning's Infinite Ambition," *Fast Company,* May 2008, p.76.
65. The Editors, "10 Emerging Technologies," *Technology Review, May/ June 2010, p. 45 and 2009.*

Chapter 6 – The Global Marketplace

66. Jose Manuel Barroso, "Beyond the Crisis," *The Economist,* April 17, 2010. p. 88.

67. Rosabeth Moss Kanter, *World Class,* (New York: Simon & Schuster, 1995), pp. 30-31.
68. Ohmae Kenichi, *The End of Nation State,* (New York: Harper Collins, 1994).
69. Alibaba.com is a global leader in e-commerce for small business and is the flagship of the Alibaba Group. Source: Internet, August 18, 2008.
70. Austin Carr, "Fast Cities 2010," *Fast Company,* May 2010, p. 84.
71. Jack Gage, "The Best Countries for Business," *Forbes,* March 18, 2009.
72. James Davidson and William Rees-Mogg, *The Sovereign Individual,* (New York: MacMillan Publishing Company, 1997), pp. 185-206.
73. David Mercer, *Future Revolutions,* (London: Burler and Tanner, Ltd., 1998).
74. Miniwatts Marketing Group, Site Surfing Guide, Source: Internet, December 31, 2009.
75. Gary Hamel and Jeff Sample, "The E-Corporation," *Fortune,* December 7, 1998, pp.53-63.
76. Ibid.
77. Ibid.
78. Chris Anderson, "The Internet is Dead. Long Live the Internet." *Wired,* September 2010.
79. Chris Anderson, "In the Next Industrial Revolution, Atoms are the New Bits," *Wired, January 25, 2010, p. 59.*
80. Max Chafin, "Let's Get Started, *Inc.,* October 2009, p. 59.
81. James Quinn, Jordan Baruch and Karen Zein, *Innovation Explosion,* (New York: The Free Press, 1997). p. 200.
82. Patrick Stafford, "The Next 10 Online Trends, *Fast Company,* Online Source, February 2, 2010.

Chapter 7 – The Global Entrepreneur

83. N.M. Tichy and M. A. Devanna, *The Transformational Lerader,* (New York: John Wiley Publishers, 1986).
84. Gary Hamel, op. cit.
85. The Editors, TR 35," *MIT Technology Review,* September-October, 2010, p. 43.
86. David McClelland, op.cit.
87. Davidson and Mogg, op.cit.
88. The Editors, *MIT Technology Review,* op.cit.

89. Alexandra Cheney, Keaton Gray and April Joiner, "By the Numbers: Miles Traveled," *Inc.,* September 2009, p. 114.
90. Hannah Clark Steiman, "Making It," *Inc.,* September 2009, p. 170.
91. Noam Wasserman, "The Founder's Dilemma," *Harvard Business Review, February 2008, p. 103.*
92. Antony Tjan, "Every Entrepreneur Needs to Master these Three Rules," *Harvard Business Review, June 16, 2010.*

Chapter 8 – Developing the Global Enterprise

93. David Teece, "Capturing Value From Knowledge Assets," *California Management Review,* Vol. 3, Spring 1998, pp. 51-71
94. Tim Kyworth and Dorothy Leidner, "The Global Virtual Manager: A Prescription for Success," *European Management Journal,* Vol 18, No. 2, April 2000, pp. 183-194.
95. Al Ries, *Focus,* (New York: Harper Collins Publishers, 1996).
96. Al Ries, op.cit.
97. Ram Charan and Noel Tichey, op.cit.
98. Douglas Hall, "Ordering Out," *Business Week Small Business,* February-March 2009, p. 33.
99. Sara E. Needleman, "Entrepreneurs Find New Ways To Grow," *The Wall Street Journal,* May11, 2010, p.B5.
100. Cyrus Friedheim, *The Trillion Dollar Enterprise,* (New York: Perseus Book Publishing, 1998).
101. Heidi Brown, et.al., "The A List," *Forbes Global Business and Finance,* January 11, 1999, p. 44.
102. Robert Stuart and Pier Abetti, "Start-up Ventures: Towards the Prediction of Initial Success," *Journal of Business Venturing,"* No. 2, 1977, pp. 215-230
103. Martin Zweilling, "Ten Ways to Measure a Start-ups Progress," Forbes. com., June 30, 201

Chapter 9 – Developing the Personal and Business Wealth Plan

104. Joshua Levine, "Cannibal Cycleworks,", *Forbes Global,* July 22, 2002, pp. 78-79.
105. Christopher Rhodes and Erik Portanger, "How an American Helped Torpedo the Dresdner Deal," *The Wall Street Journal, April 28, 2000. p. 1*
106. Clayton Christensen, *The Innovator's Dilemma, op.cit.*

107. Truls Erikson, "Entrepreneurial Capital: The Emerging Venture's Most Important Asset and Competitive Advantage, *Journal of Business Venturing,* No. 17, 2002, pp. 275-290.
108. Rossana Weitekamp and Barbara Pruitt, "U.S. Venture Capital Industry Must Shrink to be an Economic Force," The Kauffman Foundation, Kansas City, MO, June 20, 2009.
109. Martin Zwilling, "Ten Ways to Attract Angel Funding," *Forbes.com.,* October 27, 2009.
110. Gordon Shaw, Robert Brown and Philip Bromiley, "Strategic Stories: How 3M is Rewriting Business Planning," *Harvard Business Review,* May-June 1998, pp.41-50.
111. William Gurley, "Got a Good Idea? Better Think Twice," *Fortune,* December 7, 9998, pp. 109-110.
112. Guy Kawasaki, "Needbucks.com.," *Forbes Global,* January 10, 2000. p. 188.

Chapter 10 – An Emerging New Global Economy: Creativity, Innovation, Growth, and Sustainability

113. James Quinn, Jordan Baruch, and Karen Zien, *Innovative Explosion,* (New York: The Free Press, 1997).
114. Barbara Pruitt and Andrew Kalish, "Kauffman Foundation Analysis Emphasizes the Importance of Young Businesses to Job Creation in the U.S.," Kauffman Foundation, Kansas City, MO, August 23, 2010.
115. Matt Ridley, *The Rational Optimist: How Prosperity Evolves,* (New York: Harper & Row Publishers, 2010).
116. Clayton Christensen and Michael Raynor, *The Innovator's Solution, op.cit.*
117. Everett Rogers, *Diffusion of Innovation,* (New York: The Free Press, 1995).
118. Nathan Myhrvold, "The Big Idea: Funding Eureka!" *Harvard Business Review,* March 2010.
119. Wendy Kennedy, *op.cit.*
120. Gary Hamel, *Leading the Revolution,* (Boston, MA: Harvard Business School Press, 2000).
121. James McGregor, "China's Drive for Indigenous Innovation," Executive Summary by the U.S. Chamber of Commerce, October 25, 2010.
122. Norihiko Shirouza, "Trains Makers Rail Against China's High-Speed Design," *The Wall Street Journal,* November 18, 2010, p.1.

123. Jeremy Page, "China Raises Drone Output. Surprising the West," *The Wall Street Journal, November 19, 2010, p.a1.*
124. Jason Dean, Andres Browne and Shai Ouster, "China's State Capitalism Sparks a Global Backlash," *The Wall Street Journal,* November 16, 2010, p. 1.
125. Niall Ferguson, *Civilization: The West and the Rest,* (London: Penguin Press, 2010).
126. Bill Powell, "The Global Economy," *Fortune,* December 6, 2010, p. 161.
127. Eric Gregoine and Laua Narviaz, op.cit.
128. Michael Ardt and Bruce Einhorn, "The 50 Most Innovative Companies," *Bloomberg BusinessWeek,* April 25, 2010, p.35.
129. Rana Foroohar, "How to Build Again," *News Week,* July 19, 2010, p.15.
130. Robert Atkinson, "Information and Economic Prospects," Information Technology and Innovation Foundation Research Document, Source: Internet, July 28, 2010.
131. Kevin Kelly, "The New Socialism," *Wired Magazine,* May 22, 2010, p. 116.
132. Tyler Cowen, "Create Your Own Economy," *Fast Company,* July-August 2009, p.37.
133. Ram Nidumolu, C. K. Prahalad and M.R. Ragaswami, "Why Sustainability is Now the Key Driver of Innovation, *Harvard Business Review,* September 2009, p.57.
134. These authors say that becoming environmental-friendly lowers cost because firms end up reducing the inputs they use. In addition, the process generates additional revenues from better products and enables companies to create new business ventures.
135. Tom Friedman, *Hot, Flat and Crowded, op.cit*
136. *Ibid.*
137. Jared Diamond, "What's Your Consumption Factor?," *The New York Times,* January 2, 2008.
138. John Elkington and Pamela Hartigan, *The Power of Unreasonable People: How Social Entrepreneurship Create Markets That Change The World,* (Boston MA: Harvard Business School Press, 2008).
139. Michael Elliott, "China Cranks Up the Innovation Machine: Can Government Really Mandate Creativity and Innovation, *Fortune,* November 1, 2010, p. 66

About the Author

Ervin Williams, Ph.D.

Ervin Williams is an entrepreneur, author, consultant, and former Professor of Strategic Management and Entrepreneurship at Georgia State University in Atlanta. He was also a Visiting Professor of Entrepreneurship at the University of South Africa in Pretoria and an Entrepreneur in Residence at Savannah State University. Dr. Williams has served as a consultant and corporate trainer for major U.S. and international organizations. His entrepreneurial experience includes nine start-ups on three continents.

He has lectured extensively on entrepreneurship and leadership in a number of countries including Belgium, England, Finland, Hungary, Russia, Switzerland and South Africa. His consulting and training in the U.S. includes leadership courses for companies such as General Motors, Coca-Cola, Ford Motor Company, Georgia Power Company and other major business corporations. He has conducted leadership training for Andersen Consulting (Accenture) in Europe, Deloitte and Touché in South Africa and Courtaulds Textiles in England. He served as a consultant to the GetAhead Foundation in South Africa, an Entrepreneurial Center started by President Nelson Mandela.

His education includes a Bachelors Degree from Georgia State University, a Masters Degree from Georgia Institute of Technology and a Doctorate from The Ohio State University. He is the author of a book entitled *The Global Entrepreneur* and is writing a book on corporate entrepreneurship. He is Chairman and CEO of *Best*Medical, Inc.; is Chairman and President of World business Enterprises, Ltd.; and is Chairman and CEO of i»*Create* Foundation, Inc. He is also a former Vice-President and member of the Board of Directors of Ariel Savannah Angel Partners, LLC. Dr. Williams currently resides on St. Simons Island, Georgia, USA, and he can be reached via his web site: www.entrepreneurshipsource.com.

Index

D

E

F

G

M

N

O

T

U

V

W

Y

CPSIA information can be obtained at www.ICGtesting.com
Printed in the USA
235695LV00001B/4/P